Chief Daniel Bread and the Oneida Nation of Indians of Wisconsin

The Civilization of the American Indian Series

Chief Daniel Bread and the
Oneida Nation of Indians of Wisconsin

Laurence M. Hauptman
L. Gordon McLester III

University of Oklahoma Press : Norman

Also by Laurence M. Hauptman
(coedited with Jack Campisi) *Neighbors and Intruders: An Ethnohistorical Exploration of the Indians of Hudson's River* (Ottawa, 1978)
The Iroquois and the New Deal (Syracuse, 1981)
The Iroquois Struggle for Survival: World War II to Red Power (Syracuse, 1986)
Formulating American Indian Policy in New York State, 1970-1986: A Public Policy Study (Albany, 1988)
(coedited with Jack Campisi) *The Oneida Indian Experience: Two Perspectives* (Syracuse, 1988)
(coedited with James Wherry) *The Pequots in Southern New England: The Fall and Rise of an American Indian Nation* (Norman, 1990)
Between Two Fires: American Indians in the Civil War (New York, 1995)
The Iroquois in the Civil War: From Battlefield to Reservation (Syracuse, 1993)
Tribes and Tribulations: Misconceptions about American Indians and Their Histories (Albuquerque, 1995)
A Seneca Indian in the Union Army: The Civil War Letters of Sergeant Isaac Newton Parker (Shippensburg, Pa., 1995)
Conspiracy of Interests: Iroquois Dispossession and the Rise of New York State (Syracuse, 1999)

Coedited by Laurence M. Hauptman and Gordon McLester III
The Oneida Indian Journey: From New York to Wisconsin, 1784-1860 (Madison, Wis., 1998)

Published with the assistance of the National Endowment for the Humanities, a federal agency which supports the study of such fields as history, philosophy, literature, and language.

Library of Congress Cataloging-in-Publication Data
Hauptman, Laurence M.
    Chief Daniel Bread and the Oneida Nation of Indians of Wisconsin / Laurence M. Hauptman, L. Gordon McLester III.
    p. cm. — (Civilization of the American Indian series ; v. 241)
    Includes bibliographical references and index.
    ISBN 978-8061-9553-7 (paper)
    ISBN 978-0-8061-3412-3 (hardcover)

    1. Bread, Daniel, Oneida chief, 1800-1873. 2. Oneida Indians—Kings and rulers—Biography. 3. Oneida Indians—Relocation—Wisconsin. 4. Oneida Indians—Politics and government. 5. Indians, Treatment of—New York (State) I. McLester, L. Gordon III. II. Title. III. Series.
E99.045 B74 2002
977.5'00497—dc21

2002019177

Chief Daniel Bread and the Oneida Nation of Indians of Wisconsin is Volume 241 in The Civilization of the American Indian Series.

The paper in this book meets the guidelines for permanence and durability of the Committee on Production Guidelines for Book Longevity of the Council on Library Resources, Inc.∞

Copyright © 2002 by the University of Oklahoma Press, Norman, Publishing Division of the University. All rights reserved. Paperback Published 2025. Manufactured in the U.S.A.

To the memory of our friend
Bernie Cornelius

Contents

List of Illustrations	ix
List of Maps and Tables	xi
Preface	xiii

Part 1: Oneida Castle
  Chapter 1: Chief Daniel Bread:
                   The Man and the Myth   3
  Chapter 2: Childhood in the
                   Land of the Standing Stone   16
  Chapter 3: Land, Land, Land   26

Part 2: Duck Creek
  Chapter 4: Trapped in the
                   Land of the Wild Rice People   43
  Chapter 5: Chief Lobbyist   63
  Chapter 6: Two Missionaries   88
  Chapter 7: Nation-Building   99
  Chapter 8: Founding Father   117
  Chapter 9: Things Fall Apart   127
  Chapter 10: The Fall from Grace   141

Abbreviations	163
Notes	165
Bibliography	185
Index	203

Illustrations

Following page 77

Chief Daniel Bread, 1831
Oneida Chief [Bread], his sister, and a missionary, 1860s
Chief Daniel Bread, 1854
Chief Daniel Bread
Eleazer Williams as a young man
Eleazer Williams in later years
Chief Oshkosh
James Duane Doty
Daniel Whitney
John P. Arndt
Morgan L. Martin
Hobart Episcopal Church
Bishop Jackson Kemper
Chief Elijah Skenandoah
Edward A. Goodnough
Chief Cornelius Hill
Chief Cornelius Hill as Episcopal priest

Maps and Tables

Maps

1. Oneida country after the American Revolution   2
2. Oneida removal to Wisconsin and Ontario, 1820–1845   42
3. "New York Indian" lands in Michigan Territory in 1823: Lands jointly occupied with Menominees and Winnebagos under the Treaties of 1821 and 1822   49
4. Oneida Indian Reservation under the Buffalo Creek Treaty of January 15, 1838, and Amended United States–Oneida Treaty of February 3, 1838   97
5. American Indian communities in Wisconsin today   161

Tables

1. Oneida Indian population in New York State, 1800–1855   23
2. Population of Oneida and Madison Counties, New York, 1790–1830   24

3. Oneida Indian population in Wisconsin,
   1838-1872 — 103
4. Population in Wisconsin, 1836-1870 — 105
5. Episcopal missionary Solomon D. Davis's
   census of Oneidas in Wisconsin in 1844 — 111

Preface

Chief Daniel Bread (1800–1873) was the most important Oneida Indian leader of the nineteenth century. He was an articulate voice, using both the Oneida and English languages to defend his people's tribal interests during a crisis caused by their removal from New York State and adjustment to new surroundings in Michigan Territory, now Wisconsin. In Chief Bread's obituary, published in the *Green Bay Advocate* in 1873, an anonymous friend wrote that: "a most profitable and interesting volume might be made for the record of the events, circumstances, speeches and acts of his busy career."[1] Despite this recommendation, no biography of Bread has existed until this one, although he was the person most responsible for transplanting Oneida Indian existence to Wisconsin, for rooting his community in midwestern soil. In effect, Bread was the founding father of the Oneida Nation of Indians of Wisconsin.

A warrior in his youth, Bread was no Tecumseh fighting the Long Knives at every turn. Nor was Bread a Handsome Lake or a Wovoka who led a revitalization movement modifying Indian religion to adjust to the Euroamerican invasion. The Oneida chief was a politically shrewd and complex man whose life appeared to have been filled with contradictions. He wore many hats during his lifetime—warrior, orator, runner, subchief, pinetree chief, diplomat, and principal chief. Finally, he assumed the embarrassing role of deposed chief.

The chief was no idealist or utopian. He drew inspiration from the Oneida past and tried to avoid the pitfalls of what had happened to his people in central New York. He was a quick learner who operated in the hard-boiled real world of nineteenth-century America with its prejudice against Indians. He was also a masterful tribal politician, skilled at building coalitions with his former enemies or relentlessly punishing those who crossed him. In his position as "principal chief" from the early 1830s onward, Bread amassed substantial political power and acquired financial rewards that led to a tribal reaction to his leadership, eventually causing his political demise. Hence, this biography in many ways takes the form of a classical tragedy, tracing the rise of an individual from obscurity to the heights of power and status to his ultimate fall from grace.

This book attempts to fill a major gap in the historical literature. Anthropologists and historians have devoted too little attention to prominent Iroquois leaders.[2] Instead, biographers have focused largely on southwestern or Plains Indian warriors of the nineteenth century, such as Geronimo and Sitting Bull, giving a limited view of the ways Native Americans developed sophisticated survival strategies to counter the overriding negative effects of westward expansion.

Several caveats must be pointed out at the beginning. Chief Bread did not leave diaries, journals, or family correspondence. This biography, like all similar works, is affected by the size and scope of the documents that have survived the winds of time. There is no one collection of Daniel Bread papers. Many of his own writings and tribal petitions are scattered, found in the records of the Michigan superintendency as well as in the Green Bay and New York agencies in the National Archives; other materials are in

Preface

the New York State Archives, the State Historical Society of Wisconsin in Madison, the Neville Museum of Brown County, and the University of Wisconsin Area Research Center in Green Bay.

Although the public man's career is relatively easy to follow, Bread's private life was rarely shared with anyone. We know next to nothing about his parents, his sister, his marriages, or his numerous children because the Oneida chief never wrote about them; his surviving correspondence is mostly of an official nature.

In order to compensate for gaps or bias in the surviving documents, we have carefully gathered information in a variety of ways and from diverse sources. Besides archival and manuscript materials found in Washington, D.C., Albany, Madison, and Green Bay, Wisconsin, we have made use of travelers' accounts that described the Oneidas in both New York and Wisconsin. Our interviews with Chief Bread's descendants at Oneida, church records of the Oneidas' Holy Apostles Episcopal Church, linguistic analysis, and the four major portraits of Chief Bread all contributed to our better understanding of the Oneida leader.

We have made use of oral history collected by the Oneida Indian community members who took part in the Oneida Language and Folklore Project, originated by Professor Morris Swadesh at the University of Wisconsin, conducted by Dr. Floyd Lounsbury, and supported by the Works Progress Administration's Federal Writers' Project from 1938 to 1941. The participating Wisconsin Oneidas collected several volumes of tribal folklore and history. It was quite different from other WPA Federal Writers' Projects. The WPA Indian-Pioneer history of Oklahoma had whites interviewing Indians; moreover, whites interviewed African Americans in accumulating the famous WPA slave narratives. But at Oneida, native speakers listened to fellow tribal members, and then went back to translate the stories and develop an orthography and hymnal that contributed to their ability to write their native language. The project also furthered Oneida community cooperation and pride and created employment for Indians during the economic crisis of the Great Depression. In addition to serving the social needs of an Indian community, the project furthered scientific research that had a far-reaching impact on applied linguistics and promoted the scholarly interest in Iroquoian languages.[3]

This book could not have been written without the stories Dr. Floyd Lounsbury's Oneida "students" collected during the New Deal. We remember him fondly as a decent, humble man willing to share his knowledge with anyone willing to listen—his legacy in Iroquoian linguistics is unparalleled. Moreover, the authors would like to thank four linguists trained and/or strongly influenced by Dr. Lounsbury for their help in this project: Professors Blair Rudes of the University of North Carolina at Charlotte, Marianne Mithun of the University of California at Santa Cruz, Cliff Abbott of the University of Wisconsin-Green Bay, and Dr. Gunther Michelson of Ottawa, Ontario.

The writing of this biography has been a collaborative effort, with a clear delineation of responsibilities. Laurence M. Hauptman did the bulk of the writings and archival research in New York and Washington, D.C., and L. Gordon McLester III uncovered valuable materials at Oneida and Green Bay, researched Wisconsin newspapers for information about Chief Bread, arranged interviews with Bread's descendants, and helped secure access to Oneida oral histories and to the records of the Holy Apostles Episcopal Church at Oneida. The authors jointly researched Bread's life at the University of Wisconsin-Green Bay Area Research Center, at the Neville Museum of Brown County, at the University of Wisconsin-Madison, and at the State Historical Society of Wisconsin.

Many members of the Oneida Nation of Indians of Wisconsin contributed to the authors' efforts. Woodrow Webster and Blanche Powless, descendants of Daniel Bread and Cornelius Hill, allowed us to interview them. Marie Hinton

Preface

and her brother, the late Amos Christjohn, have done much to preserve the Oneida language and have produced an invaluable modern Oneida language dictionary that we consulted. Cory Habeck's computer skills were most helpful. Both of us have increased our understanding of Oneida history and politics as a result of discussions with Gerald Hill, the former Oneida tribal attorney; Judy Cornelius, the Oneida tribal treasurer; and Loretta Metoxen, the former vice chairman of the Oneida Nation of Indians of Wisconsin.

Research visits to numerous repositories proved beneficial. We would like to thank these archivists: Harold Miller of the State Historical Society of Wisconsin at Madison, Deborah Anderson of the University of Wisconsin-Green Bay Area Research Center, Louise Pfotenhauer and Mary Hueselbueck of the Neville Museum of Brown County, and James Folts of the New York State Archives. Paul Mercer and Hank Ilnicki of the New York State Library Manuscript Division provided valuable assistance. Rebecca Johns Karst of the Madison County Historical Society of Oneida, New York, helped us locate a daguerreotype of Chief Bread.

Many others contributed to the undertaking of this project. Three Wisconsin academics were most helpful in discussions about the project: Professors David Wrone of the University of Wisconsin-Stevens Point; Ronald Satz, Dean at the University of Wisconsin-Eau Claire; and Herbert S. Lewis of the University of Wisconsin-Madison. Dr. Lewis recently discovered a new cache of WPA Oneida interviews and generously made them available. Laurence M. Hauptman also acknowledges the assistance of several colleagues at the State University of New York at New Paltz. President Roger Bowen, now president of the Milwaukee Public Museum, encouraged Hauptman's research from its beginning in 1996. The college's administration also awarded Hauptman two travel grants and a sabbatic leave to finish this project. Jo Margaret Mano of the Department of Geography graciously shared her expertise on early New York State land records. Heriberto Dixon of the

School of Business suggested ways to approach this biography. Joan Walker, the former secretary of the Department of History, typed all the numerous letters of inquiry required in the research. Three staff members at the Sojourner Truth Library at SUNY, New Paltz, contributed much to the completion of this biography: Marylou Kisselburg, Leslie Masker, and Chris Raab. We especially thank Ms. Kisselburg, who generously contributed her time and energies to help photocopy barely readable microfilm, assistance much needed by aging researchers trying to decipher nineteenth-century handwriting in correspondence and petitions.

Three other individuals deserve special acknowledgment. Mr. Todd Larkin of Las Vegas, Nevada, aided us with information gathered in his many years of unraveling Oneida genealogy. Dr. Jack Campisi, the foremost ethnohistorian on Oneida history, listened to both authors ramble on about Chief Bread and suggested ways to approach the research for this biography. Our friend, David Jaman of Gardiner, New York, provided us with frank and helpful editorial comments about the manuscript.

Most importantly, we would like to thank our wives, Ruth Hauptman and Betty McLester, who tolerated our compulsive work habits and "strange" fascination with Chief Daniel Bread and Oneida history of the nineteenth century.

Part 1
Oneida Castle

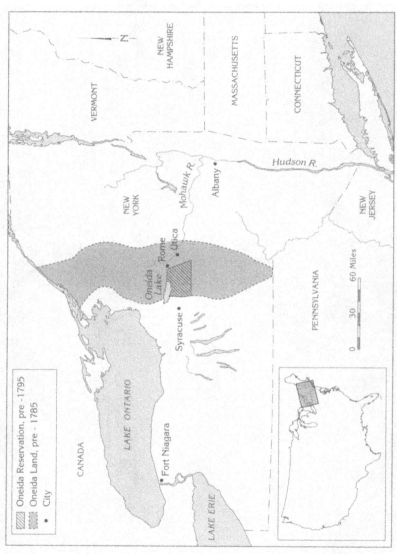

Oneida country after the American Revolution. From a map by Ben Simpson.

Chapter 1

Chief Daniel Bread

The Man and the Myth

In May of 1814, a military detachment of over 120 irregulars, mostly Oneidas but including a sprinkling of Brothertown, Onondaga, and Stockbridge Indians, made their way through the rough terrain north of Oneida Lake, unaware that their forced march would lead to a dramatic American victory at Sandy Creek. The expedition then shifted westward, reaching the American fort at Oswego where they were supplied with cartridges for their rifles, firewood, scissors, United States Army-issued rations, and were outfitted with blankets, vermilion cloth, shirts, and two pairs of shoes for each man. The Indian company was led by Adam Skenandoah, a prominent Oneida and relative of Skenandoah of American Revolutionary War fame, and by Peter Elm, formerly known as "Pagan Peter," a leading voice of the non-Christian Oneidas. This contingent was soon sent to serve as a shoreline escort for an American supply convoy of bateaux heading for Sackets Harbor.[1]

Armed with their own hunting rifles brought from their homes, these Indians going off to battle had long heard elders recount stories of their military exploits, their warriors' heroism at the Battle of Oriskany in the summer of 1777, their loyal commitment to General Washington and their admiration for the Marquis de Lafayette, who helped recruit them for military service in the American Revolution. Around council fires, they had listened to Oneida veterans talk about the greatness of Blatcop, Peter Bread, Hanyerry, Hanyost, Two Kettles Together, and the boy warrior Peter Powless, all famous Oneidas who had fought for the Long Knives in the "War of Brothers" that raged from 1775 to 1783. Attempting to replicate that warrior experience, Oneidas enlisted in President Madison's army in 1813, hoping that their Great Father in Washington would finally carry out past treaty commitments of friendship and protection.[2]

Included in the Indian detachment that May was a septuagenarian Oneida, the wizened Henry Cornelius, a veteran of the Battle of Oriskany who had been in American military service throughout the Revolutionary War, as well as Tekayá·tilu (Tega-wir-tiron, Tekaweiatiron, or Tekawyati:ron), translated in English as "Leaning Body," a fourteen-year-old Oneida. For the first time, this boy warrior was on the warpath, a time-honored route to manhood. No one then could predict that Tekayá·tilu would become the most prominent Oneida Indian of the nineteenth century.[3]

Tekayá·tilu and his fellow Indians were a vital part of the overall defense of Sackets Harbor, the only American-held ship-launching center on Lake Ontario during most of the War of 1812. The port was slowly being strangled by an effective British blockade. In the dead of night on the evening of May 28 and into the early morning hours of May 29, American Master-Commandant Melancthon Woolsey attempted to break the blockade by sneaking nineteen bateaux transporting naval guns and heavy cable past the British naval forces. The American supply "fleet" pulled into Sandy Creek to await an escort of troops being dispatched from Sackets Harbor. British Commander Stephen Popham learned of the attempt to resupply Sackets Harbor and dispatched a force of three gunboats, four smaller craft, and nearly two hundred sailors and marines to thwart the Americans.

The British contingent soon spotted the masts of the American bateaux, which had now sailed up some distance into Sandy Creek away from its entrance on Lake Ontario. Unaware that the American supply vessels were protected by numerous American-allied Indian riflemen hidden on the banks of the creek, Popham, going against orders, directed his force to pursue the American bateaux into Sandy Creek. The British navy was soon ambushed by these Indians coming from the south and by other American marines, dragoons, and riflemen on the north shore of the creek coming from Sackets Harbor.

The British forces were cut to pieces in the firefight—known in history as the Battle of Big Sandy or Sandy Creek—that soon ensued. Fourteen British sailors were killed and twenty-eight were wounded. Popham's three gunboats, which contained Congreve rockets, were captured by American forces. Subsequently, the much-needed American supply bateaux reached Sackets Harbor. The heavy cable and naval guns were then used to help outfit the U.S.S. Superior, the sixty-two-gun warship, which was launched and which weakened the British control of Lake Ontario. To this day, contemporary Oneidas have an oral tradition of this momentous battle, the day they defeated the mighty British navy, and changed the course of the War of 1812.[4]

This battle also launched the meteoric rise of Tekayá·tilu, better known by his Christian name, Daniel Bread. Bread was born on March 27, 1800. His entire career was largely determined by the first twenty-nine years of his life, spent at his birthplace, Oneida Castle, in today's central New York.[5]

Because of the changes in the spelling of Oneida names, the use of the same surname by different individuals, and the matrilineal descent practiced by this Indian community, it is difficult or nearly impossible to reconstruct a full Bread genealogy. According to one unsubstantiated newspaper account, Bread was the son of an Oneida named Williams, and when his father died, he was adopted by an Indian named Daniel Bread, who gave his stepson his own name.[6] We do know that his mother, or stepmother, was Dinah Bread, who accompanied him to Wisconsin in 1829 and who died there in 1835. We also know that Bread had a sister, since she was painted by George Catlin in a group portrait, and that she accompanied Bread on at least one of the chief's official trips to Washington; however, despite checking cemetery, church, tribal, and federal records and interviewing present-day Oneidas, her identity remains a mystery.[7]

More likely, in light of his meteoric rise to influence among the Oneidas' First Christian Party, Bread was a descendant of one of the major Oneida families. His family was clearly tied to Reverend Samuel Kirkland's Presbyterian mission, established in the years before the American Revolution. The Bread name appears frequently in the last quarter of the eighteenth century onward. For example, although his connection to Daniel Bread is not clear, a Peter Bread (Kaunaudauloonh) had served in the American Revolution and had been cited for his heroism at the Battle of Saratoga. Kaunaudauloonh infiltrated enemy positions, led Oneida warriors into battle, and captured enemy soldiers. He was a member of Reverend Samuel Kirkland's Presbyterian Church and, on occasions, was delegated to represent and speak for the Oneidas' First Christian Party in negotiations with Albany. Kaunaudauloonh's name appears on several state treaties, including those ratified in 1795 and 1807.[8]

Although frequently described as a "sachem," "head chief," or "principal chief" of the Oneidas, Bread was not an officially condoled chief and held no hereditary position within the Oneida political structure, earning respect through meritorious actions, leadership skills, and oratory. As a pinetree chief, he was often referred to as a "big man." A Wisconsin Oneida WPA story, told by Stadler King, suggested that Bread, upon becoming chief, was dubbed

Chief Daniel Bread: The Man and the Myth

"yo h ne hdah nýo·uh," which "in English would mean a pine tree grown in from without." In effect, "yo h ne hdah nýo · uh" was an honorific name later bestowed on Bread because of his outstanding leadership.⁹

In the same WPA story, which was critical of Bread and his leadership, King explained that in order to be worthy of the honor of being selected a chief, "a man must be just, he must be honest, he must have equal respect to all people, he must be wise and alert to the traditions of the tribe and he must have moral respect for himself and his conduct." He continued by stating that the Oneida word for *chief* is "la di gwa·nʌ́h se," which means "the big man." King elaborated: "They call them this because chiefs are thought to be big men that is they are high in standing. They are wise and hold big offices."¹⁰

Few members of the twelve-member council of chiefs in Bread's tenure as principal chief of the Wisconsin Oneidas were hereditary claimants since the clan system had eroded.¹¹ Their success in administering the business of the nation had previously been in their ability to satisfy the majority of the warriors, formerly controlled in New York by the clan mothers. These matrons, according to Stadler King, were called "gu d na·ja nú hne," or, in English, "women who look after the kettle" because their key role was to "look after the interest and well-being or welfare of the tribe." The "work and traditions or the welfare of a tribe are thought to be like it were packed in one solid kettle of which these mothers are looking after."¹²

The Oneidas modified their traditions to fit the circumstances after resettlement in Wisconsin.¹³ In an ad hoc way, new positions had to be created. They formed a council of twelve, comprised of chiefs, with one additional chief serving as the nation's principal voice. The chiefs were from the First Christian and Orchard parties, largely drawn from the leadership of the Episcopal and Methodist churches on the reservation. Into this remarkably adaptive and fluid political order came Daniel Bread, the greatest of the council chiefs. As principal chief of the Wisconsin Oneidas from 1832 onward, Bread had to deal with a wide spectrum of concerns, including the following: delays by the federal government in paying required annuities due these Indians under treaties; failures by the New York State legislature to reimburse the nation for expenses incurred in the removal to Wisconsin; numerous internal tribal conflicts that threatened continued Oneida existence in Wisconsin; the devastating effects of the alcohol trade in and around the Oneida lands, and incessant outside pressures to get at Oneida lands and the nation's timber resources; and finally, and importantly for Bread, the white push to force the Oneidas to leave Wisconsin and take up lands in the Indian Territory.

In Wisconsin, Bread was an active member of the Hobart Church (now the Holy Apostles Episcopal Church), the largest and historically most powerful church on the reservation. The ethnohistorian Jack Campisi has accurately noted that for a pinetree chief to have been effective as an Oneida leader of a political group before the 1860s, "it was necessary that an individual be a 'good Christian' and a church leader. He was expected to be temperate and generous in his behavior, giving to the needy as the occasion demanded."[14] Until the Civil War, these were the qualities that Bread emanated and used to cement his political power.

In the early years in the West, Bread's Christianity—he was a lay reader and a leading congregant of the Hobart Church—set the tone for his leadership. He promoted temperance among his people and acted as lay reader and sang in the Episcopal Church choir. Because of his financial success—he established a successful merchandise store, shoe shop, and blacksmith shop—Bread generously hosted church members every Christmas and Fourth of July, at which time he made many speeches about Oneida Indian military contributions, especially during the American Revolution. He stressed these Indians' continued loyalty to and alliance with the United States. In the first decades of his life in Oneida, Wisconsin, Bread saw no contradiction in promoting the tribal sovereignty and treaty rights of his Indian people while at the same time accepting the white man's religion, holidays, schools, and role of "Great Father" in Washington. For Bread was a political pragmatist, not necessarily committed to spiritual concerns or idealistic principles.

Chief Daniel Bread's lengthy political career—he dominated Oneida politics for four decades—has largely been overshadowed by the popular as well as scholarly writings about Eleazer Williams, the charismatic but eccentric Mohawk Indian clergyman who is generally "credited" with leading the Oneida Indians to Michigan Territory, now Wisconsin. Shortly after the end of the War of 1812, Bishop John Henry Hobart of the Episcopal Church appointed Williams as a lay reader and catechist. In 1817, Williams became a missionary to the Oneida Indians, converting many from the Presbyterian to the Episcopal sect. An eccentric man, later proclaiming himself, in bizarre fashion, the Lost Dauphin, Louis XVII of France, Williams expanded a plan first proposed by Jedidiah Morse, the famous minister, geographer, and congressman. The Mohawk cleric proposed that all of the Six Nations from New York State resettle in Michigan Territory. In 1820-22, Williams led delegations of the Iroquois and other Indians from New York State to Green Bay, where treaties were negotiated with the Menominees and Winnebagos, "securing" millions of acres of land and settlements in the Fox River Valley at Little Chute and along Duck Creek near Green Bay.[15]

Although Williams is a major figure in the history of the removal of the so-called New York Indians—the Brothertown, Oneida, and Stockbridge—his central role in Oneida history was temporary, quickly fading after the mid-1820s. His legend, nevertheless, is bigger than life because the Indian missionary was a self-promoter, and the strange story of the Lost Dauphin continues to captivate the fancy of readers and more recently opera aficionados.[16] The story also tends to negate the Oneidas' role in the events, treating them as helpless children under the spell of the missionary Williams.

Williams's assistant, Albert G. Ellis—journalist, federal surveyor, land speculator, lumber mill entrepreneur, Indian agent, and enemy of Daniel Bread—also helped foster the "greatness" of the missionary's reputation by his articles in such prestigious scholarly outlets as the Wisconsin Historical Collections, the official publication of the State Historical Society of Wisconsin. Ellis's biased writings have been accepted at face value, especially his interpretation that Williams dominated Oneida tribal existence until he was overthrown by disloyal Oneidas led by Bread in 1832. In these writings, Williams's less desirable qualities are minimized while his magnetic leadership is stressed. The Mohawk missionary's hallowed role as a pioneer figure in the history of Green Bay was played up by Ellis in his writings. Coversely, the myth plays down the extraordinary story of Bread and his Oneida community-building that followed in the half-century after removal.[17]

Despite this Williams myth, Bread was a most impressive voice of the Oneidas until the American Civil War. George Catlin, who painted Bread twice over a thirty-year period, described the Oneida chief in 1831, after they had met in Washington, D.C.: "He is a shrewd and talented man, well educated—speaking good English—is handsome, and a polite and gentlemanly man in his deportment."[18] Later, in 1851, the Episcopal missionary Solomon Davis wrote: "He [Bread] is an enterprising and influential chief of his tribe and was highly instrumental in their removal from the State of New York to their present location in Wisconsin."[19] In the same year, Bread's major protagonist, Judge James Duane Doty, agent of the American Fur Company, leading land speculator, territorial governor, and a founding father of Wisconsin statehood, characterized Bread as "a man of excellent character, honest and upright, and his statements are entitled to credit upon any subject— whether he is interested or not—upon which he professes to be informed. I do not know a better man in the country in which he lives."[20]

Although Bread can be judged as a political opportunist who benefited financially from his position as principal chief, the major motivation of his life was to prevent another Oneida removal. There is no direct evidence to tie Bread to criminal activities or fraud; there are only accusations to that effect. Bread took determined stands against white advocates of Indian removal, from Andrew Jackson to Wisconsin's governors, who urged Oneida transferal from Wisconsin to lands in the Indian Territory. He was severely criticized at different times because of his overwhelming economic and political power, his support for acculturation and missionary schools, his ability to cooperate effectively with most Indian agents, and his advocacy of allotment, fee simple Oneida land ownership, and United States citizenship after the Civil War. However, Bread was too complex to fit any mold. He also deserves the major credit for permanently establishing the Oneidas in Wisconsin.

The oral history of the Wisconsin Oneidas provides further insights into Bread's life, not found in Ellis's writings on these Indians or in other writings. This history provides conflicting interpretations of the chief and his leadership. Several WPA Oneida Language and Folklore stories suggest that Bread's residence was the first place Oneidas came to after their arrival at the Duck Creek Reservation in Wisconsin, and that the chief provided succor for those Indians who had been removed from New York. In one WPA story told to Ida Blackhawk by Mrs. Mark Powless, the chief's great granddaughter, Bread was "recognized by the Government as the head of the Tribe that moved here [Wisconsin]." In revealing fashion, Powless stated: "So he [Bread] was considered the head chief and *Eleazer [Williams] was his assistant.* He received the payment [treaty annuity] from the Government, but he gave the Oneidas some of the money" (emphasis ours). His great granddaughter added information confirmed in two contemporary interviews with Bread's distant kin: the chief lived in "a big house with three stories" that was burned down and later rebuilt on the same spot, where the present Episcopal Church parish hall and cemetery now exist on the Wisconsin Oneidas' reservation. The proximity of his residence to this church, the power center of the Oneida community, tells much about Bread and his influence.[21]

Other Oneida WPA stories provide important information about Bread. Tillie Baird informed Sarah Summers that Bread's house was her family's first stop upon their entrance into the Wisconsin Oneida community after they left New York because they did not want to come under the state's jurisdiction and "they didn't want to become [United States] citizens."[22] In another story, Sarah Summers told Ida Blackhawk that Daniel Bread initially took Summers' family in when they left New York for Wisconsin. They rested "until they went on to another man's place."[23] Ida Blackhawk, whose grandmother was Bread's niece, noted that the chief also helped her family. Blackhawk's family had settled at the Six Nations Reserve along the Grand River in southern Ontario after the American Revolution. Bread helped them come to Wisconsin and resettle there.[24] With a sense of great pride, Levi Elm told Ida Blackhawk that his grandmother was a sister to Daniel Bread, "who became very prominent among the Oneidas." Elm indicated that the chief and Bread's sister owned the lane "where the mission is, including the Parish Hall, hospital, church, and cemetery." This building, which burned down, was "so large that several families to occupy [sic] the building."[25]

Much less flattering observations about Chief Bread were made in two other WPA Oneida stories. At the beginning of one of them, Stadler King described how the chief accomplished his remarkable rise to leadership. Bread was presented as a tribal peacemaker at a heated lacrosse match near the Methodist Church. He intervened in a major melee that ensued and was successful in stopping the fray. The story went on to show that, although he was not "a decendent [sic] of a chief" and "not in line to become a chief," Bread convinced the two combatants and their teams to obey his wishes to stop fighting. King explained why and how Bread became principal chief of the Oneidas. Bread was seen as "very wise" and having "good ideas for transacting business for the Oneidas." Soon the "Head Chief whose name was [Jacob] Cornelius took much interest in Daniel Bread and they became great friends." Cornelius then recommended Bread to the other chiefs and "asked them to take him in because they could be benefited by his wisdom."[26]

According to King, soon Bread was delegated to transact business with the government in Washington because it "was said that he was wiser than any other chief"; however, he feathered his nest since he had the opportunity "to make the deals in his favor" and obtain moneys for himself that were owed to the tribe. King accused him, without proof, of using his position to acquire wealth, especially by keeping treaty annuity moneys and even by selling "a strip of land which runs from the Town of Ashwaubenon, including the town it self [sic], which they [some Oneidas] said was part of the reservation." The economic disparities between Chief Bread and his neighbors caused resentment and led to further recriminations against him. According to King, he built two expensive houses, the site of "all the picnics and celebrations," but both of these elaborate structures burned to the ground. In conclusion, King insisted: "So the wisdom of this chief did not do much good to the tribe, because he was doing this business in an underhanded way and did not tell the truth to the tribe and also kept the proceeds of the transactions he made for them."[27]

Equally critical was the WPA story told by John Skenandore. He recounted the Oneida oral traditions concerning Bread and his leadership. First, Skenandore described the chief's role in the removal of the Oneidas from New York. He called Bread a prominent chief who brought his people from New York to Wisconsin, a well-honored man and the first Oneida "to put up a real house on the reservation." The impressive log house, built on the east side of the Episcopal cemetery below the hill, had a large stone basement. When fire destroyed his residence, the chief, then financially well-off, rebuilt his home, this time constructing a frame house on the same foundation. Disdainful of the chief, the storyteller noted that the "Government" gave him "thirty thousand dollars for transporting the Oneidas and some time later [he] got another sum of twenty thousand dollars."[28]

Skenandore then went on to deprecate Bread. The Oneida described the chief as a "big shot" who never had to work, and had hired hands to do his farming. Bread was also pictured as a dandy who wore expensive clothes, had the best horses, "liked his fire water" too much, a thirst that led him to light up ten-dollar bills and throw "the flaming bill[s] back into the fire place." The storyteller then recounted Bread's final days: "When Daniel got older and his money had [been] exhausted then he had renters in his place as the house was big enough for [a] few families and by the time he died he was so dam [sic] poor that he was even lousy." Although not completely sure of the facts, the Oneida added that Bread probably was an Episcopal Church member because he lived "right near it" and was an educated man because he had to "be able to understand the contracts he had with the Government."[29]

The controversial nature of Bread's leadership can be explained. Much of what he accomplished was away from the Oneidas' reservation in Wisconsin, namely in Albany and Washington and behind closed doors in Green Bay. As a tight-to-the-vest Indian politician, he had few confidants. Most contemporary Oneidas did not understand as he did the powerful forces at work in the non-Indian world attempting to rid New York and later Wisconsin of *all* of its Indians. Although no saint or holy man, and an individual who definitely benefited materially by his leadership role, Bread had to contend with tribal politics that often sought to fix blame within the tribe rather than to see the larger picture of territorial, state, or federal policies that were disastrous to the Indians. Moreover, much of the "bad press" attached to his name came from non-Indian enemies such as Albert G. Ellis or from Indian political rivals such as Cornelius Hill, the popular Oneida chief who had married Bread's granddaughter and who later helped overturn Bread's leadership.[30]

To his credit, Chief Bread kept his highly divided Oneida community together until the mid-1860s. He fully understood that the Oneidas needed to speak with one voice, which was the only way for them to prevent another removal.

In large measure, Bread's skills rested upon his intellectual brilliance and his cooperative relationship with Indian agents and religious leaders, which allowed him to secure special favors for both himself and for his political supporters within the Oneida Nation. By favoring schools and working to promote the Episcopal faith on the reservation as an active member of the Hobart Church, he won admirers in the non-Indian world, including the agent George Boyd, the missionary Solomon Davis, and the Episcopal bishop Jackson Kemper. Importantly, a major reason for his ultimate fall from power was his break in the 1860s with the missionary Edward A. Goodnough, a clergyman who encouraged and supported the rise of Cornelius Hill in Bread's place.

Bread was forever shaped by his first three decades of life in central New York. He was determined at all costs to prevent the Oneidas from being removed again once they arrived in Wisconsin in the 1820s. Bread's alliances with both whites and Indians and his frequently shifting positions, which appear on the whole contradictory, were largely an outgrowth of this fear of removal.

Chapter 2

Childhood in the Land of the Standing Stone

Oneida Indians refer to themselves as "On∧yotaʔa·ká·"—the "People of the Standing Stone." According to Oneida beliefs, a granite boulder unlike any other stone in central New York State suddenly appeared at their village near Oneida Lake. Whenever they moved within the vicinity, the stone, unaided by any human hands, followed them, appearing every time. Finally, when Oneida Castle was established, it remained there. To a young boy growing up in the years before the War of 1812, the stone must have seemed magical, especially when its powers were related by the highly respected, wise elders of the nation.[1]

Around this sacred stone, Oneidas conducted their great councils where they resolved questions presented to them and worshipped the Creator. The missionary Jeremy Belknap, writing in 1796, stated that the followers of the Great Binding Law of the Iroquois, the non-Christian Oneidas, saw the stone as an "image of the deity" which was to be worshipped.[2] Other commentators viewed the sacred stone as a great altar at which Oneidas prayed. All Oneidas, including those in Wisconsin where the stone never reappeared, still see the stone as the symbol of the continuity and survivability of the Oneida Nation. Today a replica of

Childhood in the Land of the Standing Stone   17

the stone is in front of the Radisson Hotel on Oneida lands near Green Bay, Wisconsin.[3]

Belief in the standing stone and in other legends told by elders around council fires or in log cabins during the harsh winter months in upstate New York was part of an Oneida child's upbringing in the first years of the nineteenth century. Yet Bread was exposed to another tradition during his youth. He was an Indian well versed in the Euroamerican world from his earliest years. As a member of the small group of Christian Oneidas associated with the missionary Kirkland, young Bread had access to a Western education. Although the details of Bread's youth are largely a mystery, we do know that part of his life before the Battle of Sandy Creek was spent as a student in the mission school on the reservation, where he learned to read and write English, struggled with arithmetic, and attempted to master the rigors of the catechism.[4]

Bread excelled at his task of learning to read the New Testament. In his first correspondence with officials, he is known as "Christian Daniel." He made his mark and someone printed his name as "Daniel Tegawiatiron."[5] Despite his ability to read and write English, he clearly felt uncomfortable about his standing out from the group. Taught collective values of the community at large, he continued to make his mark rather than sign his name on all correspondence, memorials, petitions, and treaties well after he was literate in English. He continued this practice until 1828, just before his arrival in Wisconsin.

The wisdom of Oneida elders shaped Bread's education, undoubtedly more than his formal missionary training. Nurtured at Oneida Castle, Bread heard tales of great councils of the past that had helped determine international events. He had grown up instructed about council protocol and Iroquois diplomacy. Bread learned how these Indians dealt with the outside world in the past, playing off Europeans against each other and adopting, using, or manipulating weaker eastern Algonkian and Siouan Indian refugees. Bread was inculcated with the pride of being an Oneida, a member nation of the great Iroquois League of Peace and Power with its long-established history. His later life in Wisconsin was shaped by these nationalistic forces that influenced his diplomacy with various Indian nations as well as with federal and state governments. As participants for centuries in forest diplomacy with other Indian nations as well as with major European powers—Holland, France, and England—and now with their successor the United States, the Oneidas and other members of the original Five Nations viewed themselves as sovereign nations, even long after their military power had waned.[6]

Bread, like most Oneida children, spent his youth rollicking in the beautiful surroundings of Oneida Territory in central New York. The area around Oneida Castle was a child's paradise, a natural wonderland that can hardly be appreciated today. Indian boys then and now would be seen in the clearings playing the stick game—lacrosse—imitating the exploits of their adult counterpart heroes. The surrounding forests of basswood, beech, chestnut, elm, hemlock, maple, oak, and pine were perfect hiding places for youngsters. The boys could go fishing at Oneida Lake, on Fish Creek, or on Wood Creek, where bass, pickerel, salmon, and whitefish were plentiful. There was also a limitless supply of eels that could be skinned and brought back to Oneida Castle, where their skins were fashioned by the Indian women of the village into headbands or watertight containers. Bread and his boyhood friends could go out hunting with their blunt-tipped arrows and bring back "mighty" game—rabbits and squirrels—for the round-bottom cooking pots always simmering with food in their villages. They could climb to the tops of trees, imitating the exploits of their fathers and grandfathers who spied out intruders in the same forests, especially in the high-ground area around Steuben, between today's New Hartford and Clinton, New York. Yet, a cloud of uncertainty surrounded all Oneidas. A young boy growing up could not ignore the troubles discussed by elders in council because the "moccasin telegraph" spread news throughout the community, especially in the small numbers of Oneida families devoted to Samuel Kirkland's Christian mission.[7]

Kirkland's presence contributed to the divisions and helped shape the Oneida world long after the mission waned in the 1790s and early years of the nineteenth century. Besides his influence in bringing most of the Oneidas to the American side during the Revolutionary War, encouraging acculturation to the white man's ways, and introducing Christianity, Kirkland reinforced already existing divisions within the community between warriors, mostly his supporters, and sachems. Thus, at the end of the American Revolution, the pro-Kirkland warriors who had been allied to the Americans and who had become converted to Christianity, later referred to as the First Christian Party, largely resided at Oneida Castle (Kanaʔalóhaleʔ), Daniel Bread's birthplace, twelve miles south of the easternmost section of Oneida Lake; while the sachems and their supporters, now organized as the "Pagan Party," resided at Oriskany (Old Oriske), eight miles west of present-day Rome, New York. This deep schism was never healed in New York, and, in 1805, the Oneida lands were partitioned officially by the two parties.[8]

Prior to Bread's birth in 1800, Skenandoah, or "Running Deer," a Susquehanna Indian adopted by the Oneidas, a reformed alcoholic and a devout follower of Kirkland, had served as a "spokesman" for the First Christian Party, made up of Oneida Christian converts, including Daniel Bread, who attended Kirkland's church. Unfortunately, most contemporary accounts picture this pinetree chief as the archetypal "noble savage," overstating Skenandoah's power and influence among the Oneidas. Using an accommodationist approach to white land pressures and following Kirkland's lead, Skenandoah signed most of the Oneida land cessions to the state in the 1780s and 1790s.[9] Consequently, by the 1790s, he had lost significant influence among his people.

Any Oneida Christian growing up at Oneida Castle could see that economic disparities had arisen. Their "spokesman" had "benefited" by his connections to the white power structure. He lived in a well-made house built in a Dutch style with a hearth on one side. His residence, elaborate for Oneidas of the time, was situated on the edge of the village, commanding an extensive view all round. The aged Skenandoah, who had become blind and who was perhaps over one hundred years old when he died, had in his home gifts from prominent whites, including an elegant silver pipe presented to him by Governor Daniel D. Tompkins of New York State.[10]

Skenandoah died in 1816 when Bread was only sixteen. The old chief's tragic fall from influence taught the youngster valuable lessons. Too much collaboration with outsiders could lose you respect within your own Indian community. Too much economic disparity with your neighbors would engender resentment, jealousies, and even charges of being a sell-out.

The Oneidas faced other problems besides political and class divisions in this period. Epidemics of yellow fever and increased cases of tuberculosis weakened and depopulated them.[11] Oneidas were especially affected by alcohol and alcohol-related problems in the first three decades of the nineteenth century.[12] After the Indians received their state annuities on June 1 of every year, some individuals began binge drinking, and at times, violence resulted. Alcoholism also led to excessive timber stripping on reservation lands to pay for drinks at the local tavern and deaths, caused when drunken Indians fell down and froze to death along the road on their way home in winter. The full effect on a child growing up in this dysfunctional setting cannot be measured. Significantly, Bread dealt with these same problems in his years as principal chief in Wisconsin.

Oneidas themselves readily admitted these problems. In 1810, in a poignant appeal to close the taverns and stop the alcohol trade in their midst for the sake of the children and the community's overall welfare, Christian (Chrisjohn/

Christjohn), an Oneida Indian, responded to a missionary by stating that he wanted a tavern removed from his community since it had caused "great injury to us." He added that "our warriors and *our children* will go to it." Christian went on, insisting: "The land is ours, and this tavern makes confusion among us. It breeds quarrels. In particular on the Lord's day, our men often stop there while on their way to church, and they cannot get away; and they often stop too in going from church."[13] Six years later, Skenandoah, just before his death, repeated much of Christian's observations, stating that alcohol had contributed to losses of parts of the Oneida homeland time and time again.[14]

Less than two years before Bread's birth, a Mohawk prophet arose along the Grand River in Ontario. In his interpretations of his visions, he claimed that the "Upholder of the Skies or Heavens" had been neglected by the Indians, and that, as a result, the Creator brought epidemics, famines, and unpleasant days upon the Iroquois. He urged the revival of ancient ceremonies that had been abandoned. The Mohawk prophet emphasized "temperance, universal love, domestic tranquillity," and respect and sympathy for one another. In his eclectic message, combining traditional and Christian teachings, he also advised the Indians not to reject openly all the teachings of their missionaries and to follow the Bible's words.[15]

A second holy man, Handsome Lake, the Seneca prophet, also stirred Iroquoia in 1799 and 1800, changing it forever. He was to preach the message of *Gaiwiio*, the Good Word, one that condemned whiskey, witchcraft, love potions, and abortion. All wrongdoers had to confess and repent their wickedness or be punished. Handsome Lake's three visions were to have a profound influence on the Iroquois, who were faced with disaster in the aftermath of the American Revolution. In part, the origins of the Handsome Lake religion stemmed from the splintering of the Iroquois Confederacy, substantial loss of Indian land, constant land pressures from whites, social disintegration as reflected in the increased alcoholism and murder rates, and growing economic dependence on the non-Indian world.[16]

Handsome Lake brought moral and social reform, advocating the punishment of wrongdoers: wife-beaters, drunkards, gamblers, witches, sinners. Although Handsome Lake never preached among the Oneidas, his message spread there. Handsome Lake combined his teaching with an emphasis on family values, condemning gossip, philandering, abortion, and alcohol, all of which were rampant among the Indians at the time. The Seneca prophet also promoted men's participation in horticulture, which traditionally had been the women's domain.

Julian Ursyn Niemcewicz, a snobbish Polish visitor to Oneida Castle in October 1805, sarcastically noted Handsome Lake's influence. The Pole praised what he referred to as the "pretended" prophet for helping to instill temperance, hard work, and racial separation to prevent the "total extinction of the Indian race."[17] It is important to point out that, although few Oneida men in New York plowed the fields in 1800, most Oneidas did so in Wisconsin after the removal. When Bread settled in Wisconsin, he became one of the more prosperous farmers in the Oneida community.

A little over four months after Bread's birth, John Maude, a British traveler with a curious bent, passed through Oneida Castle. Maude noted that the Oneida Reservation was twelve miles square and that six hundred Oneida Indians resided there. He stayed the night at Wemp's (Wemple's) Tavern, which served as a way station for travelers and a dispensing station for Indians buying alcohol. The Englishman commented on the riches of the Oneida territory. He described the Oneida-owned woods as being "excellent." These forest lands were filled with beech and sugar maple and provided an exquisite natural home for the "whip-poorwill and hoot-owl." Coming upon Oneida Castle, which was on the main New York State transportation route—the Western Inland Lock Navigation Canal and the Great Western Turnpike Road (also known as the Genesee or

Table 1
Oneida Indian Population in New York State, 1800-1855

1800	600
1805	750
1819	1,031
1839	578
1855	161

Based on traveler accounts by Maude and Niemcewicz cited in the bibliography; New York State Legislature, Assembly Document 90 (1819); Annual Reports of the United States Commissioner of Indian Affairs; and the New York State Census of 1855.

Seneca Turnpike)—Maude dined at a local inn on salmon caught in nearby Wood Creek. He then pointed out the "good mills, built for the Oneida Indians," an Oneida woman and youngster conversing in their native language, and "a boarded house, the only one I saw in the Castle."[18]

Two years later, Friedrich Rohde, a German-American geologist born near Cologne, Germany, visited the Oneidas, whom he estimated as being six hundred in number. His was a scientific expedition in which he sought to collect specimens of mineral deposits found in central and western New York. Citing a gazetteer, Rohde described this region as "one of the most productive in all America, because one acre produces 36 to 40 bushels of wheat, where otherwise a harvest of 25 bushels is regarded as considerable." Rohde spent the next week in and around the Oneida Reservation. With a scientific eye, he commented about the purity of the water as well as the rich fishery of the Oneida Lake-Fish Creek-Wood Creek area with its abundant supply of salmon and the extensive and varied types of trees—beech, fir, and maple—in this region. Rohde also pointed out that the Oneida Indians' concern for the forest and the fishery led them to stipulate that when the lands were "sold" at state treaties, "the woods for 1/2 mile wide on either side [of the lake] should not be cut down, because they believe that denuding the creek of woods would harm the fishing."[19]

The astute Rohde was not just making random thoughts. The Oneida concerns about preserving forest lands and about the productivity of the tribal fishery continued throughout the nineteenth century and were especially important to the council of chiefs once their government was reestablished in Wisconsin. Tribal leaders such as Bread had witnessed the despoliation of Indian lands in and around Oneida Lake and did not want to repeat the mistakes of the past. Unfortunately, even in Wisconsin later, Bread did not have the power to stop these same forces.[20]

Thus, both Indian and non-Indian observers of Oneida Territory in the first years of the nineteenth century, the formative period of Daniel Bread's life, described a society in crisis. Despite federal guarantees to protect the Oneidas in 1784 in the Treaty of Fort Stanwix as well as in the Treaty of Canandaigua and in the United States-Oneida Treaty of 1794, the Oneidas were dispossessed of nearly six million acres of their territory from 1785 to 1846 by state officials intent on building the Empire State on profits from Indian cessions.

Table 2
Population of Oneida and Madison Counties,
New York, 1790-1830

Year	Oneida	Madison
1790	1,891	——
1800	20,839	8,036
1810	30,634	25,141
1814	45,627	26,276
1820	50,997	32,208
1825	57,847	35,646
1830	71,326	39,038

Based on the New York State Census of 1855.

In 1790, less than two thousand non-Indians resided in what was left of Oneida Territory, now Oneida and Madison Counties; however, by 1825, over eighty-three thousand non-Indians lived in the two-county area. The Oneidas found themselves overwhelmed by transportation pressures brought by whites, rapid white settlement in and around their historic territory, social disintegration caused by alcohol, and intratribal rivalries that at times resulted in bitterness and even bloodletting.

These crises produced a spiritual searching for answers. Oneidas wondered whether their society would be able to cope or even survive, since they had lost such outstanding leaders as Good Peter, Beechtree, Captain John, and others who had tried to deal with earlier crises in the 1780s and 1790s. Few could predict the rise of Daniel Bread, who would try to fill this vacuum in Oneida leadership.

Chapter 3

Land, Land, Land

Bread's emergence as a major Oneida political leader stemmed from skills that he developed well before his permanent relocation in the West. His fighting skills as a young warrior during the War of 1812 had helped him achieve recognition; however, in the decade and a half after this conflict, his language skills helped him attain the rank of pinetree chief in his Oneida community.[1] As one of the few Oneida leaders who was literate in English, Bread could serve as a vital go-between with the white world. His ability was not just in reading and writing English, but in translating it into the various Iroquoian languages required by the Oneida chiefs. Indeed, most of the petitions and memorials by the Oneidas in the decades after 1829 were drafted and signed by Bread. Almost all of the other Oneida leaders before the Civil War signed documents with a mark, rather than a signature.

The young chief was also the most renowned Oneida orator of his day. Lewis Henry Morgan observed in 1851: "By the cultivation and exercise of this capacity [of oratory], was opened the pathway to distinction; and the chief or warrior gifted with its magical power could elevate himself as rapidly, as he who gained renown upon the warpath."[2] This skill served Bread well in New York as well as later in Wisconsin.

Bread's speaking abilities augmented his role as a runner, bringing news and information back to New York from Michigan Territory, and gave him a position of particular influence at the council fires of the people of the Standing Stone. The importance of runners in Iroquois history should not be underestimated. They were not merely gifted athletes intent on winning personal rewards. Iroquois runners summoned councils, conveyed intelligence from nation to nation, and warned of impending danger. It is also important to note that the Iroquois use the term *runner* to describe a person who serves the council as a conduit for the conduct of essential business, and who is accorded respect as a community leader worthy of other higher positions of authority and prestige in the nation. Significantly, runners even today convey official messages and carry stringed wampum to symbolize their official role, diplomatic protocol, and/or truth.[3] In 1820, Bread was delegated to serve as a runner, bringing valuable information about Michigan Territory back to New York.

Bread was, nevertheless, an early opponent of the removal of the Oneidas from New York. In one of his more famous speeches before the governor of New York State, Bread clearly expressed this view:

Father, the white men are powerful and they are rich. You can turn the rivers of the waters; you can dig away the mountains; why then do you want the little spot that we have? It is but a little time since, and we possessed the whole country; now you have gained all but a few spots. Why will you not permit us to remain?[4]

Reluctantly, Bread came to accept removal as a fait accompli and was the Indian most responsible for the overall administration of the move to Michigan Territory. He stayed behind in New York to accomplish this result and helped evacuate the Oneidas from New York, guiding them west, arranging their transportation, and providing temporary shelter and food for each wave of Oneida emigrants to Wisconsin.[5] This service to the Oneida Nation as a whole, not just to the Episcopal or Methodist Indian relocatee, clearly brought him respect and political power among his people and won admiration from government officials and missionaries alike. Later, in 1835, representatives of the First Christian Party praised Bread for his wisdom and vigilance in helping the Oneida Nation secure "title to our lands," establishing "a great portion of our people located at Green Bay."[6] The same year, the Episcopal missionary Solomon Davis reiterated the Oneidas' view of Bread, as a man of "unbinding integrity," who, the clergyman insisted, always expressed "kindness to his people."[7]

One cannot completely fathom the pressures facing the Oneidas to make the decision to move and resettle in Michigan Territory. In 1805, Robert Sutcliff, an English traveler who visited the Oneidas by following the route of the Genesee Turnpike, predicted that this thoroughfare, one that became the first state road, "may, in a few years, be as thickly inhabited as some parts of Europe are at this time."[8] Sutcliff's prediction was an accurate one since the Oneidas were "convinced" to sell over sixty-five thousand acres of their remaining homeland between 1805 and 1817.[9]

Thurlow Weed, the prominent New York State politician, wrote in 1818 about the pressures on the Oneidas and other Iroquois. In his newspaper the *Albany Register*, Weed insisted that the Indians in New York were "beset by greedy and unprincipled advisers" and their grievances were "unredressed." He sadly noted that "if they meet in council with our countrymen, debate invariably ends in the abrogation of some right or privilege, or the ceding of additional territory." Weed concluded: "The condition of the Six Nations, residing within this state, is truly lamentable. Their reservations have become very valuable, and every species of intrigue is put in operation to wrest these lands from the confiding occupants." Reading his crystal ball, Weed predicted that, in a "few years," whites "will undoubtedly drive them from these possessions."[10]

Six years later, Weed, while traveling west by stagecoach, passed through Oneida Castle, stopping at Vernon and Westmoreland, New York. The politician-journalist, who later helped found the Whig Party in New York State, presented a depressing portrait of what had befallen the Oneidas as a result of what he sarcastically dubbed the "advantages of civilization." Weed wrote in his journal that this "civilization" process had contributed to undermining Oneida existence by introducing taverns that freely dispensed whiskey and created Indian dependence instead of self-sufficiency: "Full two thirds of the tribe had ceased to hunt or to fish, or to cultivate their lands, than which none more fertile were to be found in the State. Large numbers of both sexes were idling about the tavern, all or nearly all of them endeavoring to sell some trinket for the purpose of whiskey." Importantly, Weed wrote that this "process of demoralization went on until the few who did not die prematurely were induced to emigrate to Wisconsin."[11]

Pressures for Oneida land cessions began a decade and a half before Bread's birth. In state "treaties" at Fort Herkimer in 1785 and at Fort Schuyler in 1788, the Oneidas were dispossessed of over five million acres, lands south of Oneida Castle to the Pennsylvania border. By 1794, the Oneidas still had nearly a million acres of land left in their homeland; nevertheless, pressures continued to accelerate. The year after two federal treaties of 1794 guaranteed their remaining Oneida land base, these Indians "ceded" a portion of their land on the south side of Oneida Lake and half-mile sections along the north shore, totaling 246,165.13 acres. In clear violations of the federal Trade and Intercourse Acts, New York State officials continued to negotiate for the Oneidas' homeland. Except for state treaties of 1798 and 1802, no federal commissioner required under these laws was present, and no United States Senate treaty ratification occurred in the thirteen other state treaties with the Oneidas made from 1807 through 1829.[12]

Taking advantage of the wide cracks in the Oneida polity, Albany officials periodically played on Indian weaknesses to the state's advantage. At this desperate time of crisis, individual family survival took precedence over Oneida national and cultural integrity. Any young Oneida boy growing up, and brought up on stories of past Iroquois glory, could not ignore the present conditions and the weakness and ineffectiveness of Indian leadership in meeting the challenges of the early nineteenth century.

By 1809, the chiefs of the First Christian Party pleaded with Albany policymakers, asking them for a moratorium on future land cessions. Writing to Albany policymakers after another "cession" of 7,500 acres of their lands, they posed an intriguing question. They asked the white officials whether they would "like that we [Oneidas] should buy the town of Albany from a few of any white men we could persuade to sell it. And we, then come and take it, whether you be willing or not [?]" The Oneida chiefs answered their own question: "You would not like this and we do not like it." Insisting that both Indians and whites were children of a common Creator, they poignantly observed: "We feel when we are hurt, just like white men."[13] Yet, these cessions continued as a result of state land pressures and the actions of individual Indians such as John Denny, not a tribal official but an Oneida Indian entrepreneur who had become a United States citizen. He operated an inn and had choice lands along the Genesee Turnpike. Despite threats to his life by other Indians because he was seen as a traitor, Denny illegally signed off on land cessions well into the 1820s, reserving choice lots for himself and his family members.[14]

On January 22, 1816, Alexander Dallas, the United States

secretary of war, wrote Daniel D. Tompkins, the governor of New York State and soon-to-be-elected vice president of the United States, about the future of the Iroquois residing within the empire state. Dallas saw these Indians, all allied to American interests as a result of the Treaty of Canandaigua in 1794, as serving the United States as well as their own tribal interests by agreeing to relocate out of New York to the west, specifically Michigan Territory: "it is believed that the settlement of a friendly tribe of Indians in that part of the country, bound by the ties of interest and friendship to the United States, will have a beneficial influence upon the conduct of their savage friends in the event of another war with England."[15]

In the aftermath of the War of 1812, during which Oneidas excelled in the defense of the American flag, these Indians were now presented with federal pressures of removal westward. No longer could the Oneidas expect any federal support to remain in New York State. Indeed, with the nomination and appointment of John C. Calhoun as secretary of war in President James Monroe's cabinet in 1817, Oneidas, almost as a whole, saw that their days in their central New York homeland were numbered. Now federal officials began an active dialogue with all of the Six Nations about removal. This new policy was pushed by prominent clergymen such as Jedidiah Morse and Bishop John Henry Hobart, land speculators such as former Congressman David A. Ogden, territorial governors such as Lewis Cass of Michigan Territory, and so-called local experts "on the ground" such as Indian subagent Jasper Parrish and Eleazer Williams, the newly appointed Episcopal catechist-missionary to the Oneidas. Calhoun and Monroe attempted to convince the Six Nations to accept removal. Ogden lusted after Indian lands and suggested removal westward or concentration of all of the Iroquois to the Allegany Indian Reservation in the isolated southwestern corner of New York State. Morse, with long experience among the Iroquois and as a sometime federal policymaker, believed migration westward was for the Indians' own good. Indeed, it was Morse who first suggested Green Bay and environs in Michigan Territory as a possible alternative for site resettlement of the Six Nations.[16]

As early as February 1, 1817, Charles Jouett, a federal Indian agent in Illinois Territory, saw the possibility of moving the Six Nations to the upper Midwest as a way to "destroy the British influence with the Indians north and west of the settlements" and also free up rich agricultural lands in New York for white settlement.[17] Later, in 1820, Lewis Cass, the territorial governor of Michigan, favored this move: "Their [Six Nations'] habits and pecuniary ties, which bind them to the United States would ensure their fidelity, and they would act as a check upon the Winnebagos, the worst affected of any Indians upon our border."[18] Hence, land interests in New York and national defense concerns converged to force the Oneidas westward. The religious rhetoric of helping the Indians escape the ravages of white frontier society, with such attendant vices as alcohol, covered up the real reasons to relocate the Oneidas.

With this new policy of removal presented to the Indians as "inevitable," the Oneida First Christian Party chiefs wrote Governor De Witt Clinton in November, 1818. Although expressing annoyance at being forced into removal, the sachems and warriors of the Oneida Nation petitioned Governor Clinton of New York, asking for time to prepare for the inevitable migration westward. Insisting that "the most respectable part" of the Oneida Nation had formerly been opposed to this course of action and the issue had become "the source of many quarrels between individuals and the nation, these leaders expressed their understanding "that the government of the United States has determined on our removal." They were particularly "grieved" by this change of federal policy that "threatened" them with expulsion from their remaining lands because they had rendered such valuable service to the Americans in the

Revolutionary War. The Oneida leadership requested that Clinton help them intervene with the federal government to delay the removal until they were better prepared to move.[19]

Between 1818 and 1821, Bread became a major figure in the Oneida polity. By the latter date, he was putting his mark on documents as a "chief" of the First Christian Party.[20] With this party's ceding of another 562 acres in 1815 and the rival Pagan Party, now known as the Second Christian Party, exchanging 1,356 for 678 acres with the state, many Oneidas came to the sad realization that they could not prevent removal.[21] Although Bread eventually came to this conclusion, he was no advocate of this policy and reluctantly agreed to it. This difficult decision helped shape his future course. His entire career in Wisconsin after 1829 was premised upon preventing an Oneida removal from the environs of Green Bay to west of Missouri into the Indian Territory, an alternative considered and pushed by some Wisconsin and federal officials. Bread's final acceptance of removal from New York only came in 1824 when he signed the New York State–Oneida Treaty, one of three major state accords he signed between 1824 and 1829.[22]

In 1816, Eleazer Williams arrived at the Oneida Reservation. A member of the St. Regis Mohawk band, Williams was appointed by Bishop Hobart as a lay reader, catechist, and schoolmaster for the Oneidas. Besides his role in the conversion of the First Christian Party from Presbyterianism to Episcopalianism, he secured the conversion of members of the old Pagan Party who publicly professed Christianity, becoming known as members of the Second Christian Party, who ceded land to the Mohawk missionary to build an Episcopal Church. Yet, Williams's greatest influence and support remained with a few influential members of the First Christian Party. As the historian Karim Tiro has recently written, "The image of him [Eleazer Williams] leading hundreds of Oneidas to Wisconsin is simply inaccurate. It was not Williams' pull that brought the Oneidas to Wisconsin so much as the push provided by large-scale Canal Era immigration of non-natives to the Oneida homeland." Tiro pointed out that "Williams' principal accomplishment was to gather about him a handful of Oneida supporters who provided the removal enterprise with a veneer of credibility, however thin."[23] Indeed, as early as October 1821, Williams had alienated a sizable number of Oneidas with his meddling and his overbearing style.[24] In leaving New York, the Oneidas were not merely pulled by the charisma of Williams but by the sense they had few other alternatives to deal with land pressures, fractionated political behavior, the whiskey trade, and poverty.

Williams pushed for removal of the Oneidas and other members of the Six Nations from New York. Despite his specific instructions simply to help the Oneidas get the best deal they could to secure their future, Williams soon saw himself as a self-styled Moses, albeit an unstable and corruptible one. White federal, state, church, and business leaders saw him as a convenient agent to get the Iroquois west and/or to secure their remaining lands in New York.[25] Williams, it should be noted, was closely tied to and in the pay of the Ogden Land Company in his removal efforts.[26]

In the summer of 1820, Bread, the "runner," was chosen as a delegate to explore Michigan Territory and negotiate with the Menominees for land in the Fox River Valley. The delegation included three Oneidas, including Bread, a Mohawk, and missionary Williams, who were sent west to negotiate with the Menominee Indians. When they reached Detroit, they found they couldn't get water "passage up the Lakes." They were even more disappointed when they learned that John Bowyer, the Indian agent at Green Bay, had concluded a federal treaty with the Menominees for the very same lands—the Fox River Valley from Lake Winnebago to Green Bay—that the New York Indians had been promised.[27] Before this treaty could be finalized and ratified by the United States Senate, Bowyer died; however, the Oneidas began to fear that if the United States secured these lands by treaty before the Oneidas could negotiate with the Menominees, they would not have much choice about which lands and/or the size of the land base they could obtain. At Detroit, they met with the missionary-geographer-federal commissioner Jedidiah Morse, who was at the time investigating the conditions of the Indians nationwide for Secretary of War Calhoun. The Indians informed Morse that they had misgivings about federal governmental officials and their intentions.[28]

Bowyer's secret negotiations with the Indians of Michigan Territory had accentuated Oneida fears about their future. Once again, they suspected that Washington officials were "selling them down the river." Memories of broken federal promises—the alliance of the American Revolution, the Treaty of Fort Stanwix (1784), the Treaty of Canandaigua (1794), and the Oneida Treaty (1794)—weighed on Oneida leaders' minds and required them to take the initiative to prevent another disaster. Morse assured them that they should proceed and negotiate with the Menominees, a move recommended by Monroe and Calhoun.

While at Detroit, Bread and the Six Nations delegation there sent a formal protest on August 12, 1820, to Lewis Cass, Michigan's territorial governor, as well as to the territorial secretary. Writing to Cass, they insisted that they wished peace as well as "a place to set one foot on peaceably and to live in friendship with our brothers of the west and our Great Father the President." They asked for a fair resolution, for President Monroe to "remove these obstacles out of the way that your children" might benefit and gain respect for the rule of law.[29] In the second letter the same day, the delegates, except for missionary Williams who did not sign the letter, indicated that the Indians had decided to return to Buffalo, asking the territorial secretary to help them obtain passage back to New York.[30] Soon after, they secured passage and returned to Buffalo and home to Oneida Castle. Much to their pleasure, they were informed that the Bowyer treaty had failed to win support in Washington.

Bread did not return to Michigan Territory for another six years. One can only speculate what happened in the aftermath of the exploring party's return in 1820. With Williams serving as an adviser, John Anthony (Antone), John Skenandoah (Skenando), Cornelius Baird, Neddy Archiquette (Otsiquette), and other leaders of the First Christian Party went west in 1821 and negotiated treaties that year and in 1822 with the Menominees and Winnebagos—treaties allowing for the establishment of two Oneida settlements there.[31]

Bread and Williams grew apart after 1822, long before the Oneida chief helped ostracize the clergyman from the Duck Creek community in 1832. Williams continued to play a role and interfered in Oneida affairs until 1832 but was increasingly marginalized by his actions and by the reactions of the Oneidas to them. Although Bread clearly tried to create distance between himself and Williams, at other times he defended the Mohawk cleric. The two apparently used each other. As Williams used the Oneidas for fame and profit, Bread learned from Williams about power and the importance of building political connections to the white world.

On April 5, 1824, Iroquois warriors wrote Secretary Calhoun, making it clear that Williams had no authority to speak for them or their nations.[32] Two years later, when Williams was accused of fraud because of his involvement in New York State–Mohawk negotiations, Bread and the Oneida chiefs of the First Christian Party defended him but clearly indicated that he had no power of attorney to negotiate for them.[33]

There were several reasons for this growing split. The Mohawk missionary's acquisitiveness became more apparent as he obtained special benefits, including land in one New York State treaty.[34] More importantly, Williams became suspect and his motives were questioned because of his association with the nefarious David A. Ogden in the removal westward.[35] Williams also ingratiated himself with the power elite of Green Bay and built his ties through marriage to the Franco-Menominee Indian world of Brown County, all of which further alienated him from the Oneidas.[36]

When some powerful Menominees such as Oshkosh began to challenge the legitimacy of the two treaties signed in 1821 and 1822 with the New York Indians, Williams's ability and loyalty to the Oneidas were called into question by even more Oneidas. Oshkosh labeled these accords as fraudulent documents and attempted to void them by petitioning to Washington. Many Oneidas also began to question Williams's skills and his impartiality since they had entrusted him with these important negotiations. Moreover, he was never able to win full acceptance of these treaties from Washington officials.[37]

Consequently, against the backdrop of Williams's declining influence in the mid-1820s, Bread's role expanded. Bread became the key Oneida in the difficult administration of the Indian removal to Michigan Territory. Fortunately, we have an affidavit of his closest Oneida political ally, Henry Powless, describing Bread's activities in the period 1824 to 1838. On August 26, 1824, Bread went to Albany, spending two weeks negotiating with New York State officials. In order to pay for the Indian lands obtained in Michigan Territory in 1821 and 1822, the Oneidas ceded two tracts, totaling 1,900 acres of land of their central New York homeland; in return, New York State gave them $1,150 and a $300 annuity.[38]

In late 1826 and early 1827, Bread, now serving as chief more than as delegate, was placed in charge of twenty-five or thirty Oneidas whom he escorted to Buffalo, where they embarked on lake packet boats for Green Bay. In his new position as pinetree chief and as the Oneida agent in charge of administering Oneida removal, Bread helped resettle them in Michigan Territory. He also brought supplies to the Oneidas already based there, spending the entire winter with his tribesmen exploring the territory.[39] He learned about Menominee discontent over the 1821 and 1822 treaties with the New York Indians, a major problem that he was forced to deal with for another decade.

Bread was also involved in two other state treaty negotiations. On February 13, 1829, in Albany, the First Christian Party Oneidas "ceded" lands west of Oneida Creek and north of the Seneca Turnpike, a sale of 1,810 acres of land. The Oneidas were to receive $1,500; two hundred of these acres were to be sold off and the profits, plus 6 percent interest, were to be used to create an Indian educational fund to support a teacher among the Oneidas in Michigan Territory. Shortly after Bread relocated to the west, he returned and signed a state treaty in October 1829 at Albany that ceded an additional six hundred acres for a $1,000 payment.[40]

Bread's role in these negotiations, which were never ratified by the United States Senate, cannot be completely ascertained because no formal transcript of the proceedings exists; however, a careful analysis of the provisions of the treaties and the young chief's later actions in protesting the accords reveal much about them. The 1824 state treaty reserved two hundred acres for Eleazer Williams and his family and two hundred acres for the Denny family.[41] The October 1829 accord awarded ten acres of land to John Denny. Besides payoffs to these Indians, both the February and October 1829 state treaties provided title to lands totaling 150 acres to two whites, Timothy Jenkins and Peter Augustine, who had been leaseholders on Oneida lands.[42] Oneida lands that were "bought" by the state in 1829 for eight dollars per acre were almost immediately sold off for twenty-two dollars per acre soon after their "purchase."[43]

Dependent on state annuities to survive in Michigan Territory, Bread could not offend the powers-that-be in Albany. He had no leverage to demand overturning treaties because the omnipotent Albany Regency, the Van Buren machine, controlled New York politics throughout the 1820s and 1830s. He could not force these officials to return lands to these Indians, stop their push for tribal land cessions, or even require them to pay out annuities "guaranteed" in past state-Oneida treaties. To make matters worse, he could not even rely on certain missionaries to intercede on the Oneidas' behalf. Distrustful of the scheming Williams, Bread had previously protested the actions of the Northern Missionary Society, the major religious organization that had obtained a lease from the Oneidas in a state treaty in 1798 but whose title to these lands was suspiciously "confirmed" by state actions in the 1820s.[44]

The skilled Bread attempted two methods to counter these moves, although both strategies failed to achieve the necessary relief. After spending the first year in Michigan Territory, he wrote Silas Wright, then comptroller of New York. In the letter, Bread indicated that the Oneidas were "satisfied" with their new home in Michigan Territory, and that "the country is well calculated for the home of the Indians." Thanking the comptroller for his "kindness and liberality toward us," Bread indicated that in a short time "our condition will be much better here than it had ever been in the State of New York." In effect, Bread was begging for prompt payment of the annuities under past state treaties.[45]

In seeking over $17,000 compensation under the two 1829 treaties, the Oneidas under Bread's leadership appealed to the New York State legislature. With the aid of their Episcopal missionary, Solomon Davis, they pointed out that the enabling legislation required "a fair price for the lands" and they maintained that an "injustice had been done to them in the state surveyor's appraisal." They insisted: "The State of New-York is rich, the red man is poor—in his need he but asks justice from the full hand."[46] Instead of granting compensation to the nation, the legislative committee praised "the patriarchal influence of Daniel Bread" for his Herculean influences in administering and straightening out the "embarrassment" heretofore attending the removal to Green Bay; the legislature then allocated some moneys—$1,400—to reimburse Bread personally.[47] Frustrated, the Oneidas continued to appeal for further relief from the legislature at least through the Civil War.[48]

Sadly for Bread and his Oneida people, the same pressures that had forced them to leave their central New York homeland were to reappear in the west. Instead of dark clouds coming from Albany, two new storm fronts were on the horizon: one arising in and around Green Bay, namely the appointment of Indian agent Samuel C. Stambaugh, and the other from Washington in the form of Andrew Jackson. The two unfavorable weather patterns were to converge in the summer of 1830 and nearly bring the ruination of the Oneida Nation.

Part 2
Duck Creek

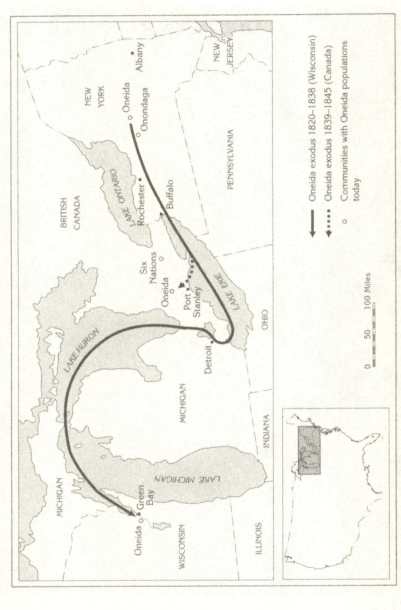

Oneida removal to Wisconsin and Ontario, 1820–1845. From a map by Ben Simpson.

Chapter 4

Trapped in the Land of the Wild Rice People

In June 1829, Chief Daniel Bread, accompanied by his mother, Dinah, his wife, Electa, his son John, and possibly four other young children, left Oneida Castle headed for Green Bay.[1] Chief Bread was the leader of an emigrating party of 106 Oneida Indians.[2] Bread, a seasoned traveler who had journeyed this route two times before, had planned for this evacuation for upwards of five years. The Oneidas depended on the abilities of their young chief to bring them safely to Michigan Territory, an unknown and scary world to these refugee Indians.[3]

The Oneidas had reason to fear what lay ahead in the environs of Green Bay. As Alice Smith, the distinguished historian of Wisconsin, has written, the "state had its full quota of speculators." She added that by 1830 "Green Bay probably furnished as good a sampling as could be found anywhere of local land speculators."[4] What had been a sleepy fur depot, largely composed of Franco-Menominees with fewer than five hundred people and fifty houses in 1820, was soon to become transformed.[5]

Although Green Bay still had the flavor of a fur trade and military frontier at the time of Bread's arrival, the city's fathers, including Daniel Whitney and James Duane Doty, engaged themselves in laying out and selling lots across from Fort Howard, establishing mercantile enterprises, building lumber mills and cutting timber, and promoting transportation schemes that would further their land speculative efforts. By 1832, two roads had already been laid out by soldiers from Fort Howard: the first following the Fox River to Fond du Lac at Lake Winnebago and thence to the Fox-Wisconsin Rivers portage, and the other running southeast from Fort Howard to Manitowoc and thence along the shore of Lake Michigan to Chicago. It was along these two corridors that the Territory of Wisconsin, established in 1836 (carved out of Michigan Territory), developed, and it was no coincidence that two Green Bay entrepreneurs, Doty and his first cousin, Morgan L. Martin, were to lead the way.[6]

Soon after his arrival in 1829, Chief Bread realized that the Oneidas had been "snookered" into coming to the environs of Green Bay. The same transportation, land, and timber pressures that his Oneida tribesmen had faced in New York were apparent in Michigan Territory. Less than two years later, Bread, in his most famous speech in council, attended by Michigan's territorial governor, reflected on the broken promises made by federal, state, and territorial officials as well as by the missionary societies. Bread claimed that he had always feared that the promises given to the Oneidas in New York about a permanent home in Wisconsin were empty ones: "We have just settled in this country; have hardly laid down the packs from our shoulders and recovered from the fatigue of our journey here, when you wish us again to remove. It is discouraging," Bread maintained, not only for the new arrivals but for "those left behind." He asked why the United States government, which has "taught us to cultivate our lands," now wanted the Oneidas to move again. "If we are like the feather, we may soon be blown beyond the Rocky Mountains." Distressed about working lands that might be taken from them, Bread wondered why the whites needed any more lands from the

Indians since they had taken so much already, amounting to "a greater country than Great Britain," and had allowed Indians "but a few spots." Adamantly insisting that he and his people did not want to move beyond the Mississippi to lands he claimed were occupied by the Six Nations' former enemies, Bread pleaded, stating that the Oneidas were a loyal people who had no objection to living at peace with their white neighbors.[7]

The Indian world that the Oneidas encountered in the environs of Green Bay in the early 1820s was also a very strange and forbidding one. Although these new lands were on the same latitude as their homeland in New York, the Oneidas were now face-to-face with culturally distinct indigenous peoples, who still relied on hunting and gathering for their subsistence, in addition to mixed Franco-Indian populations of Roman Catholic faith and French trappers with economic ties to the old fur port at La Baye, dating back to the end of the seventeenth century.

The Menominees, the "People of the Wild Rice," had first been French allies in the colonial wars and then served the British in the Revolutionary War and the War of 1812 against American interests. This Algonkian-speaking group had successfully secured, through war, the vast territory around Green Bay and much of the Fox River Valley from the Siouan-speaking Winnebagos (Ho-Chunks), whom they had pushed westward and southwestward, where they remained. It is important to note that, despite their military prowess, the Menominees shared joint occupancy on some of their lands with the Ojibwa, Sac, Winnebago, and Sioux Indians that extended as far as the Mississippi River. Moreover, the Menominees had been involved as allies of the Three Fires People—Ojibwas, Ottawas, and Potawatomis—enemies of the Iroquois in the late seventeenth century, a fact that did not help matters in the early-nineteenth-century negotiations with the Six Nations. Now, the Menominees, a proud and powerful people, had to deal with the Long Knives and their Indian allies, the so-called New York Indians, who, besides the Iroquoian-speaking Six Nations, included Algonkian-speaking Stockbridge and Brothertown Indians.[8]

Although a remarkably adaptive people, the Menominees faced a major crisis after 1815. They feared American reprisals because of their alliance with the British and major involvement in British victories at Prairie du Chien (Fort Shelby) and Mackinac Island in 1814. In the wake of the war, four American warships landed at Green Bay on August 8, 1816, and soon an American fort, Fort Howard, was established nearby to counter British fur interests to the north and the British navy on the Great Lakes. Moreover, the historian Patricia Ourada has written that after the war, "Menominee leadership was on the verge of collapse." Wee-kah, a chief, was killed in battle in 1814; Tomah, the Menominees' "grand old orator of the tribe and tutor for the future leaders," died in 1818; and their principal chief, Cha-wa-non, who had been chief since 1778, died in 1821 at the age of 100.[9]

The coming of the United States military brought American entrepreneurial interests, most significantly John Jacob Astor's American Fur Company. Tensions arose between Astor's men and the French and Franco-Indians with ties to the British fur interests based in the Lake Superior country; later, however, many of the major traders, such as the Grignon and Porlier families along with the British John Lawe, saw the great profits to be made by an association with the American Fur Company. Much of the attention of company officials and their political allies in the environs of Green Bay would turn to land and land speculation by the 1820s and after. In this time of change, during the two decades after the War of 1812, farming replaced fur trading as the major occupation of the region. While the small trappers were constantly complaining about declining fur sources, an elite developed, comprised of the older major fur trade families, headed by John Lawe and Augustin Grignon, and the new American entrepreneurs, Whitney and Doty, tied to the American Fur Company. This emerging elite had dreams of making Green Bay the major center on

Trapped in the Land of the Wild Rice People					47

the upper midwestern American frontier.[10] In the age of the Erie Canal, completed in 1825, they envisioned a navigable water route from Green Bay on Lake Michigan to the Mississippi River. This would result in a continuous waterway from Green Bay to New Orleans, ensuring the future success of "Ancien La Baye," making it one of the most important and prosperous cities of the United States. However, there was one major problem, namely how to wrest it from the Indians, be they Menominees, Winnebagos, or the new indigenous people in town—the New York Indians.[11]

Much to the Oneidas' surprise, the same forces (as well as the same people) at work in New York State were soon manifest in Wisconsin. In the 1790s, Astor's men had shifted much of their fur enterprise in central New York to land speculation. In the 1820s, with declining fur sources in Wisconsin, the agents of Astor's American Fur Company once again switched their focus from the fur trade to land acquisition. Importantly, many of the original white settlers of the Fox River Valley, the vicinity of the Oneida lands, were from central New York State, the Oneida homeland. With the building of the Erie Canal route from 1817 onward, completed in 1825, many central New Yorkers, including the well-connected Doty, sought their fortune on the Wisconsin frontier. Hence, the land rush that affected the Oneidas in New York was soon repeated in almost the exact way in their new Wisconsin home.[12]

While this "big picture" was largely unknown to most Oneidas at the time, Bread clearly understood the forces at work and the unsure nature of Oneida existence in Wisconsin in the 1820s and 1830s, but he had little power to change external white politics. Bread was especially distrustful of so-called friends of the Indians. Throughout the 1820s and after, he was especially suspicious of missionary Williams and his assistant Ellis because of their increasing ties to the Green Bay power elite, centered at Christ Episcopal Church of Green Bay, whose vestrymen included John Arndt, Henry Baird, as well as Doty, Ellis, Lawe, and Whitney. Fearful of challenging them, Bread carefully attempted to deal with them in a delicate manner for four decades until his death in 1873.[13]

As a chief, Bread had to deal with problems generated by the negotiations of Williams and the New York Indians with the Menominees and Winnebagos in 1821 and 1822. The New York Indians, in August 1821 and again in September 1822, had made agreements of joint occupancy with the Menominee and Winnebago Indians. In the first treaty in 1821, the New York Indians paid $1,500 for a small tract of land in the area of the Fox River between the Menominee and Winnebago villages. In the second treaty in 1822, the New York Indians paid $3,950 in goods, receiving from the Menominees and Winnebagos joint occupancy with the two Indian nations of 6,720,000 acres of land, an area 140 miles in length and 75 miles in width, a vast territory lying between Green Bay, Sturgeon Bay, and the Fox River.[14] If the lands of the two treaties were combined, according to historian David R. M. Beck, the New York Indians in effect received the right to jointly occupy these lands at a "steal," namely for a penny, they would receive 13.4 million acres of land! In the past, the Menominees and Winnebagos had made similar accords of joint occupation with other Indian nations. Therefore, the 1821 and 1822 accords cannot simply be looked at just in terms of the financial consideration or in the framework of western contract law. Beck appears to have overstated his case because there were other tribal reasons for these western Indians' generosity.[15]

Menominee protests against the two treaties were led by Oshkosh and Josette Carron, who claimed that their nation had no principal chief at the time of the signings of the two accords. Moreover, the French trappers and their families on the newly purchased land feared that they would lose out and be thrown off lands soon to be occupied by the New York Indians.[16] These fur trappers, as well as the Menominees and the New York Indians, began lobbying in earnest to protect their interests. On March 13, 1823, President

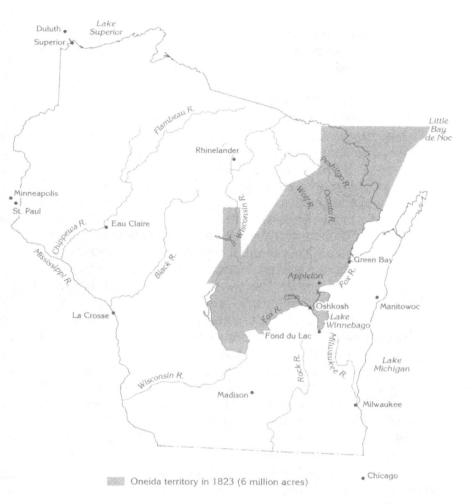

"New York Indian" lands in Michigan Territory in 1823: Lands jointly occupied with Menominees and Winnebagos under the Treaties of 1821 and 1822. Sources: Oneida Nation of Indians of Wisconsin.

Monroe recognized the New York Indians' right to occupy two million acres of this land; the president's decision, one which he had modified from his initial determination of six million acres, came after intensive lobbying by Ogden Land Company interests who knew that few Oneidas and other Iroquois would leave their New York lands and come to Green Bay if there wasn't a sizable land base to entice them. The more members of the Six Nations who would migrate to Wisconsin, the more likely Ogden and his associates could purchase Indian lands in New York because they held the preemption rights to much of the Iroquois land base in the Empire State.[17]

The Menominee and Winnebago leaders saw the 1821 and 1822 treaties as fraudulent. They further presented these accords as going against Menominee custom because no principal chief signed the two treaties. The Menominees later claimed that, although Pine Shooter (Ocquo-ne-naw) and other chiefs and war chiefs had signed the treaty, only a "great chief" could cede their land. With the death of the great chief Cha-wa-non, Oshkosh's grandfather, they insisted that no Menominee chief had the authority to sell land. They attempted to void the provisions of the treaties of 1821 and 1822. The Oneidas tried to counter these arguments, insisting that the treaties were legally binding and that the land base acquired was purposefully large to encourage all of the Six Nations in New York to emigrate to Wisconsin, a move encouraged by the federal government and New York State officials, as well as land speculators and missionaries of the age.[18]

In 1830 and early 1831, Calvin Colton, an eastern theologian and journalist, visited the relocated New York Indians in Michigan Territory, later accompanying them on their lobbying trips to Washington, D.C. His is an extraordinary account, one quite sympathetic to the Oneida and Stockbridge Indians, that clearly shows what happened between 1822 and 1831. To Colton, the entire controversy between the New York Indians and the original Indian inhabitants of the Green Bay area, the Menominees and the Winnebagos, was a conscious policy whereby "one set of Indians was set in array against the other, for the destruction of the rights of both" since the ultimate aim was to create a state out of Indian lands ceded in Michigan Territory. Colton noted that the New York Indians acquired a large territory far away from white settlement at the recommendation of the United States. He astutely observed:

The white man came. He fixed his eyes on this desirable country, and coveted it. But could he lift the title of the New York Indians? On examination, he discovered "a flaw in the indictment." It could be shown, that the title covered an unreasonable extent of territory. Consequently there must have been fraud in the negotiations. The title must be impeached. The wild tribes [Menominee and Winnebago Indians] must be alarmed; they must be told, that these New York Indians have caught them in a snare, and will ultimately eject them entirely from their own country; and that this is their intent. They must be urged to sue for the recovery of their territory, which the Government will undoubtedly grant, through our instance. And when this is accomplished, we can purchase of these wild Indians on our own terms, and without difficulty. That is: we can manage, that the Government shall do it for us, with the view of forming this North-West Territory into a new State.[19]

Bread and his Stockbridge counterparts, John Metoxen and John Quinney, fully understood this strategy, as their later statements before the federal commissioners in 1830 attest. Throughout the crisis, they did not take on the Menominees or Winnebagos as enemies but attempted to seek an accommodation—compromise and peaceful relations—in their discussions. With a larger view of governmental-Indian affairs gained from their tragic experiences in New York State, these leaders of the New York Indians understood that the forces at work in Michigan Territory did not originate simply from speeches at Menominee or Winnebago tribal councils but in meetings among powerful whites in Green Bay and Washington. Bread had also seen how Indian divisions in New York had contributed to Oneida removal, and the Stockbridge people had been removed at least two other times from their original Mohican homeland in the Hudson Valley of New York. All feared the renewed talk of removal heard once again as a result of the election of President Jackson.

While this debate was raging in the summer of 1823, the first Oneidas began arriving from New York and settling on this disputed land. Led by Neddy Archiquette, a chief of the First Christian Party, they took up residency near Little Chute on the Fox River. In 1825, another wave of Oneida emigrants left New York and settled at Duck Creek. This later settlement, which was just a few miles west of Green Bay on lands "8 or 9 miles wide and 12 miles long," with extensive fish and fowl in its environs, was named after the stream that flows through it, and, to this day, is the home of the Oneida Nation of Indians of Wisconsin. Later, Oneidas from the Little Chute community consolidated with this Duck Creek settlement.[20]

In the midst of a dense forest of pine, oak, chestnut, and maple, these Oneidas carved out a new home in the 1820s, struggling to survive, ironically in the manner of most Wisconsin pioneers of the time. Having come from the same latitude in upstate New York, they had been conditioned to overcome the harshness of winters; however, they were unprepared for events emanating out of Green Bay, Detroit, and Washington that threatened their continued existence as a people.

With a carefully worked-out strategy of survival, to prevent removal from Duck Creek to Indian Territory, Bread even sought help from former enemies. He and the Oneidas knew that New York land and transportation interests, as well as Empire State officials, were committed to encouraging and/or forcing all the Indians to go west. These interests needed a place to "dump"/relocate the Indians. Until 1838, that place was the environs of Green Bay, Wisconsin. For this was Bread's only leverage—working with "the devil," lobbying the New York State legislature and the governor of New York to get more money from Oneida land cessions in order to put more and more Indians into the region around Green Bay. Acting as a cooperative Indian with his former enemies in New York, he attempted to assure a place for Oneidas in Wisconsin.[21]

The ever-present fear of Oneida removal from Michigan Territory predated Bread's arrival there. The fight over the federal government's acceptance of the 1821 and 1822 treaties with the Menominees and Winnebagos appeared to the Oneidas as a never-ending struggle. In 1827, the Treaty of Butte Des Morts, which involved the Menominees, Winnebagos, and Chippewas, and the federal government, but not the New York Indians, left the controversy in the hands of the president of the United States and the issues largely unresolved. Article II of the treaty stated:

Much difficulty having arisen from the negotiation between the Menominee and Winnebago tribes, and the various tribes and portions of tribes of Indians of the State of New York, and the claims of the respective parties being much contested, as well with relation to the tenure and boundaries of the two tracts, claimed by the said New York Indians west of Lake Michigan, as to the authority of the persons who signed the agreement on the part of the Menominees, and the whole subject having been examined at the council this day concluded, and the allegations, proofs and statements of the respective parties having been entered upon the journal of the commissioners, *so that the same can be decided by the President of the United States;* it is agreed by the Menominees and Winnebagos, that so far as respects their interest in the premises, *the whole matter shall be referred to the President of the United States, whose decision shall be final. And the President is authorized, on their parts, to establish such boundaries between them and the New York Indians, as he may consider equitable and just* [emphasis added].[22]

The United States Senate ratified this treaty in 1829 but qualified its acceptance by resolving "that the said treaty shall not impair or effect any right or claim which the New York Indians, or any of them, have to the lands, or any of the lands, mentioned in the said treaty."[23]

Faced with a need to settle the issue of the New York Indian claims in the Michigan Territory, President Jackson, on June 7, 1830, appointed Michigan Territorial Secretary John S. Mason and two New York legislators, Erastus Root and James McCall, as federal commissioners to establish the boundaries for the "accommodation and settlement of the New York Indians."[24] The three commissioners were generally sympathetic to the Menominees and Winnebagos. Influenced by their official instructions written by Secretary of War John Eaton, they concluded that the New York Indians were essentially agricultural and therefore did not need as much land as the hunting and gathering Winnebagos and Menominees. Eaton had suggested that the so-called New York Indians could easily survive on 131,640 acres of land or 54 acres per individual. Hence, it was largely predetermined by the incoming Jackson administration that the 1821 and 1822 treaties would be substantially negated. The secretary of war concluded: "The New York Indians are a weak and feeble tribe [sic] peaceably disposed, and incapable to contend in war with the powerful tribes of the Lakes. It would be cruelty in the Government to send them to a new home where they would be under any feelings of dissatisfaction, and be subjected to danger." Besides this, Eaton's major "worry" was not that the New York Indians would unfairly lose out in a compromise, but that they would somehow revert from the "civilized state" to "savagery," abandoning their farming for hunting because their agricultural needs would not be sufficient in the settlement with the Menominees and Winnebagos.[25]

The commissioners first held preliminary meetings at Detroit from July 18 through August 4, 1830. On August 11, they hired Albert G. Ellis as an official surveyor for the commission. Henry Baird, a leading Green Bay attorney and land speculator in the community, served as the legal counsel for the Winnebagos, while Doty served in a similar capacity for the Menominees. Hence, from the beginning of the "negotiations," the New York Indians faced poor odds.[26]

Four days later, the commissioners held council with Winnebago Indians at Little Buttes des Mortes. On August 17, they met with Chief Metoxen of the Stockbridge Indians. Three days later, they gathered at Eleazer Williams's residence and consulted with Oneida delegates who included Daniel Bread. At Green Bay, meeting at John Arndt's tavern on August 21, the representative of all of the New York Indians insisted (1) that no Indian council be held within Green Bay's limits; (2) that only the federal commissioners and Indian delegates and chiefs be admitted to council; and (3) that a code of secrecy be observed during the deliberations. Two days later, the commissioners quickly rejected all three points.[26] Much of the early focus of the Oneidas' attention was on stemming the influence of the French and Franco-Indian trappers among the Menominees. Bread and the other delegates clearly felt these trappers worked against their interests, since the Oneidas, unlike their western Indian neighbors, were not dependent on the fur trade in Michigan Territory.[27]

On August 24, the commissioners once again met with the Oneida Indian delegates, Neddy Archiquette, Cornelius Stevens, Henry Powless (Powlis or Powles), John Anthony, and Daniel Bread. At this conference, Eleazer Williams made an appearance and indicated that he was representing only the St. Regis Mohawk tribe, an odd but telling circumstance since there were no other Mohawk Indians at the meeting and few, if any, in Michigan Territory.[28] This fact further suggests that Williams had already begun to be excluded from Oneida policy-making circles. To make this meeting even more bizarre, the federal commissioners, unaware of the Iroquoian custom of wampum and the Condolence Council, conducted the Great Lakes pipe ceremony, passing around a calumet to smoke at the beginning of the day's events, something that was unrelated to Six Nations diplomacy. Thus, even the customary style of the meeting was apparently not conducive to Oneida traditions.[29]

The next day, the commissioners met with the Menominee and Winnebago delegates. The Menominees under Oshkosh, Bear Grease, and Josette Carron and the Winnebagos under Four Legs vehemently articulated their position in favor of reducing the Oneida cession. At the same meeting, the delegates of the New York Indians, who once again included Bread, Archiquette, Anthony, and Powless, passionately insisted that they would not have left New York for this "cold and sterile region without an indemnification—without something prospectively equivalent." The Oneida delegates maintained that the treaties of 1821 and 1822 were valid agreements. They blamed the impasse on the Menominees and the "current complaints of the French people" at and around Green Bay who had unusual influence among these Indians.

Soon after, Bread and the Stockbridge chief Quinney expressed concerns about the commission's interpreter and once again mentioned what they saw as the improper influence of outsiders, presumably the French fur traders at Green Bay. On August 28, Chief Bread, hoping to win Indian acceptance, referred to the Menominees and Winnebagos as "brothers," claiming that all the Oneidas wanted was "peace and goodwill" among the Indian nations. He went further by suggesting a compromise, one which would reduce the Oneida lands but allow them to have a better agricultural, more concentrated land base.[30]

During these heated discussions, Bread and the delegates of the New York Indians saw first-hand the powerful forces at work threatening their continued existence in Michigan Territory. On September 1, Doty, acting in his capacity as attorney for the Menominees, maintained that the United States had no responsibility to repair an injustice done to the Indians in New York State by strong-arming the Menominees. Hoping to get at these Menominee lands because of his access to these Indians' leadership, Doty and his Green Bay associates became the outspoken defenders of the local Menominees against the interests of the New York Indians. By this time the commissioners had basically worked out a proposal, one not acceptable to the Oneidas, that assured the New York Indians "fixed and reasonable agricultural limits."[31]

Doty, the father of Wisconsin statehood, had migrated to Michigan Territory from Lewis County, in central New York, where his uncle, General Walter Martin, had become one of the largest holders of land in the Black River Country, purchased from land jobbers who had obtained it from the Oneida Indians. Doty and his cousin Morgan L. Martin, another adversary of the Oneidas, were clearly men on the make. Doty tied his fortunes to Astor's American Fur Company in the 1820s and 1830s. His law practice soon burgeoned, representing Indian clients, including the famous Oshkosh, in a murder trial in 1828. At the same time he was appointed a federal territorial judge, while he continued to have one eye on higher office. The judge, as he was referred to, contemplated obtaining the rich lands of the Fox River Valley. Allowing the Oneidas and future Indian refugees from New York State to settle permanently within this corridor on millions of acres of land was threatening to him and the new white power elite of Green Bay. The historian Alice E. Smith has observed that Doty's aims conflicted with the Oneidas' hopes: "the prospect of [New York] Indians cultivating the soil conflicted with the cherished aspiration of every hustling Yankee to obtain a goodly portion of that fertile valley for himself." Doty knew that "the Wisconsin tribes [Menominees and Winnebagos], uninterested in tilling the soil and related to some of the [white] settlers by marriage, would be relatively easy to dislodge." Smith concluded: "Under these circumstances it is easy to place credence in the accusations of government officials that local white men incited them to rebellion against the terms of the two treaties [1821 and 1822] and spurred them on in their insistence that the whole subject of the transfer be reopened."[32]

Doty was enamoured with the idea of making Green Bay and environs more of a regional center of trade and commerce, much in the manner of what Chicago later became. As attorney-agent for the American Fur Company, he hoped to succeed the Franco-Indian power elite that had dominated the area's commerce. Doty's aim was to go beyond fur and speculate in land whose value would increase dramatically with improved transportation networks. A native New Yorker who had left the Empire State right after the start of construction of the Erie Canal, Doty envisioned that the Fox River–Lake Winnebago–Wisconsin River corridor would be a major transportation link between the Great Lakes and the Mississippi. It is little wonder that Doty speculated in lands as far southwest as today's Madison and his cousin Martin as far south as today's Milwaukee.[33]

Doty's actions reveal much. Claiming that his years as an attorney and judge in the West among the Indians had made him an expert, he constantly lobbied federal, New York State, and Michigan territorial officials. Hoping to ingratiate himself to President Jackson and his major policy advisers in order to secure a post, such as the commissionership of Indian affairs, in the War Department, he repeatedly wrote about the need to reorganize the administration of Indian affairs.[34] Right after he met with the federal commissioners dealing with the controversy over the New York Indians' rights under the treaties of 1821 and 1822, Doty clearly presented his own views on the subject to the president: "It would not be difficult to compel most of the N.Y. Indians, who propose to establish themselves here to remove at once to another suitable portion of the country west of the Mississippi." Providing false information to the president, Doty added that he had presented this alternative to the New York Indians but "the only opposition which it has received is from one or two individuals who expect to receive a large part of the tract claims here."35

Doty strenuously resisted allowing the Oneidas to settle permanently in Michigan Territory. Writing to the territorial governor, he chided Reverend Morse's old idea of creating an "Indian Republic" in the West, arguing that the concept went against such acts of Congress as the Northwest Ordinance. He insisted that "the government might as well attempt to dismember a portion of any state of the Union." Doty's racism was clear in this letter. Calling the New York Indians "Mongrel Tribes," he stated that because of "their semi-barbarous character," he could "discover no spot for them to occupy east of the Mississippi." Doty's solution was for Congress to award them United States citizenship and encourage them to intermarry with whites, which would "terminate their wanderings." Thus, to Doty, they had "to be required to part with their national character and their national domain together."36

Doty and his cronies would do almost anything in their schemes to get Oneida lands. The judge was a master of territorial politics, as evidenced by his elevation to the governorship of two territories—Wisconsin in the 1840s and Utah in the 1850s. In a letter to then Secretary of State Martin Van Buren, he showed his stripes, recommending his cousin Martin to be Indian subagent for the New York Indians. Martin, who later served in that capacity in the 1860s, was long seen by the Oneidas as "their worst nightmare." Yet, in the 1830 letter, Doty claimed that attorney Martin was "well acquainted with the Indians" and that "he possesses the confidence of the Oneidas."37

Two memoirs throw light on territorial politics as well as on the federal commissioners' work in the summer of 1830: a journal kept by James McCall, one of the three commissioners, and one by the previously mentioned Calvin Colton.38 McCall's journal describes the incredible size and scope of these councils, citing that 1,740 Indians, including five Oneida delegates—Bread, Cornelius, Anthony, Powless, Archiquette, and Stevens—were in attendance. McCall, a state senator from southwestern New York and pioneer who had settled on former Indian lands west of Cayuga Lake in 1798, was not at all complimentary to Doty and Grignon and suspected their motives. He was even less flattering about Eleazer Williams whom he connected to white entrepreneurial interests at Green Bay. In derogatory fashion, McCall wrote that Williams had married a Franco-Menominee, "a half blood," to further his ambitions. McCall saw the Mohawk missionary as an operator: "He has the advantage of a liberal education and [is] said to be a cunning man and claims, in the right of his wife, a large tract of land, and is paid by [the] government $250 annually as chaplain for the Oneida Indians." The commissioner saw him as a problem because he expected the Mohawk missionary to create difficulty, making the New York Indians believe that "their claim is more extensive than it is."[39]

In the end, McCall and Erastus Root wrote the majority opinion of the 1830 federal commission. The two men questioned the validity of the 1821 and 1822 treaties and suggested that all of the New York Indians be awarded less than 276,000 acres, leaving the Menominees with well over 5 million acres. The Brothertown Indians would receive 20,000 and the Stockbridge 6,000 acres; 250,000 acres were to be set aside for all of the six Iroquois Indian nations, not just the Oneidas. These acres would consist mostly of lands secured by the United States from the Menominees in the Treaty of Butte Morts of 1827. John T. Mason, in a minority report, dissented, claiming that only the president and not the commissioners could determine the validity of the claim of the New York Indians under the treaties of 1821 and 1822.[40]

Colton's remarkable journal tells much about the Indians' oratory, their style as well as the substance of their presentations. Although Colton was especially impressed with Stockbridge Chief Metoxen, he commented favorably about Chief

Bread. At one of these sessions, Colton noted that "a chief of the Oneidas about thirty years old" stood up and addressed the commissioners and the Indians in the English language, frequently employing biblical stories and metaphors. After appealing both to Jesus Christ and the Great Spirit, Bread acknowledged Chief Metoxen and the Stockbridge Indians in attendance. Humbly stating that he had been asked to speak for the Oneidas even though he "did not wish to speak," Bread recounted how "discouraged" his people were, and how they were misled by official promises made before their relocation to Michigan Territory.[41]

To Bread, the formal commitment that had been made to the Oneidas by President Monroe, namely "that his white children should never come after us" if they decide to leave their New York homeland, had now been broken by subsequent presidents. Monroe had said "he had a desire to see us living by ourselves, in peace and prosperity—that it would be better for us to come out here [Michigan Territory] than to live in the state of New York." Only after promises of federal protection did the Oneidas decide to leave New York, where they had "good land, raised corn, learned the good ways of our white neighbours, had houses for our families, and a house of God." Attempting to win support from the federal commission of 1830, the young Oneida chief consciously exaggerated the positive features of Indian existence in the 1820s in New York, claiming that the Oneidas had "protection of the laws," which were enforced after appeals to "our great father" who "could see and right the wrong."[42]

Bread, formerly known as Christian Daniel, a man who had studied the Bible so thoroughly while growing up, then brilliantly employed the story of Joseph in Egypt. After a pharaoh encouraged Joseph to bring his people, the ancient Hebrews, to Egypt, they were enslaved by "another king in the land, which knew not Joseph." Instead of enslavement as in the case of the ancient Hebrews, the white people in Michigan Territory were not allowing them to build their community. Bread insisted that "the white people are surrounding us again—they are getting our lands—they will not let us have any influence over the native tribes—they fill the ears of our great father with wrong stories—and they have already threatened to drive us out." He concluded by sadly appealing to the three commissioners: "Brothers, we cannot move any more. Tell our great father, that our hearts are made very sorry by the conduct of his white children—and that we have no peace."[43]

Thus, by the late summer of 1830, Bread was now speaking as the voice of the Oneidas in the West. His great oratory, although inspirational to the Oneidas and to outside observers such as Colton, nevertheless had little influence among white policymakers in Green Bay. Surrounded by a power elite intent on driving his people from their new lands, Bread turned to Washington in a desperate appeal to save himself, his family, and his Oneida people. Instead of sending a message through these commissioners, who had already made up their minds, Bread went to Washington twice, in late 1830 and again in the winter of 1831. He spent four months of intense lobbying there, meeting with American officials, including President Jackson. These visits to the nation's capital changed Bread's life forever, educating him about American politics and political leadership, giving him a wider understanding than his other Oneida tribesmen about the impending danger of removal from Michigan Territory. Besides his council with Old Hickory, Bread encountered the famous George Catlin, the great painter who ennobled his Indian subjects with a dignity and humanity generally not found in Jacksonian America.

Chapter 5

Chief Lobbyist

Besides the establishment of the federal commission to recommend a boundary settlement of the Menominee–New York Indian controversy, President Jackson's administration had other plans for Michigan Territory. In his 1829 inaugural address and in his support of the Indian Removal Act of 1830, Old Hickory set in motion a policy that became a cornerstone of his first and second terms. By appointing Michigan territorial governor Lewis Cass as his secretary of war, he was elevating to prominence issues relating to the Old Northwest frontier.[1]

After Jackson assumed office in March 1829, Commissioner of Indian Affairs Thomas L. McKenney expressed his support for closure on the Menominee–New York Indian controversy. In a letter to Thomas L. Ogden, the brother of David A. Ogden, McKenney suggested to the principal agent of the Ogden Land Company that a final settlement of the matter would result in a few years. By ridding New York State of its Indian population and moving them west, the Indians themselves would actually benefit in the long run. McKenney urged a "*judicious* fixing of the limits at Green Bay for the New York Indians, in which as far as possible, their own views ought to be consulted," which he felt would lead to further emigration from New York. McKenney insisted that the federal policies should be designed to instill confidence in the Indians from the different communities, after which a "proper agent" could be appointed to visit them.[2] Instead of a "proper agent," President Jackson designated an interim federal Indian agent at Green Bay, Samuel C. Stambaugh, a Lancaster, Pennsylvania, newspaperman and political sycophant who had helped Old Hickory carry the state in the election of 1828. Later, in the mid-1830s, General Zachary Taylor categorized Stambaugh as being "compliant in conforming" to Jackson's wishes, overly "zealous in carrying out his principles, and executing his plans for the elevation of his favourite; for I do not believe he possesses one particle of firmness, independence, political or moral honesty."[3]

Stambaugh immediately interceded in the Menominee-New York Indian controversy, only complicating matters further. The agent told the chiefs "that no other tribe of Indians in the United States was so poor as they were; that with a wide waste of lands entirely useless to them, they had not a dollar of annuity, while many of their neighbors received annually twenty to fifty thousand dollars." The Pennsylvanian soon presented himself as their savior from "the rapacity of Indian and white sharpers from New York." He encouraged the Menominees to sell a portion of their lands to the United States, which would assure them a comfortable annuity instead "of giving away their country to the New Yorkers."[4] The Pennsylvania Democrat suggested that the New York Indians had received large annuities and were rich in comparison to the poorer Menominees and that the New York Indians had used "undue influence" in their negotiations with the impoverished Menominees in 1821 and 1822 to secure six million acres of land.[5] At a council with the Menominees in August of 1830 and without the Oneidas a party to the accord, just at the time of the federal commissioners' hearings, Stambaugh secured Menominee approval for a treaty with the United States.[6]

To carry out his plan and lobby for this treaty, Stambaugh arranged for a delegation to go to Washington. In November 1830, Stambaugh set off with fourteen Menominees, excluding Oshkosh, now the "Grand Chief"; Charles G. Grignon, an educated Franco-Menominee tied to the American Fur Company; Eleazer Williams; and Albert G. Ellis.[7] Fearing that this "official" delegation would work against their interests, representatives of the New York Indians followed them to Washington. They included Daniel Bread and his sister as well as John Anthony from the Oneidas and Chief John W. Quinney of the Stockbridge Indians. Bread's involvement in the New York Indians' visit to Washington in the winter of 1831 (late November 1830 through March 1831) and his later visit that same year (December 1831) was a turning point in his life, one that haunted him to his dying day.

The New York Indians' attempt to stop the Stambaugh treaty proved fruitless. In January of 1831, the treaty reached the floor of the United States Senate. While Stambaugh and his allies were lobbying for it, Bread and the other representatives of the New York Indians urged President Jackson to stay out "of our difficulties with the Menominees and afford the right of the New York Indians to lands at Green Bay."[8]

On February 8, 1831, the Senate approved the so-called Stambaugh treaty with the Menominees, one that clearly threatened all of the New York Indians by giving them no formal assurances of a federal commitment. The treaty refused "to recognize any claim of the New York Indians to any portion of their territory, that they neither sold nor received any value for the land claimed by these tribes." However, out of friendship and alliance with the United States, the Menominees agreed to cede 500,000 acres of lands to the federal government as the president "may direct; [which] may be set apart as a home to the several tribes of New York Indians," who had to relocate and settle there within three years of the date of the treaty. If the New York Indians refused to accept the terms, the president had the right to remove all the New York Indians already settled on these lands. Yet, this treaty also required that no more than 100 acres per family be awarded to the New York Indians by the United States in this 500,000-acre Menominee cession.[9]

The federal treaty of February 8, 1831, was subsequently modified nine days later in a second federal-Menominee treaty passed by the United States Senate. This amended accord gave the president the right of discretion to determine the exact number of acres per New York Indian family and allowed an unlimited time for these Indians to settle on these former Menominee lands.[10] In effect, by mid-February 1831, Congress had given Andrew Jackson almost total control over the controversy. The fate of the Oneidas was placed squarely at the feet of the old Indian fighter, precisely at a time when Indian treaty rights on a national level were being sacrificed for political expediency and for the goals of the states.

The whittling down of the original accords of 1821 and 1822 produced real fears among the Oneidas that their New York experience with dispossession would recur in Wisconsin. If ever-increasing Iroquois numbers arrived in Wisconsin to be resettled, would there be room for all? At a time of growing tensions between Winnebagos and whites in the lead district and in a frontier trading setting with all of its attendant evils (such as alcohol) just a few miles away at Green Bay, the New York Indians feared the worst.

Importantly, Bread's presence in the nation's capital was precisely at the same time that the Cherokee Nation of Indians was suing the State of Georgia before the United States Supreme Court.[11] The Iroquoian-speaking Cherokees from the Southeast were attempting to gain recognition of their federal treaty rights to allow them to remain in their homeland. Colton described Washington City, as it was called then, as being abuzz with talk about what the Marshall court would decide in its decision. Moreover, numerous Indians from all over the nation had gathered in the city because Jackson's administration had brought the "Indian Question" to the fore and numerous tribal delegations were at the War Department, on Capitol Hill, or at the White House, conferring with federal policymakers and/or receiving peace medals as allies of the United States. As the George Catlin painting suggests, Bread was one of those Indians receiving a peace medal, one literally split in half and shared with another member of his delegation.[12]

The Indians—Cherokees, Choctaws, Creeks, Osages, Quapaws, and various Iroquois nations—conferred with each other in secret negotiations, although they were asked to dance and sing and did so in performances before the public and on the White House grounds. On March 5, *Cherokee Nation v. Georgia* was decided with the Supreme Court holding that it had no jurisdiction, that Indian nations had no standing or constitutional rights to sue a state in federal courts based on the Eleventh Amendment, and that the Indians were "domestic dependent nations."[13] The next morning, a Sunday, Indians sadly gathered for "a day of fasting and prayer." They gathered at Brown's Hotel, where they were led in prayer by an unidentified Oneida. Later that day the Indians met at the Gatsby Hotel for an evening service conducted by an Indian clergyman.[14] According to Minister Colton, they turned to solemn Christian prayer and "that High and Almighty Providence" to cope with "adversity and public gloom, with naught but darkness overshadowing, and calamities heaped upon them."[15]

One hope for Indian redemption had come three days earlier, on March 3, 1831, when the United States Senate rejected Stambaugh's nomination to be the Indian agent at Green Bay because of his well-known partisanship and suspect ethics. Yet, Stambaugh did not bow out graciously but continued to lobby; the president, facing increasing political pressures, refused to proclaim the second federal-Menominee treaty until July of 1832.

Rewarded as a loyal Jacksonian, Stambaugh was sent on a special assignment by Secretary of War Eaton to write a comprehensive report describing this Menominee cession and its economic potential. In it, he once again pleaded the Menominees' case and represented the New York Indians as having taken advantage of their less sophisticated Indian brethren in Michigan Territory. Although Stambaugh had earlier been critical of Judge Doty and was initially criticized by Doty, the former Indian agent began to collaborate with the judge: "Any deficiency or error in the Map or in this Report, may be supplied by Colonel Irwin, Hon. James D. Doty and Morgan L. Martin, Esq. of this place, who will be in Washington during the ending session of Congress."[16]

Stambaugh's report, which was widely circulated, emphasized canals and the exploitation of natural resources. He saw the future upper Midwest with Green Bay at its core. Taking lands from the Menominees and transferring them all to the Six Nations would delay land acquisition by Green Bay interests. Stambaugh wrote that in the future the great thoroughfare between the Mississippi and the City of New York would pass through Green Bay. He suggested: "Nature has done so much for this country that there must soon be a commodious highway, connecting the waters of the Lakes with the Mississippi River; and then the whole business of Galena, the lead mines and the upper Mississippi will take this route, by which the value of property at the line of ship navigation will be greatly enhanced, and the commerce of the Lakes much benefited." To Stambaugh, both the Menominees and the more sedentary New York Indians were not suited to take advantage of these changes that in his opinion would soon lead Wisconsin to become a separate territory. He suggested that another federal treaty be consummated, opening up three million acres of Menominee lands as an "inducement to emigration" by whites.[17]

Buried in Stambaugh's report was the later basis of a settlement of the New York Indians–Menominee controversy:

a land exchange for the Oneidas and a one hundred-acre-per-family allocation. He estimated that there were no more than six thousand Indians remaining in New York State and claimed that "the quantity of land provided for them by this Treaty, will be sufficient for all their purposes as an agricultural people, for the next half century." He continued by insisting that "if they should all consent to remove to this country, which is by no means certain . . . there can be one hundred acres allotted to each soul out of this tract." Stambaugh then recommended a land exchange: "if they [the New York Indians] should desire to exchange some of their land lying along their northerly boundary, for a location further south, I presume the government can procure an extension of the purchase from the Menominees in a direction S.W. from the upper boundary of the tract given to these Tribes, by the Treaty."[18]

Chief Bread was tireless in attempting to win assurances for continued Oneida residence on this southwestern tract on available lands in the environs of Green Bay. To ensure the protection of his Oneida people, Bread went beyond his earlier efforts, hoping to win Democrat support and bringing it to bear on Jackson. On April 13, 1831, he sought help from the Oneidas' greatest enemy—the governor of New York State. He asked Governor Enos Troop for support against the "Stambaugh treaties." He insisted that New York State owed the Oneidas for moving them to a "cold region of the Northwest." He criticized the work of the federal commissioners appointed by Jackson for basing their decision not on contractual treaty law but on the principle of equity and claimed that the Oneidas did not want charity from the Menominees or anyone else. Attempting to play on guilt, Bread wrote:

It was not originally our situation or desire to emigrate. We resisted untill overcome by the superior addresses of white men who promised us what has never been fulfilled. We were to have peace and protection. A territory was to be set off for the exclusive occupancy of the remnants of tribes of the State of New York free from the destroying influences and intrusions of strangers. Instead of finding fulfilment of these engagements[,] *we are left exposed to the arts and calumnies of designing white men charged with fraud and extortion and meanness are taken to drive us from the country"* [emphasis added].[19]

To protect Oneida interests under the two Stambaugh treaties, ones that the New York Indians were not party to, Bread, along with Oneida delegate John Anthony and representatives of the Brothertown and Stockbridge Indians, once again took their case to Washington in December 1831. At considerable cost ($700) they lobbied, fearing their land rights would not be respected in any federal-Menominee treaty. Bread and representatives of the New York Indians went to the War Department to meet with Secretary Lewis Cass, the former governor of Michigan Territory.[20] Subsequently, they went to the White House, accompanied by George B. Porter, the governor of Michigan Territory, who took detailed notes of the Indians' meeting with President Andrew Jackson in late December 1831. Porter focused his attention on the young Oneida chief's interaction with "Old Hickory."

Daniel Bread then rose and addressed the President, quite intelligibly in the *English Language*—stated that he was very anxious to have this settled—that he did not deny but what there was land enough and more than enough good land and wished to know whether a piece of land could not be given to them along the south side of that tract (describing it as has been done in a former part of this report). To this the President replied that this could not be done: that the commissioners had told him the truth, when they stated that this land belonged to the Menominees, and was expressly reserved to them for agricultural purposes in the treaty of last year; and that it was not his to give:—his emphatic remark, you must remember—(I never told a red man a lie in my life: nor do I speak to you with a forked tongue—if I were to promise

Chief Lobbyist 71

to give you this land I would tell you a lie—I could not do it—I cannot deceive you.) Daniel Bread then asked this question: 'If we can make a bargain with the Menominee for an exchange of lands, giving them a piece of the north of the 500,000 acres, for a small piece on the south of the tract, will you sanction it?' The answer of the President was 'certainly—if they will agree to do this, we can have no objections'—Daniel Bread remarked 'we are afraid Father, that some of the white men will interfere and that the Menominees will not do this, unless their Great Father will advise them—the Menominees have a high respect for what their Great Father says, and if he will advise them we are sure they will make this exchange.'—To this the President answered—'You were last year told, if you would accept the land set apart for you by the Treaty, and it should be ascertained on examination, that it was not sufficient in quality or quantity for your accommodation, the Government would use their endeavors to get you more land; a person was appointed to examine this tract of country and make a report—And I now tell you in answer to your question that if there is not sufficient good land in this tract, we will advise the Menominees to make, and as his Great Father had now said that he would send good advice to the Menominees, he would agree to the settlement; and he thought that they could make an exchange sometime with the Menominees, and get what they wanted, and they could live in peace.'—Having nothing more to say they took leave and retired, apparently much pleased and not more so than the rest of us, who were present, at the prospect of having brought so near to a close, this long and unprofitable controversy.[21]

At the end of this exchange, missionary Williams arrived, claiming to represent the St. Regis Mohawks. Soon Bread's position hardened, although one can only speculate the reason for this turnabout. Porter then described:

At this meeting Daniel Bread (for the first time in my presence) spoke in his native language and Mr. Williams was his interpreter. To our great astonishment and in the face of his voluntary agreement when before the President, he [Bread] refused absolutely to consent to any arrangements unless the Government would guarantee and assure to them two hundred thousand acres on the south side of the tract of 500,000 acres set apart by the treaty of last year: In vain did I remind him of his own voluntary agreement, and of the consequences which must inevitably result if his present course were persisted in:—A repetition of all former arguments was used:— that the Government had no claim to this land; that it belonged to the Menominees—: that I have assured him of this two weeks before, and that the Government could not undertake to grant to them what they did not possess—: That he had remarked himself that he [had] no doubt, they could make an exchange with the Menominees if the President would advise them to do so; that he had agreed to do so; and that from all I could learn there would be no difficulty in accomplishing it: To all that I could say, *we heard little or nothing more by way of answer than that he [Bread] had no faith in the Government;* that they had made promises time after time: and he was determined to submit their claims to the justice of the Senate of the United States. The stand here taken and the language, as *interpreted,* being so different from any thing previously used [emphasis added].[22]

Porter, concerned, asked Williams to meet with Bread privately. Williams, it appears, urged compromise, fearing that Bread's recalcitrance might lead to reprisals against all the Indians in attendance. Porter then described:[23]

The President remarked "we'll set apart 200 acres for each family, which is more than you will ever cultivate, there will be 200,000 acres and upwards left;—can't be supposed that there is not 200,000 acres of good land in this large tract of country?"—Some conversations then took place among the Indians themselves. After which Daniel Bread remarked that "he wished to have an end to their disputes— . . . and made no other reply."[24]

Porter then concluded that Bread "understood the President to say that the lands should be exchanged as desired—thereby pledging the faith of the Government to him, to effect the exchange with the Menominees."[25] Although the Oneidas did not win any assurances or even recognition for a permanent home in Michigan Territory, they did make it clear to the president that the Oneidas would be willing to settle the issue by exchanging their claim for better, more fertile lands in the southern part of Menominee territory. Yet, fears of uncertainty still gripped the Oneidas because they knew well that Jackson was not to be fully trusted.

Before leaving Washington, Bread, along with the representatives of the Oneidas, Brothertowns, and Stockbridges, also filed a formal protest with the United States Senate in early 1832. This protest recounted the controversy from an Oneida perspective, stating that the accords of 1821 and 1822 were valid, providing joint ownership for the New York Indians and the Menominees and Winnebagos. The memorial spelled out Oneida objections. The Indians resented the Menominee claim to being "exclusive owners of the whole, without the concurrence of the New York tribes, in opposition to their wishes." The petition accused the federal commissioners and the President of the United States of ignoring their responsibilities to "dependent Indian allies," vacillating in dealing with the issue, and denying a firm commitment to "Daniel Bread, the representative of the Six Nations," concerning a permanent home in Michigan Territory.[26]

Bread made a clear statement of his position, dated January 14, 1832, as part of the protest. He reiterated what he had told President Jackson, declining the "acceptance of the tract of five hundred thousand acres, as set off by the Menominie [sic] treaty for the accommodation of the tribes." He insisted that the "situation, soil, and condition" of this 500,000-acre tract were unsuitable for the Oneidas as well as the other Six Nations. The chief suggested "an exchange of 200,000 acres on the north side of this tract for a like number to be added on the south side," a satisfactory compromise to the New York Indians. He expressed the fear that the Menominees were unwilling to make "this exchange or to sell to the New York Indians the territory required." He stated adamantly that the New York Indians had not been consulted and had "received no invitation to become a contracting party in that treaty." With a sense of humility or a politician's calculation, Chief Bread suggested that he had misunderstood the president, thinking him to say "that the lands should be exchanged as was desired, thereby pledging the faith of the Government to him to effect the exchange with the Menomonies." The chief claimed that his "imperfect knowledge of the English language, and his almost entire inability to express himself intelligibly, has, doubtless, produced this misunderstanding." He refused to totally blame President Jackson for the broken promise.[27]

A third federal-Menominee treaty was fashioned in the fall of 1832. On October 27, 1832, the United States Senate approved a modified version of the 1831 treaties, allowing for an exchange of 200,000 acres of New York Indian lands in the northeastern side of the Menominee cession to the United States, in return for 500,000 acres on the southwestern side of the tract, including lands that the Oneidas were occupying then at Duck Creek, as they are today. To satisfy the New York Indians, the third federal-Menominee treaty contained an appendix. It referred to the accord as being the "best practicable terms, short of those proposed by the Senate of the United States, which could be obtained from the said Menominies." While the body of the third treaty was signed by federal and Menominee officials, this appendix, which called for "an end to strife" and urged the Indians "to sit down in peace and harmony" in the future, was signed by federal officials and delegates of all the New York Indians, including such Oneidas as Bread, Anthony, Nathaniel Neddy, Thomas Neddy, and Cornelius Stevens. Importantly, Eleazer Williams was no longer a signatory for the Oneidas or the St. Regis Mohawks. The treaty was subsequently proclaimed by the president on March 13, 1833.[28]

While the ratification process was well underway in Washington, Secretary of War Cass sent Territorial Governor George Porter to Green Bay to win acceptance for the treaty and mitigate tensions that had arisen between two American allies, the Menominees and the "New York Indians." At the time of the Black Hawk War, and while hostilities continued between whites and Indians in the lead district of Wisconsin, Cass wanted no other military disturbances threatening stability on the frontier.[29]

On October 23, Porter first met with the Menominees. Grizzly Bear, one of the Menominee delegates and the official orator, accused the "N.Y. Indians" of being greedy and not accepting the 500,000 acres granted them. "We were then all satisfied and we thought that the N.Y. Indians there were all satisfied too. But they staid [sic] there to make objections— We don't know what they mean—We don't like it, that they act so...." He added: "Father, these N.Y. Indians have behaved so badly:- and opposed every thing [sic] that is right for so long a time; that we begin to hate them,— They are dogs—They want to take our land from us without paying for it—They hunt on our land and kill our deer:— Have they any right to do so?" Grizzly Bear's comments were followed by those of other delegates: A-yah-manta, Shaw-e-no-geshig, Cheno-ma-bee-mee, Pe-wait-e-naw, and Little Wave. One of the speakers pointed out that any exchange of lands would interfere with the maple sugar camps and the mills run by Augustin and Charles Grignon, the leading Franco-Menominee family within the territory. The last speaker, Little Wave, emphasized his people's valuable military service to the United States in the war that was then being waged against Black Hawk, undoubtedly to sway the territorial governor to the Menominees' position.[30]

Perhaps remembering Bread's confrontation with President Jackson, Governor Porter purposely snubbed Bread by failing to invite him to the first meeting on October 24 and to subsequent councils. The next day's discussions focused on the Stockbridge Indians after tribal leader Quinney offered a Christian invocation in the English language. Although Oneidas such as Henry Powless and John Anthony, Nathaniel Neddy, and Cornelius Stevens arrived on October 25, the discussions still centered on the Stockbridges. The peripatetic missionary Williams also appeared on that day, this time claiming to represent both the St. Regis Mohawks and Tuscaroras. Porter met with representatives of the New York Indians at the agency headquarters. After a Christian invocation by Quinney, representatives of the New York Indians, including the Oneidas Anthony, Powless, Stevens, and Nathaniel Neddy, confirmed their acceptance of the third Menominee treaty, after agreeing to a proviso allowing Charles Grignon to continue to operate his maple sugar camp in their ceded territory. Quinney, Bread's ally, refused to sign that proviso and insisted upon land "clear of these incumbrances." Understanding Bread's great influence among his people, Porter, upon leaving the council on October 26, advised the delegates to report back to the chief about the deliberations. On October 27, 1832, precisely the same date as the Senate ratification of the third treaty, the Menominees agreed to settle the controversy. They agreed to grant the "New York Indians" 500,000 acres on the southwest side of the tract from Duck Creek to Lake Winnebago in exchange for 200,000 acres on the northeastern side of the tract.[31] On October 29, the chiefs and head men of the Menominee and the "several tribes of New York Indians" sealed the deal at a dinner at Arndt's tavern at Green Bay, where "they shook hands and parted as friends, determining to forget and forgive all that had passed, and to live hereafter in peace and harmony with each other."[32] Yet, for Bread, all was not forgiven.

Although Bread acquiesced, he viewed the long deliberations between 1821 and 1832 over the Menominee cession as an insult to his people. Instead of being the central focus as in great councils of the past, the Six Nations were treated

Chief Lobbyist

as an afterthought, humiliated before other Indian nations, treated as "doormats" by local, territorial, and Washington officials. For the Oneida people who cherished their major role as allies of George Washington, this decade was especially painful. Responding to these difficult times, Chief Bread was to strengthen his reins of power internally in the Oneida Nation.

Chief Daniel Bread. Portrait by George Catlin, 1831. Courtesy of the National Museum of American Art.

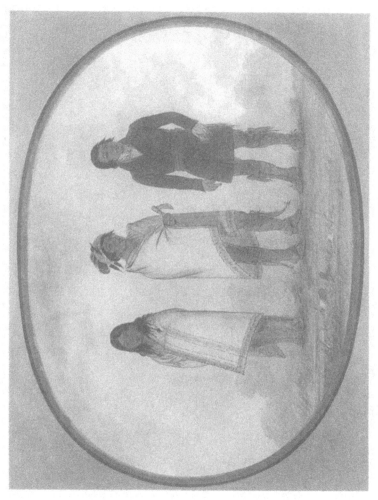

Oneida Chief [Bread], his sister, and a missionary. Portrait by George Catlin, ca.

Chief Daniel Bread. Daguerreotype, 1854. Courtesy of the Madison County (N.Y.) Historical Society.

Chief Daniel Bread. Portrait by Samuel M. Brookes. Courtesy of the State Historical Society of Wisconsin.

Eleazer Williams as a young man. Portrait by George Catlin. Courtesy of the State Historical Society of Wisconsin.

Eleazer Williams. Courtesy of the Neville Museum of Brown County (Wisconsin).

Chief Oshkosh. Portrait by Samuel M. Brookes. Courtesy of the State Historical Society of Wisconsin.

James Duane Doty.
Courtesy of the State
Historical Society of
Wisconsin.

Daniel Whitney.
Courtesy of the State
Historical Society of
Wisconsin.

*John P. Arndt.
Courtesy of the
Neville Museum of
Brown County.*

*Morgan L. Martin.
Courtesy of the
Neville Museum of
Brown County.*

The Oneidas' Hobart Episcopal Church on the Duck Creek
Reservation. Reproduced from Bloomfield, The Oneidas, 2d ed.,

Bishop Jackson
Kemper. Reproduced
from Bloomfield, The
Oneidas, 2d ed., 1909.

Chief Elijah Skenandore. Courtesy of the State Historical Society of Wisconsin.

Edward A. Goodnough. Reproduced from Bloomfield, The Oneidas, *2d ed., 1909.*

Chief Cornelius Hill.
Reproduced from
Bloomfield, The
Oneidas, 2d ed., 1909.

Chief Cornelius Hill,
Episcopal Priest.
Reproduced from
Bloomfield, The
Oneidas, 2d ed., 1909.

Chapter 6
Two Missionaries

In order to achieve consensus among his people, Bread became the great defender of Oneida interests, bad-mouthing the French traders and Franco-Menominees at Green Bay. He presented himself as an Oneida nationalist, insisting on a separate course of action from the other tribes of New York Indians, and, despite the accord of 1832, refused to deal with Chief Oshkosh and the Menominees. Bread made clear his open opposition to "mingle in council with the Menominee" and other Indians. "We have nothing to do in conjunction with them. The Oneida Nation must therefore be regarded as standing alone."[1] Even though Bread saw the Oneidas' problem as centering on the white power elite of Green Bay, any hint of cooperation by Oneida leaders with the Menominees was to be shunned.

This factor was to have a direct bearing on Oneida views of Eleazer Williams, who could no longer be trusted at all because of his connections to land speculators and to the Menominees. Moreover, Williams's assistant, Albert G. Ellis, had served the federal commission of 1830 and aided in Stambaugh's efforts to overturn the treaties of 1821 and 1822. Even before the ratification of the third federal-Menominee treaty, Bread was to banish Eleazer Williams, now considered his nation's albatross.

In an hour-long address in Oneida before an assemblage of the First Christian Party in council, Bread documented the charges against Williams. The Oneida chief showed how Williams "had failed of all his promises for long years, and how it was owing to his want of good faith, his fraud and deceit, that they were in the wilderness, utterly abandoned, without schools, churches, or religious privileges of any kind." He accused Williams of misusing missionary society funds for "entirely contrary purposes." In responses to Bread's speech, "not a dissenting voice was heard." Colonel George Boyd, the Indian agent invited to the council, was told that the missionary was *persona non grata* and the Oneidas informed officials of the State of New York and the church and missionary societies that they no longer recognized Williams "as having any authority to act for them, to speak in their name, or in any possible way meddling with their affairs." Thus, Bread confined Williams to the Iroquoian world of the "walking dead," ostracized permanently from Oneida existence. More than four decades later, Ellis suggested that Williams, then residing at Little Chute some twelve miles away from Duck Creek, had "no church under his control" at that time and the whole hijinx was orchestrated by Bread, with Boyd's support.[2]

Ellis's unconvincing defense of Williams and charges of Bread's disloyalty, repeated by Bloomfield and subsequent writers, covered up the full-blown scandal of Williams's tenure as missionary to the Oneidas. Williams, as previously stated, benefited by the New York State–Oneida Treaty of 1824 and had profited from his connections to the Ogden Land Company. Although his ties to Green Bay interests and his marriage to thirteen-year-old Mary Jourdan, a Franco-Menominee girl, offended most Oneidas, Bread apparently was disturbed by the missionary's mercenary qualities and his use of the Oneida chief's name for personal advancement. While Bread was still in New York in 1828, Williams was not above "signing" Bread's name on documents that promoted Williams's schemes, including the Mohawk clergyman's efforts to become Indian agent at Green Bay.[3] Now, finally, matters had to be resolved.

The action against Williams had the sanction of most Oneidas. The Episcopal publication *Gospel Messenger* later published a revealing letter written by Bread and his Orchard Party rival, Jacob Cornelius, concerning Williams, attempting to explain why the Mohawk missionary was ostracized from Duck Creek. The letter told church readers that Williams had been dismissed as missionary because he was more "indefatigable in his efforts to advance his own selfish views" than devoted to service as a clergyman. They went on to add that Williams had been "much more agreeable to receive his salary than to render service." Williams was accused of receiving funds for a school that never operated and of preaching at Duck Creek too infrequently—twice in one year and never more than six times per year since 1825.[4] Williams was slow to accept his firing. He "resigned" officially from his post on September 8, 1833, and left Green Bay for the Saint Regis Mohawk Reservation in October 1834, where he lived out the rest of his life.[5] Unfortunately for Bread, Williams was to reappear one more time in 1836 to bring further trouble to Oneidas.

Next, Bread turned against Chief John Anthony of the First Christian Party in a move apparently related to purging Williams's influence. There was more to this than simply a power struggle for leadership within the First Christian Party, since the rivalry between Bread and Anthony was not resolved until 1845, when Anthony lost what little influence he had and was humiliated along with his followers at a treaty council at Duck Creek.[6] There was also a hint of misappropriation of funds based on a report on Oneida emigration expenses by the New York State legislature.[7] Anthony was deposed as chief the same year as the scandal, soon after Williams's ostracism, suggesting a connection between these events. By this time, 1833, Bread's stands against Oshkosh, Doty, Stambaugh, and even Old Hickory himself, had catapulted him into a singular position of authority at Duck Creek.

Bread had shown brilliant leadership in fighting the Stambaugh treaties; however, he had no respite even after the Senate's ratification of the third federal-Menominee treaty in October 1832. In this third treaty, one problem had been dealt with, namely the exchange for better agricultural lands. A major problem remained. There was still the possibility of many hundreds or thousands of Iroquois, and not just Oneidas, who might choose to relocate or be forced west to the Michigan Territory under Jackson-Van Buren Indian removal policies. And there was no assurance that the federal government in Washington would honor past commitments and allow Oneidas to remain at Duck Creek. After all, Jackson's vice president, Martin Van Buren, had pushed for Oneida removal from New York while serving as the state's governor.

These fears became a real crisis in 1836 when John Freeman Schermerhorn, a Dutch Reformed missionary from New York, was appointed as federal negotiator to facilitate Indian removal from New York State.[8] Coming off his "success" in securing Cherokee removal under the blatantly fraudulent Treaty of New Echota, Schermerhorn now turned his attention to the Six Nations. The cleric, involved in removing twenty Indian nations westward, according to his biographer James Van Hoeven, was "indirectly responsible for provoking the Seminole War" as well as abetting factional conflicts within several Indian nations, including the Cherokees and Senecas. Van Hoeven has stated, "No appointed government official did more to implement Jackson's program of Indian removal in the field" than Schermerhorn during the Jackson era.[9] Schermerhorn was also seen as "Jackson's man" by the Indians themselves. Oneidas complained to Cherokee Chief John Ross "bitterly of Schermerhorn's past conduct towards them also." Ross claimed that *"they feel as we* [Cherokees] do, in regard to Indian affairs generally" (emphasis by Ross).¹⁰

Dogmatically judgmental and uncompromising, the New York minister fervently backed Jacksonian removal policies and viewed its political opponents as morally corrupt. Ironically, the moralist Schermerhorn was also a slimy supplicant constantly badgering his political supporters for appointments to office. While serving as Jackson's ear to the missionary societies, he frequently sought his due rewards, not final judgment. He speculated in Wisconsin lands while serving as a commissioner dealing with the Oneidas and other Indians of the Six Nations and lobbied successfully for two thousand dollars reimbursement in Article 8 of the Treaty of Buffalo Creek of 1838 with the New York Indians, three months after he had been relieved of his negotiating duties!¹¹

On September 16, 1836, at a treaty council at Duck Creek in which Bread served as principal chief and negotiator, the Oneidas were forced to conclude an accord with federal commissioner Schermerhorn.¹² Bread, aware of the Cherokee circumstances, apparently feared that the minister would recommend to Jackson Oneida removal from Duck Creek if they resisted. The preliminary agreement stated that the accord was with "several Tribes of New York Indians" and their "chiefs and representatives." Besides both chiefs of the Oneidas' First Christian and Orchard parties, only three Tuscarora Indians and the ostracized Eleazer Williams put their names to this preliminary treaty, a clear indication of misrepresentation by Schermerhorn. Williams's name on the accord is evidence—with more than a hint of suspicion—that the treaty was bogus and that the Oneidas were coerced into this agreement. In this preliminary treaty, the Oneidas reserved the following Wisconsin land base:

... Beginning at the south westerly corner of the French Grants at Green Bay and running thence southwardly to a point on a line to be run from Little Cacalin [Little Chute] parallel with the line of French Grants & Six Miles from Fox River, from thence on said parallel line northwardly Six miles, from thence eastwardly to a point on the Northeast line of the said Indian lands and being at right angles with the same.[13]

In exchange for most of the 500,000 acres of land recognized as Oneida territory in the third Menominee treaty, the Schermerhorn treaty proposed awarding moneys to the two Oneida parties: the First Christian Party was to receive $30,500 and the Orchard Party $3,000. Based on Schermerhorn's actions among the Cherokees, the vast disparity of amounts was clearly intended to produce Oneida intratribal conflict.[14]

Besides payments to the Tuscaroras and St. Regis Mohawks and payoffs to their chiefs and agents in attendance at this bizarre council, Schermerhorn's accord provided for lands west of the state of Missouri, in Kansas, then Indian Territory, to be used and settled by the New York Indians. They were to receive "as much land as they have now ceded or hereafter may cede to the United States or to the State of New York." The treaty also provided for moneys for removing members of all the Six Nations to lands adjacent to the Cherokees and Osages in Indian Territory, subsistence for the first year there, the creation of an Indian school fund, and assistance for aged and orphaned Indians.[15]

In another section, article six, the Oneidas agreed to stop migrating from New York State after the ratification of the treaty by the Senate of the United States.[16] Importantly, by the fall of 1836, parts of Wisconsin were now sought after even more than the Oneida homeland in Madison County, New York. Hence, Schermerhorn, himself a speculator in Wisconsin lands, did not want to encourage further Indian settlement there, but would push for removal to Indian Territory, then well beyond the interest of American land jobbers. Thus, Bread, in order to gain recognition for continued Oneida land rights in Wisconsin, had to make a pact with the devil, Andrew Jackson's missionary from hell.

Because of strong congressional criticism of Schermerhorn's handling of Cherokee negotiations at the Treaty of New Echota of 1835, the missionary was forced to resign in 1837 as federal commissioner to treat with the Six Nations. He was replaced by Ransom Gillet, the former law clerk of powerful Democrat Silas Wright, from Ogdensburg, New York.[17] Despite the change of negotiators and the lack of Iroquois representation at the 1836 Indian council that produced the preliminary "accord," this Schermerhorn treaty was in many ways the precursor of things to come.

What eventually resulted was the Buffalo Creek Treaty of January 15, 1838, with the Six Nations. Wisconsin had become extremely valuable with the opening of the Erie Canal in 1825, resulting in a major land rush in the next quarter-century, prompting heightened tensions with the Winnebagos, a major war with the Sac and Fox, and a realization that the United States had to find a much more isolated region for the remaining eastern woodlands Indians. With its rising white population, Wisconsin split off from Michigan Territory and became a separate territory in 1836. Kansas lands in the Indian Territory seemed a more logical choice to place the rest of the New York Indians. By 1838, all of the Five Civilized Tribes and Delawares, Shawnees, and Ohio Senecas and Cayugas had already been removed to the Indian Territory. Thus, instead of treating to remove the rest of the Six Nations to Wisconsin, the authorities in Washington decided to "encourage" them to go to Kansas.

The resulting Treaty of Buffalo Creek permanently affected all of the Iroquois as well as the Stockbridge-Munsees. The treaty resulted in the loss of the Buffalo Creek Reservation, the center of Iroquoian life in New York at that time. Under this fraudulent "accord" consummated as a result of bribery, forgery, the use of alcohol, and other nefarious methods, and containing the signature of missionary Eleazer Williams, the Senecas ceded all their remaining New York lands except the one-mile-square Oil Spring Reservation to the Ogden Land Company and relinquished their rights to Menominee lands in Wisconsin purchased for them by the United States. In return, the Six Nations accepted a 1,824,000-acre Kansas reservation set aside by the federal government for all the Iroquois as well as for the Stockbridge-Munsees. These Indian nations had to occupy the Kansas land within five years or forfeit it. For a total of 102,069 acres in New York, the Indians were to receive $202,000, $100,000 of which was to be invested in safe stocks by the president of the United States; the income earned was to be returned to the Indians. The United States was to also provide a modest sum to facilitate removal, establish schools, and purchase farm equipment and livestock for the Indians' use.[18]

The treaty had other far-reaching results. Some of the Indians in this Iroquois version of the Trail of Tears died en route to or in Indian Territory of cholera, exposure, and starvation. In addition, the bitter in-fighting in tribal politics after the treaty's consummation eventually led in 1848 to the creation of a new political entity, the Seneca Nation of Indians. Moreover, the reaction to the treaty resulted in a Quaker-directed campaign to restore the Indian land base in New York, leading to the United States Senate's ratification of the Supplemental Treaty of Buffalo Creek in 1842. The Senecas regained the Allegany and Cattaraugus, but not the Buffalo Creek and Tonawanda, Reservations. Only in 1856 was the Tonawanda Band of Senecas finally "allowed" to purchase a small part of its reservation back from the Ogden Land Company. This land purchase, as well as the confirmation of federal reservation status, was acknowledged by the United States and the Tonawanda Band in a treaty concluded the following year. American Indian claims, including those of the Oneidas, under the Treaty of 1838 were not settled until the 1890s in a major United States Court of Claims award. Thus, in effect, the Buffalo Creek Treaty was the basis of federal-Iroquois relations throughout much of the nineteenth century.[19]

The treaty had a major impact on Bread's Wisconsin Oneidas as well. Because their Six Nations kin were no longer planning to resettle at Green Bay and environs, the federal government, realizing that their land base had been conditioned upon this possibility, reduced the size of their territory to 65,654 acres, 100 acres for each individual then allegedly in Wisconsin. On February 3, 1838, the United States Senate ratified this separate federal-Oneida accord, in effect an amended agreement to the Buffalo Creek Treaty of January 15, 1838. The Oneida's First Christian and Orchard parties ceded to the United States "all their [Wisconsin Oneida] interest in the land set apart for them in the 1st article of the treaty with the Menominies of February 8, 1831, and the 2d article of the treaty with the same tribe of October 27, 1832." Each Oneida individual was to receive one hundred acres and the federal government agreed to pay the Orchard Party $3,000 and the First Christian Party $30,500; the latter party could use $3,000 to pay their missionary and erect a church and a parsonage. The rest was intended to cover expenses of the treaty and "remuneration of the services of their chiefs and agents in purchasing and securing title to the land ceded in the 1st article."[20]

This latter provision and the payment of annuities to the chiefs and big men alone, not the people directly, became a sore point and led to attacks on Bread and other leaders well into the second half of the nineteenth century. Moreover, when some Oneidas on their way west to the Indian Territory under provisions of the Buffalo Creek Treaty decided to stay in Wisconsin in 1839, they found themselves landless people because they could not obtain lands legitimately under this federal-Oneida accord of February 3, 1838. The tragedy of these Oneidas, often referred to as "Homeless Oneidas," became an issue in tribal politics from 1839 until well after Daniel Bread's death in 1873. Furthermore, despite the federal assurances in the February 3 treaty to recognize the Oneidas' land base in Wisconsin, the existence of these Indians' remained precarious.

Oneida Indian Reservation under the Buffalo Creek Treaty of January 15, 1838, and Amended United States-Oneida Treaty of February 3, 1838. Sources: Oneida Nation of Indians of Wisconsin.

Bread, who had helped his people through this difficult transition and who had shown that he was a man of principle during the crises of the 1830s, had by the end of that period established himself as the singular voice of the Oneida people in the West. Now was the time to rebuild his community and create the Oneida Nation of Indians of Wisconsin. Although the Oneidas in Wisconsin in 1838 had only a small fraction of the lands they had purchased in the 1821 and 1822 treaties with the Menominees and Winnebagos, they no longer had to worry about whether the influx of thousands of members of the Six Nations would inundate, weaken, and destroy their ability to survive at Duck Creek. Nevertheless, the question lingered: Would the outside white world allow them to remain as culturally distinct Oneida Indians on lands guaranteed by treaties in 1838?

Chapter 7
Nation-Building

Even before the Treaty of Buffalo Creek, Chief Bread's focus was on rebuilding the Oneida Nation in Wisconsin. The noted anthropologist William N. Fenton has written that Iroquois Indians traditionally saw their society as a "body of relatives, 'my people'," who reside in a specific village. They consider themselves a nation, "literally 'a native land,' a concept that is once kindred and territorial."[1] While always remembering their central New York homeland and the tribal divisions that had contributed to their removal west, Bread helped redefine the Oneidas' concept of nationhood at Duck Creek.

Fearing what he considered a strange and threatening world—the rapidly changing Wisconsin frontier—Bread developed strategies to cope with new challenges and threats to Oneida cultural existence. From the beginning, he followed a careful course, overthrowing Williams and neutralizing his political rivals in the First Christian Party. Most importantly, he developed a remarkable alliance with his former political enemies within the Orchard Party that lasted two decades, and he worked effectively with local federal Indian agents and key clerics to stymie efforts intent on ridding Wisconsin of all Oneidas.

By aiding refugee Oneidas, be they Episcopal or Methodist, to get established in Wisconsin, he presented himself as a good Christian Indian serving the Creator and his people at the same time. Portraying himself as an Oneida nationalist intent first on stopping removal from New York State, then administering the logistics of resettlement in Wisconsin, and finally opposing removal from the environs of Green Bay to Indian Territory, he cemented his role as the single most important voice in council; however, he had other motives.

Bread, a complex individual with human foibles, was not simply driven by this "humanitarian" streak. He frequently sought financial compensation for his actions. The Powless affidavit shows that Chief Bread sought ten thousand dollars for his extensive services to the Oneida Nation from 1820 to 1838, specifically for his extensive travels as a lobbyist in defense of Oneida rights and claims "as the general agent or businessman of the nation" who acted for the "benefit of all." For decades he beseeched Albany and Washington officials for personal as well as tribal monetary compensation. Yet, at times, as Powless stated, Bread rejected payments as well, instead insisting that his impoverished nation use the money allocated from the federal and state treasuries to pay off tribal debts.[2]

Although this defense of the chief was written by Henry Powless, his most ardent supporter at the time, other aspects of Bread's political career from the late 1820s onward throw light on both his tribal leadership and the motives behind his actions. By "burying the hatchet" with Chief Jacob Cornelius' Orchard Party for a twenty-year period, Bread, at this critical time in Oneida history (1832–52), built a viable political coalition to help his community's survival. While the Oneidas' Indian neighbors were being disastrously affected by territorial and federal policies—the Brothertowns were being terminated, the Stockbridges divided into citizen and noncitizen parties and removed from the Lake Winnebago area to north-central Wisconsin, the Menominees forced to cede millions of acres, and the Winnebagos forced out of Wisconsin—the Oneidas under Bread's leadership successfully fought off these efforts. He carefully attempted to heal the splits between his First Christian Party and the Orchard Party, to bridge the chasm that had helped bring about tribal ruin in New York.

In part, Bread's success was conditioned by the nature of Oneida society and politics in the 1830s. Oneidas continued to arrive and their basic needs had to be met. In some ways, the Oneida pinetree chief served as a "padron," a conduit, facilitating resettlement and winning their allegiance at the same time. Bread also had to contend with major problems in the political order that were brought to Wisconsin by the Oneidas. He proved remarkably capable of overcoming them for a period of two decades.

Oneida political disunity and religious schisms were carried west. Numerous sets of so-called chiefs, self-proclaimed or otherwise, are listed in the historical documents for the Oneidas in the 1820s, both in New York and later in Michigan Territory. Challenges to a chief's legitimacy were often made because few chiefs who went west to Michigan Territory were officially raised in the customary way.[3] Into this clear power vacuum came the shrewd and aggressive Daniel Bread, emerging out of the shadows.[4]

In the early years in Wisconsin, both Chiefs Bread and Jacob Cornelius of the Orchard Party were forced to cooperate.[5] Each worked to head off tribal fissures that both chiefs knew might contribute to another Oneida removal. Both men had to face a myriad of problems of resettlement in the early 1830s caused by waves of impoverished Oneidas arriving in the environs of Green Bay from New York State. Even though each man operated as the singular voice of his party and sought separate compensation from Albany officials under New York State treaties, the two joined together on many other issues. These included petitions for the payment of federal annuities under the Treaty of Canandaigua, claims for compensation under the Treaty of Buffalo Creek, and relief for struggling members of each party, newly arrived from New York State. They took joint stands against removal from Wisconsin, supported several federal subagents at Green Bay who were favorable to the Oneidas' interests, and opposed the appointment of others who were seen as enemies of their people. Importantly, both men signed the Oneidas' amended Treaty of Buffalo Creek of February 3, 1838.

By 1836 and 1837, Bread's alliance with Jacob Cornelius was set down on paper when both men were designated to speak for the entire Oneida Nation in negotiations. On August 31, 1836, long-time First Christian Party chiefs Neddy Archiquette and Elijah Skenandore gave Bread an unqualified vote of confidence for his policies and actions, insisting that the thirty-six-year-old chief was "a fine expression of our views."[6] Two days later, Bread and Cornelius formally made a pact, one that proved invaluable in the decade and a half that followed.[7]

Bread prepared the groundwork for the accord with the Orchard Party by carefully administering two waves of Oneida emigration from New York in 1833 and 1834. On his first trip, he went to Oneida "and assembled a party of his people to remove to Green Bay and acted when at home as their general agent commissioner of the nation."[8] The next year, Bread went back to New York, this time to make another appeal for relief funds from New York State legislators and to guide First Christian Party members and the large bulk of Jacob Cornelius's Orchard Party to Duck Creek. Bread's work on behalf of the Indian refugees of both parties was acknowledged in a report made by the New York State legislature in 1835. The report categorized his relief efforts as "meritorious," stating that he was "prudent, wise and energetic" in facilitating the administration of removal for both First Christian and Orchard Party Oneidas.[9]

The accommodation of Bread and Cornelius is even more remarkable because their two neighborhoods on the reservation operated separately, almost as autonomous units, each with its own set of pinetree chiefs, its own church, its own singing and mutual aid societies, its own missions school, even its own lacrosse team. Campisi has written that a "quid pro quo soon developed between the groups; each managed the affairs of its sector, and each represented in tribal councils in proportion to its membership." The ethnohistorian added: "The Episcopalians generally controlled two-thirds of the political positions."[10] At the time, in the late 1830s, the First Christian Party had 440 members and the Orchard Party had 184.[11] Although intermarriage between the members of the parties was discouraged, the leadership of both groups was similar, composed of the "more successful and prosperous farmers with similar views toward a work ethic and Christian morality." Indeed, their separate residence patterns "consisted of individual farms strung along the main roads, and it was common for sons to establish homesteads near those of their fathers. The neighborhoods were integrated at one additional level: one was a Southender [Orchard Party] or a Northender [First Christian Party]."[12]

Threats to Oneida existence continued throughout the first two decades of Bread's leadership. With the opening up of a federal land office in Green Bay in 1834 and the formation of a separate Wisconsin Territory in 1836, much of central and southern Wisconsin became prime land for

Table 3
Oneida Indian Population in Wisconsin, 1838-1872

1838	624
1844	720
1853	978
1865	1,064
1872	1,279

Based on the *Annual Reports* of the Commissioner of Indian Affairs; and the correspondence of the Office of Indian Affairs, OIA, M234, RG75, NA.

settlement.[13] Baird, Doty, Martin, and Whitney urged Indian land cessions as well as Indian removal from the territory. They pushed for Wisconsin statehood, which served their pockets as land speculators because it required mass emigration to the territory. The influx of easterners from New York and New England would further their political and economic goals, making the land "acquired" from the Indians extremely valuable. From the time Wisconsin became a separate territory in 1836 until 1850, two years after statehood, its population increased by 2,414 percent, compared to a 51 percent population growth for the entire country![14]

Pressures on the Oneidas stemmed from demographic changes as well as the direction of national Indian policies of the Jackson-Van Buren era. First, Washington policymakers favored removal, especially after the Indian Removal Act of 1830 was passed by Congress. Second, two Indian conflicts—one with the Winnebagos in the iron district of Wisconsin and the other a major Indian war with the Sac and Fox in 1832 in southern Wisconsin—gave added support for the wholesale removal of all Indians from the upper Midwest.

Immediately after a separate Wisconsin Territory was achieved in 1836, renewed talk of Oneida removal increased. The governor of Wisconsin Territory, Henry Dodge, who wore a second hat as federal superintendent of Indian Affairs for Wisconsin Territory, advocated this "solution" in his reports to Washington. On October 18, 1839, he suggested an exchange of Oneida lands at Duck Creek for other lands in the Indian Territory. Casting the move as inevitable, the governor wrote that since initial white settlement, "history has shown that the Indian never prospered in the vicinity of the white man." For their own betterment and protection, Dodge argued, they had to be removed because of the rapidly increasing white population in and around Green Bay. Although at the time the Oneidas were having to deal with internal disputes, Dodge exaggerated the split, claiming that the Oneidas were divided in half,

Table 4
Population in Wisconsin, 1836–1870

Year	Population
1836	11,683
1840	31,000
1850	305,000
1860	776,000
1870	1,055,000

Based largely on Alice E. Smith, *History of Wisconsin*, Volume 1, and on the United States Department of Commerce. Bureau of the Census. *Historical Statistics of the United States*.
Author's Note: Wisconsin Territory was created out of Michigan Territory in 1836. Wisconsin became a state in 1848. The statistics for the period from 1840 to 1870 were rounded off to the nearest thousand by the Bureau of the Census.

with one group favoring removal and the other advocating United States citizenship.[15]

A year later, Dodge added other arguments to his advocacy of Oneida removal. On October 18, 1839, after referring to the Oneidas and the other New York Indians as being "more a civilized than a savage people, in their habits, manners, and customs," the governor stated that these Indian nations were few in numbers and loyal allies of the United States. The Oneidas deserved protection and United States citizenship, Dodge maintained, since their present settlement will eventually be lost because their lands were of the "first quality." He referred to the Indians' presence as an obstacle because their community was in the "immediate vicinity" of white settlement.[16]

The push for Oneida removal continued into the 1840s, well after the end of the Jackson and Van Buren presidencies. Judge Doty succeeded Dodge as territorial governor and federal superintendent of Indian Affairs for Wisconsin. Not surprisingly, considering his history, Doty took a position in favor of Oneida removal. On October 11, 1843, he wrote T. Hartley Crawford, the United States commissioner of Indian Affairs, pointing out that, under the Treaty of Buffalo Creek, the Oneidas were given land "much larger than they required for the purposes of agriculture or hunting." He observed that "their tract is so large that it prevents the sale and settlement of the country north of Green Bay." Doty urged the commissioner of Indian Affairs to hold treaty negotiations for a land cession: "The interests of the Territory and of the government, it is believed, would be advanced, by reducing their possession to those of farms of the ordinary size, and allowing them to hold in severalty."[17]

In part, the Oneidas' "success" in dealing with these threats was the result of factors unrelated to the alliance made between Bread and Cornelius. Their success in overcoming this push could largely be attributed to the efforts to get at more valuable lands of the Brothertowns and Stockbridges, who originally settled around Lake Winnebago, as well as the extensive lands still held by the Menominees north of Green Bay. Yet, some credit in thwarting these forces must be given to Principal Chief Daniel Bread and his sophisticated strategy of dealing with these threats.

Bread's political skills, great presence, and oratory helped the Oneidas articulate their position in Wisconsin and become rooted in the West. Unlike their neighbors the Winnebagos, who were removed from Wisconsin four times, even as late as 1874, the Oneidas under Bread successfully resisted this harrowing fate. Indeed, fear of another removal was Bread's great motivation after he arrived in Wisconsin and found a chaotic situation similar to the one that had beset the Oneida polity in New York State. Seeing the strong possibility of a repeat of the situation that led to removal to Wisconsin, Bread fervently worked to rebuild the Oneida Indian community. Working with the local Indian agent and advocating a course of acculturation, he attempted to prevent another Oneida removal. By the end of the decade of the 1840s, with the beginning of Wisconsin statehood, the Oneidas had much greater roots in

Wisconsin, and Daniel Bread, in many ways, was the leading Oneida gardener, planting the seeds of a new home.

Bread cultivated his power base in other ways. He used his position as vestryman in the Hobart Church to win support. He supported the construction of a first permanent Episcopal Church.[18] When this Hobart Church was finally dedicated on September 2, 1839, he arranged for the visit of Jackson Kemper, the Episcopal bishop, to Duck Creek. As the Oneida spokesman, Bread extended the "chain of friendship" to the bishop, metaphorically adopting the cleric into the Oneida Nation.[19] This friendship lasted until after the Civil War and served both Bread and the Oneidas well because of Kemper's special feeling for this particular Indian community and the Oneidas' affection for the bishop. The bishop, who visited Duck Creek on many occasions, served as the Oneidas' protector, the counterweight against powerful anti-Oneida forces emanating from Green Bay.[20]

After the Treaty of Buffalo Creek, Bread and the Oneidas faced a major challenge within the nation. The January 15, 1838 federal treaty, not the February 3 amended accord, had provided for lands in Kansas, then part of a large Indian Territory. Two separate but interrelated groups arose to challenge Bread's authority to speak for the Oneidas: the so-called Woodman Party and the Missouri Emigrating Party. After the Amended Treaty of 1838 that recognized an Oneida common land base of 65,400 acres, approximately one hundred acres per person at the time of the accord, Indians from New York and Canada, not included in the treaty, continued to arrive in the environs of Green Bay. This group of late arrivals was known as the Woodman Party, after their missionary William Woodman, who had accompanied them from the East. These Indians were also referred to as "Homeless Oneidas" because they had no land rights under the treaty and were not accepted as equal members of the community until 1887.[21] These Oneidas frequently petitioned for land rights, became pawns in tribal politics, and some even collaborated with or joined a second opposing group to Bread's leadership, known as the Missouri Emigrating Party, which was committed to leaving Wisconsin for Indian Territory.

The Missouri Emigrating Party was formed by deposed First Christian Party chief John Anthony. Anthony's supporters included disaffected members of First Christian, including Baptiste Powless, the brother of Henry Powless, a leading chief of the First Christian Party who remained loyal to Bread; and John Denny (John Sundown), largely considered a tribal outcast for his family's involvement in land sales in New York.[22]

In October 1838, the Missouri Emigrating Party, in a petition of 196 signatories sent to President Van Buren, insisted that they wished to exchange their 100 acres per person allotted to them under the February 3, 1838 Amended Treaty of Buffalo Creek for 320 acres west of Missouri. They explained that they wanted to be "out of the reach of the white settlement; and those malign influences which overcome and overreach the half civilized Indian relative to their property and moral habits." They maintained that Bread was not a legitimate chief since he had the support of no more than four (First Christian Party) chiefs, two of them whom he controlled, "old and infirm and superannuated."[23]

The Missouri Emigrating Party pursued their campaign with intensity well into the 1840s. As early as March 12, 1838, members leveled another charge against Bread: They objected "to Daniel Bread's having so large a share [under the Treaty of Buffalo Creek] as is said to be awarded to him."[24] Six days later, in a letter to the Secretary of War, Anthony and his allies advocated the need for a new federal-Oneida treaty, claiming his followers could no longer live in peace with the followers of Daniel Bread, "who want to stay in Green Bay and become as white man citizens of the country." They added that Bread and the First Christian Party chiefs were getting all the annuity money and had, in effect, become "chiefs of the white man." Members of the Missouri Emigrating Party continued to present themselves falsely as representing the majority of the Oneida Nation.[25] The party leadership soon besieged federal, state, and local officials with appeals for a new treaty that would lead to an exchange of tribal lands at Duck Creek for those south of the Missouri River. Whether this movement was orchestrated by Baird, Doty, Ellis, or Whitney and the elite at Green Bay who lusted after Oneida lands is unclear; however, it did result in a movement that culminated with an Oneida treaty council with Governor Henry Dodge and other federal commissioners in November 1845.

Bread's political skills helped him thwart the Missouri Emigrating Party. The chief attempted to build on his cooperation with federal Indian subagents George Boyd and David Jones as well as with Chief Jacob Cornelius to weaken the Woodman and Missouri Emigrating Party threats. These disruptive movements weakened the Oneidas, fed into Green Bay interests pushing for Oneida removal from the territory, and took six years of Bread's incredible leadership to defeat.

Subagent Boyd, the son-in-law of former President John Quincy Adams, was well known for "feathering" the nests of his family and associates. One contemporary historian of the Menominee has labeled him as "the most corrupt of the pre-reservation agents of the [Menominee] tribe." He apparently lost his mental faculties in the late 1830s and was ultimately dismissed from office by early 1842.[26] To Bread, it appears, a corrupt and mentally deficient Indian agent was better for his Oneidas than one who represented Green Bay's leading families.

Boyd, who referred to Bread as his "friend" in his correspondence, used the Oneidas for his personal rewards, but also was clearly used by Bread to defend Oneida tribal interests.[27] Throughout the decade of the 1830s, Bread worked with Boyd, Stambaugh's successor at Green Bay, despite the subagent's anti-Catholic, anti-French, anti-Menominee views. Bread supported schools and western education and public health efforts such as vaccination for his people, cooperating with Boyd at every turn.[28] Moreover, because of the constant expenses of feeding, housing, and resettling Oneidas from New York in Wisconsin, complicated by their arrival at different times, the climate of the upper Midwest, and periodic epidemics, including cholera, Boyd periodically asked for special federal funds to help what he considered his impoverished wards.[29]

Boyd frequently defended the Oneidas. In one annual report in 1838, he called the Oneidas and Stockbridges the "best and most practical farmers in the country" and stated that he would "be sorry to see them removed" to Indian Territory. His attitude was in sharp contrast to that expressed by Doty, Ellis, and their associates. Boyd, who hated the Grignons and Martin most, recommended no forced removal and believed that only Indians who desired emigration should be aided.[30] Not surprisingly, on February 14, 1840, Bread came to the subagent's defense, calling him an "honest man" and saying that the New York Indians had no complaint against Boyd, whom they considered "our friend."[31]

The next subagent at Green Bay, Col. David Jones, basically continued Boyd's cordial relations with the Oneidas. Jones was clearly impressed by the Oneida community. In his annual report of September 16, 1844, he wrote favorably about the Duck Creek community. The subagent considered the Oneidas "civilized," in contrast to the Menominees and Winnebagos, because they had two churches, two schools, and had adopted "the language, dress, manners and agriculture of the white men." The agent claimed that they lived in comfortable houses and cultivated large farms on rich, fertile, and well-watered land, producing a "large surplus of wheat, oats, barley, corn, etc." Yet, there was a hint of things to come in Jones's report. He observed that the Oneidas had "rich forests of white pine, sugar maple and other valuable timber" and their "farming land in this section of the country" was "susceptible of supplying all the wants of the white as well as the red man."[32] By the 1850s, these rich Oneida resources would be the object of Green

Nation-Building

Table 5
Episcopal Missionary Solomon Davis's Census of Oneidas

Number of families	150
Number of souls	722
Frame Houses	20
Block Houses	43
Log Houses	84
Frame Barns	51
Log Barnes	38
Wagons	30
Sleighs	87
Ploughs	69
Harrows	51
Fanning mills	15
Threshing machine	1
Horses	104
Oxen	200
Cows	181
Calves and young cattle	110
Hogs	561
Domestic fowls	1,298
Sheep	5
Clocks	17

Authors' note: According to Davis, 2,213 acres of Oneida lands at Duck Creek were under cultivation. The Oneidas had two sawmills, one grist mill, and one blacksmith shop. most of the rest of the 65,400-acre reservation "was covered with a heavy growth of timber."

Bay entrepreneurs and would help undo much of Bread's work.

In early February 1844, Bread reported to Jones what the chief considered removal schemes, pushed by Whitney and Baird, that misrepresented Oneida views. Whitney and Baird suggested new negotiations for a treaty of removal, claiming that a large portion of the tribe was anxious to sell them lands and move into Indian Territory.[33] On February 28, Jones informed the commissioner of Indian Affairs of this plot by outside meddlers, naming Baird and A. I. Irwin, the postmaster at Green Bay. He claimed they were promoting a treaty in clear violation of the federal Trade and Intercourse Acts.[34] Hence, it was no surprise that because of Jones's defense of Oneida interests and criticisms of the subagent's actions by the Green Bay establishment he was subsequently fired in 1845 and replaced by Albert G. Ellis, Bread's long-time enemy.

Before Jones's firing in the summer of 1845, the Oneidas petitioned the commissioner of Indian affairs, calling Jones "kind and faithful," a man who "watched over our best interests." Hearing the rumor that Ellis would be appointed in Jones's place, they insisted that Ellis was a dishonest man who "has smooth words; but we fear, a bad heart. These are two bad things when connected in one man." The Oneidas added that, because of this, Ellis would filter information to Washington which would confuse and complicate the situation. Ellis would "stand between our nation and the President of the United States." Using the traditional metaphors of Iroquoian diplomacy, the petition, one apparently drafted by Bread, concluded: "We can never know through him how to understand each other's words, and it will require a great deal of rubbing and scouring to make the chain of friendship bright between you and us [emphasis added]."[35] Despite this petition, President Polk nominated Ellis to be the agent at Green Bay. As it turned out, Bread's decade-long alliance with Jacob Cornelius would help save the Oneidas from the same fate that they had experienced in New York State. Now he had to do battle with his old enemies at Green Bay and their new point man, Bread's old nemesis, Albert G. Ellis.

As soon as he assumed office, subagent Ellis began to push his agenda. On September 24, 1845, in a report to Governor Dodge, he advocated citizenship for the Oneidas, a seemingly beneficial strategy on its surface. This policy initiative, pushed by Whitney, had slowly worked to paralyze and divide the Brothertown and Stockbridge Indians into citizen and Indian parties and led to their land cessions from 1839 to 1856. Alluding to the Missouri Emigrating Party of the Oneidas, Ellis added that a "considerable portion of the [Oneida] tribe has for some time been desirous of emigrating to Missouri."[36]

On November 19-21, Dodge met in council with the Oneidas at Duck Creek. Morgan L. Martin, another appointed federal commissioner, was unable to attend; however, Ellis and Henry Baird, serving as secretary to the commission, were in attendance, along with Bread and Cornelius and representatives of the First Christian and Orchard parties. Dodge informed the conferees that as a federal commissioner he was there because "it was the wish of a part of the Oneida Nation to sell their lands." President Polk, "their Great Father," was willing to allocate them 320 acres per person to relocate them west of Missouri and pay a "fair value for their lands" and "for their improvements" in Wisconsin."[37]

Bread, the first Indian to respond on November 19, politely stated that the council would come to a final decision the following day. Perhaps hoping to clarify Dodge's statements for other Oneidas at the council, he inquired whether the federal government wished "to purchase and pay for our lands here, or only to exchange for lands south of Missouri; and whether the lands west of the Mississippi would be given to them in addition?" Dodge quickly responded by repeating that the Oneidas would be paid for their lands and their improvements on these lands and that the Oneidas would obtain lands west of the Mississippi if they agreed to sign the federal treaty.[38]

The next day, Bread, deferring to the Orchard Party chiefs, let Chief Cornelius open the council by recounting the Oneidas' experience as allies of George Washington during the American Revolution. Then Cornelius bluntly stated "We have always thought that when we bought the lands at this place [Duck Creek], we had a right to them." He added: "We are perfectly satisfied with this our home, and we know no other." After recounting the move from New York and the Oneidas' struggle to build a community at Duck Creek, Cornelius insisted that "the country [Wisconsin Territory] and its climate are good and we do not want to leave." Although angered, the chief revealed a sense of humor, exclaiming that Wisconsin was "the proper place for us; that a warmer climate [Kansas and the rest of the then-existing Indian Territory west of Missouri] would not agree with us." All the Oneidas wanted, he maintained, was for the federal government to provide schools for the children and leave the Oneidas alone, which would "make us happy."[39]

Working in tandem with Chief Bread, Cornelius concluded that the Oneidas were satisfied with their present lands, "and have *all* agreed not to sell; and we hope you will not think hard of us in refusing to sell [emphasis added]." Being a realist after surviving the New York experience and specifically countering the Missouri Emigrating Party argument, the Orchard Party chief insisted that Oneidas could never get away from white settlement, even if they were resettled nearer the Rocky Mountains; if they were removed to far-off places, he astutely observed that they would be "compelled to move again before many years." The only way was to stay and become friends of the whites and "not object to live near them. We are now taught and instructed by whites— There is good and bad among them." Despite the acceptance of acculturation, Cornelius concluded by affirming Oneida sovereignty under federal treaties and the guarantees to the 65,654-acre reservation in and around Duck Creek.[40]

On November 21, the final day of the council, Chief Bread arose and dominated the discussions. He informed Dodge that John Anthony had been deposed as a chief as early as 1833 and that Adam Swamp had replaced him on the council of chiefs. He then went about discrediting one by one the other Oneida leaders of the Missouri Emigrating Party—Henry Bear, Baptiste Powless, John Metoxen (not the Stockbridge chief of the same name), Metinus King, and

Isaac Wheelock, suggesting that all exaggerated their positions within the Oneida Nation and that they had falsely presented themselves as chiefs, or were designated chiefs "not in the regular way."[41]

Bread then thanked Dodge and the federal commissioners for following Oneida protocol. "Everything has been done in a just and proper manner and through the chiefs." In effect, what Bread was saying was that Dodge and the commissioners had correctly consulted with the recognized leadership of the Oneida Nation, especially Chief Cornelius and himself. Hoping to win points with the commissioners, Bread then asked that President Polk send them an American flag "as a remembrance of the 4th of July, the Birthday of Independence." In a sly, self-effacing way because Dodge had been a well-known enemy of the Oneidas, Bread stated that the Oneidas were pleased that "our Great Father has sent so good a man for commissioner."[42]

By the end of the meeting, only 87 out of 770 Oneidas had signed up supporting the federal treaty of removal.[43] Without the support of Cornelius or Bread and with the approaching international crisis leading to war with Mexico, efforts to push Oneidas out of Wisconsin stalled. Ten days after the council at Duck Creek, Dodge wrote Commissioner of Indian Affairs William Medill that the Indians pushing for removal west, the Missouri Emigrating Party, "were entirely unauthorized by the chiefs and head men of the Oneidas" and that "King [Adam], Powlis [Baptiste Powless] and Denny [John] are men of no standing in the Nation here."[44] Thus, Bread's strategy of cooperation with Jacob Cornelius had worked, leading to the defeat of another threat to Oneida existence. Although Ellis remained in charge of the federal Indian subagency at Green Bay for another three years and continued to lobby for Oneida removal, the Oneidas now had a slight respite to strengthen their community and dig deeper roots in Wisconsin.[45]

The victory of 1845 and the community-building efforts that followed produced a rosy view of the future. It appeared as if the displaced Oneidas finally had become rooted in Wisconsin largely as a result of a level of tribal cooperation not found in earlier days in New York. Yet, despite the optimism, they were still faced with having to deal with their long-standing enemies among Green Bay's elite families. Moreover, the relationship between the First Christian and Orchard parties was tenuous at best. The question was whether it would last. Could Chief Bread continue to build on this connection for the betterment of his people?

Chapter 8
Founding Father

In the summer of 1849, Alfred Cope, a wealthy Hicksite Friend and Quaker philanthropist from Philadelphia, visited Duck Creek. Cope had accompanied Thomas Wistar, another Philadelphia Quaker, who had been sent by President Zachary Taylor to Fort Howard to distribute forty thousand dollars to persons of mixed Menominee and white ancestry for partial payment of some of their Wisconsin lands.[1] While on assignment, Cope recorded his observations of the Oneidas led by Bread.

Cope's memoir reveals much about Bread and Oneida life in Wisconsin at mid-nineteenth century.[2] Upon first viewing the Oneida Indian Reservation at Duck Creek, Cope noted the "unpretending but substantial habitations of the Oneidas as far as the eye can reach," as well as the "green fields and snug buildings so prettily situated," which were the "result of their own labor and good management." After describing the umbrella-carrying Oneida women, who wore Menominee-styled headgear, Cope commented favorably on the menfolk and their farming abilities. He was struck with the respectability of their appearance and equipages." Comparing the Oneida farms with those of his native Pennsylvania, Cope insisted that "their horses, wagons and harness could have been creditable" to his home state. He added that the Oneida horses "were superior in appearance and spirit" to those commonly found in Pennsylvania and that the Indians "had better teams than any other country people about the [Green] Bay."[3] Once again drawing comparisons, Cope noted:

The buildings of the Oneidas were by no means equal to those of the Brothertowns, nor were their fields in as nice condition nor their horned cattle as carefully bred as those of the Stockbridges. Yet, in all these respects they would bear pretty well to be put in comparison with most communities of whites of as recent date. In one particular—the height, material, and firmness of their fences—they excelled. No such fencing was seen elsewhere. The height seemed needless, unless for the exclusion of deer. It was asserted that these people formed the most important part of the agricultural population of this vicinity, were quite superior . . . in industry and productiveness to the farmers of French descent, and, in fact, brought to market more corn and beef than anyone else.[4]

Cope observed that the Oneida houses were of unpainted wood, "well-proportioned and neatly constructed," and built along a main corridor, and that, even as early as 1849, most of the timber on the lot had been cleared, leaving no shade on these homesites. The "most conspicuous buildings" on the reservation were the Episcopal church and the home of Daniel Bread. The church wore "the pleasant face of a New England village meeting-house." Cope claimed that there were between seven hundred and eight hundred Oneidas, and that five hundred were members of the Episcopal Church and one hundred were Methodists. Each church ran schools for Oneida children and, in 1848, fifty students, more than half girls, attended.[5]

The Philadelphia businessman then described the July 4, 1849, celebration at Oneida, at which time it was customary to invite the tribe and their guests to the head chief's

(Bread's) house. Over one hundred attended the feast, which included venison, fresh pork, beef, rice pudding, and coffee. Much as in other American communities, fireworks were set off. The meal was followed by a lacrosse match between teams selected from members of the Episcopal and Methodist churches. Fully reporting the match, the pacifist Cope cringed at the combative nature of the game but delighted at the players' great agility and overall prowess. What disturbed Cope at the match was the ever-present liquor trade, which he now noted had been somewhat reduced from past times. Indeed, tribal council regulation forbade "grog shops in the Nation."[6]

Bread apparently scripted Cope's visit. The only sense of discord presented was in the lacrosse match. Bread was inaccurately described as a sachem, living in a "spacious, double house painted white and set back a considerable distance from the road," although his residence, like many other Oneida residences, had no trees to protect it from the "noonday sun," nor steps to bring a guest up to his front door easily. Here was the great man welcoming Indians to feast at his house. To show his magnanimity, Bread invited a visiting delegation of Oneidas from the Thames in southern Ontario to join their brothers at Green Bay and environs permanently.[7]

As the Cope memoir reveals, the Oneidas had made a remarkable adjustment at Duck Creek by midcentury. Largely through Chief Daniel Bread's leadership, they had accomplished much over a quarter century. They had relocated several hundred of their tribesmen from central New York to the Wisconsin frontier, survived the threats of new removals, established themselves on farms, and worked out political compromises between former bitter enemies, the First Christian and Orchard parties.

Despite territorial, state, and federal efforts to absorb these Indians into the American polity and inculcate them with Euroamerican ways and values, the Oneidas at Duck Creek maintained their separate identity; however, these

Indians had lost much. Their traditional social organization with its structure was fading. Moreover, the Oneidas' traditional political organization based on the leadership of condoled chiefs and warriors controlled by clan matrons was a thing of the past. Despite rapid cultural changes, the Oneidas rebuilt their nation under Daniel Bread's aegis. He and the rest of the Oneidas did so by taking cultural elements of the past and modifying them to serve the Indians' needs at Duck Creek. The modifications went far beyond the creation of a twelve-member tribal council composed mostly of non-condoled "big men," pinetree chiefs, with Bread as its head.

Campisi has succinctly summarized the ways Oneidas adapted to their new surroundings:

It is difficult to determine the degree to which the traditional Iroquois belief system permeated the culture of the Wisconsin Oneidas or was incorporated into their Christian religious attitudes. It seems certain that the Oneidas of Wisconsin performed none of the calendrical ceremonies, nor were any followers of Handsome Lake. It is equally clear that the great epics of Creation and the Peacemaker, which validated the traditional sociopolitical system, were no longer recited, nor was the condolence of sachems performed. However, the ceremonial giving of names appears to have been continued, although it took place during Fourth of July celebrations. . . . clan and moiety arrangements atrophied when the emphasis shifted to religious and neighborhood affiliations and to nuclear family and bilateral kindred membership. A few Iroquois beliefs were integrated into Christianity, losing much of their original meaning. Thus the good twin in the Iroquois Creation, Thaluhyawa·ku (He Who Holds Up the Sky), became synonymous with Jesus Christ. In another example, the Oneidas collected water before sunrise on Easter morning. This water, called *kanekka·nol* (holy water), was thought to have therapeutic powers. The Oneidas brought with them to Wisconsin the complex of beliefs associated with individual health, societal well-being, and balance and equilibrium in the universe, and these continued to exert influences throughout the nineteenth century. In addition, the medicine societies continued curative practices well into the twentieth century.[8]

The Oneidas' world had definitely changed after their relocation to Wisconsin, but their modus operandi had not. As the proud descendants of a once-powerful Iroquois Confederacy that had negotiated with representatives of kings, the Oneidas adapted their Condolence Council ritual, at the core of their culture, into the Wisconsin setting. They did this through the annual commemoration of Independence Day. As Cope described, every July 4th, Oneida chiefs made their formal addresses to their people and to invited guests in a conscious diplomatic attempt to soothe Oneida-white relations within the Brown County region and to build bridges with key members of the surrounding white community. By recalling the past, Oneida leadership and accomplishments, and reminding their own people and these outsiders of the need for ties to bind them, these chiefs, especially Daniel Bread, were in effect adapting elements of the Iroquois Condolence Council to the mid-nineteenth-century Oneida world at Duck Creek.[9]

The Oneidas' commemoration of Independence Day was not simply the fruit of acculturative white forces working to absorb them. Their Revolutionary War alliance with the American colonists had cost them dearly in lives, and their communities had been devastated. The war had also strained their relations with pro-British elements within the Six Nations; however, the Oneidas were proud of their role as loyal warriors of General Washington. Right up to the present time, July 4th is the date of the Oneida Nation pow-wow, at which time the Indian nation's veterans are always honored. It is no surprise that Bread, as the great orator and principal chief of the Oneidas in Wisconsin, addressed gatherings on that hallowed day, remembering these Indian Revolutionary War warriors and their sacrifices.

These annual speeches served to remind Indian and non-Indian alike of those who had come before and the responsibilities of the living to the dead as well as to the seven generations that were to follow. In effect, the Condolence Council Ceremony lived on at Duck Creek every July 4th. Bread's achievement in this regard can only be understood by examining the role of the Condolence Council historically in Iroquoian culture.

Fenton has noted: "The ritual paradigm that governed the proceedings [of forest diplomacy] guided the behavior of Iroquoian and Algonquian speakers alike throughout the lower Great Lakes; it survives today in the program of the Iroquois Condolence Council."[10] This council was for mourning dead chiefs, lifting up the minds of bereaved relatives, and installing their successors. The ceremony is essential for understanding the Iroquois and their diplomacy with other Indian and Euroamerican nations. It consists of rites known as the Roll Call of the Founders, the Welcome at the Woods' Edge, the Recitation of Laws, the Requickening Address, the Six Songs of Requiem, and the Charge to the New Chief. Invited guests gathered at the woods' edge and were welcomed into the village where the chiefs read the Roll Call of the Founders, recounting the sacrifices of past leaders. Dead chiefs were recognized for their service to the nation, mourned, and their successors raised and validated, "requickened in the titles of the founders so that the league may endure."[11] Then the face of the new chief was revealed and he was charged in his new duties to carry out the people's will.

The ritual of mourning and installation of chiefs was also filled with numerous metaphors that attempted to "strengthen the house [nation]."[12] Dispelling the clouds and restoring the sun were metaphors used to emphasize the importance of this bereavement and installation ritual. To create alliances of the gathered participants, there were references to keeping the path open by clearing rivers, rapids, and roads; polishing a chain; and maintaining a perpetual fire to bind.[13]

The Iroquois' expectation was that all the guests/outsiders observe and respect these Indians' traditions and learn the proper forms of the ritual. Fenton has written that, through the seriousness and religiosity of the Condolence Council, the Iroquois attempted to manipulate the foreboding white world to their own advantage. Knowing their great power had waned by the eighteenth century, the Iroquois Confederacy saw alliances as indispensable for survival. Whether weaker Indian nations such as the Munsees, Nanticokes, Saponis, Tutelos, or Tuscaroras, or more powerful Europeans such as the English or French, one thing was clear, as Fenton has observed: "Whoever came to the Iroquois came on their terms."[14]

The hospitality and generosity of the Six Nations during this Condolence Council Ceremony was exceptional. It included the "passing of wampum belts, the distribution of presents and the enormous expense of the expected feast." Besides social dancing that always followed the end of the ten-day period of the Condolence Council, a lacrosse match was held, which was intentionally planned as part of the rite. For lacrosse was more than a game. It was a "game that anciently discharged social tensions" by discouraging intervillage warfare, keeping the warriors fit, and cheering the depressed relatives of the deceased.[15] Thus, the ceremony, in effect, reinvigorated Iroquois existence, renewed political forms, restored society, and built or strengthened alliances.

Chief Bread was the central figure in transforming the Iroquois Condolence Ritual into an annual Independence Day ceremony at Duck Creek. Through his brilliant oratory, Bread used the traditional elements of Iroquoian ritualism, modifying them to meet the political circumstances of the day. In typical Iroquoian diplomatic fashion, he attempted to educate both his people and friendly whites to the great Oneida leaders and accomplishments of the past and their contributions to the American nation. For nearly four decades, Bread helped make Independence Day an essential part of Oneida identity.

Three of the Oneidas' July 4th celebrations—in 1849, 1854, and 1857—reveal much about this adaptation and Bread's role in the process. Each festivity contained a chief's addresses (although the 1849 one was not fully recorded or reported on), a feast, a lacrosse match, and, at least in one instance, social dancing. The reporting of these festivities, all made by outside, non-Indian observers, focused on the good times, the foods, and the lacrosse match, more than on the meaning of the day to the Oneidas.

With little understanding of the spiritual meaning in the address, or of Oneida pre-Revolutionary War history, the *Green Bay Advocate* wrote about Bread's Independence Day speech of July 4, 1854:

> The custom is an excellent one, as it tends to promote harmony between the two races, a result which cannot be too highly appreciated by either party. Visitors are entertained, and invited to partake of viands cooked in the most tempting style; the audience are then usually addressed by the chief through an interpreter, and a reply made by any person present; the day then closes with athletic games by the Indians.[16]

In this same speech on July 4, 1854, Bread stated deferentially, much in the manner of Grand Council protocol: "If you observe anything on our [Oneidas'] part (as you undoubtedly will), which may appear to you unseemly, you will please to excuse us; and as well [we] shall endeavor to entertain you to the best of our ability, and of the best which we have we offer to you." He then continued by mentioning that the Oneidas had "forsaken many of the customs of our fathers"; however, Bread carefully indicated that despite significant changes there was still "a wide difference between us." This observation was a conscious effort to teach the outsiders that Oneidas were not willing to be made into carbon-copy whites, but, in the traditional Iroquois metaphor, they paddled a separate canoe down the river. They could not completely enter the white man's canoe and could not straddle with one foot in two canoes.[17]

In the next segment of the address, Bread recounted the history of the Iroquois and the major role the Oneidas played in the American Revolution: "But the Oneidas, ever friendly towards your fathers, could not be alienated from them either by the threats or persuasions of their foes." In their commitment to General Washington, they "painted their tomahawks red in blood of the enemies of your people." The chief pointed out his people's sacrifice: "Many of their bravest warriors were slain, but their own children knew not the resting place of their bodies. There are no monuments erected to show where they fell." Renewing the chain of friendship, he reaffirmed his people's loyalty to the Americans and looked to the president of the United States, "our Great Father in Washington, who will act as the eagle watching over the Oneidas" to protect them "whenever we are in danger of trouble."[18]

On July 4, 1857, Bread once again held forth. In the speech, Bread recounted the history of the Oneida people, while lauding American progress; however, in the same address in which he diplomatically praised certain past enemies of his people, including his archnemesis, Andrew Jackson, now an American icon, he pointed a finger at some of his local Brown County enemies, "a certain class of citizens" of Green Bay, for their continued hostility toward his Duck Creek community.[19] A reporter for the *Green Bay Advocate* noted: "Our neighbors, the Oneida Indians have an old, time-honored usage of celebrating our national holiday every year, by a sort of Festival, in which they are joined, not only as spectators but participants by their pale-faced brethren."[20] Viewing it as an excellent way "to promote unity and harmony between the two races," the reporter praised Bread's and his Oneida people's hospitality since the assembled were entertained and invited to share a "sumptuous feast." After the address by Bread in the

Oneida language, which was interpreted and replied to by any person present, the day closed, as in other years, "with athletic games by the Indians."[21]

Bread's July 4th addresses were his way of reaffirming Oneida identity and, at the same time, dealing with the world beyond Duck Creek. Besides extending "chains of friendship" just as he had done earlier with Bishop Kemper, symbolically adopting the clergyman as his people's own and bringing him into the Iroquois circle, Bread consciously reached out to build alliances with whites every July 4th. As a proud Oneida with knowledge of the Condolence Council Ceremony, he adapted it to the needs of the mid-nineteenth-century Wisconsin Oneida community. Whether it was using the metaphors of the past, "chains of friendship," or the ancient game of the Iroquois people—lacrosse—Bread, in a calculated way, ran the affairs of the Oneida Nation. His sophisticated leadership served his people well for decades.

The chief fervently worked to rebuild his community in the West and modified Oneida customs to meet his people's needs; nevertheless, the Oneidas were soon to be faced with new threats to their world at Duck Creek. Bread's skills were to be tested, and this time they were to fall far short of their mark.

Chapter 9
Things Fall Apart

By the 1850s, the Oneidas had made a remarkable adjustment to Wisconsin; however, they did not fully possess all the means necessary to ward off all threats to their Wisconsin community. Campisi has observed that the Oneida political system from the 1820s to 1870 "never had time to solidify; the precipitous changes in the surrounding white society which in the 1870s controlled the political destinies of the tribe precluded any adjustment."[1]

According to traditional Iroquois thinking, a chief had to have "skin seven thumbs thick" to deal with tribal affairs, especially internal politics of the nation. Chiefs were often brought down to mere mortal status by a process that is still characteristic of Iroquois politics. At times it was a petty and demeaning process; on other occasions, it was intended to bring forth the wishes of the clan mothers or the community at large and was a sincere expression of the nation. Bread's political life over the decade and a half after Alfred Cope's 1849 visit to Oneida must have appeared to him as part of this traditional leveling process; nevertheless, he successfully walked the gauntlet and survived every test, however weakened, through the Civil War.

Chief Bread, with the cooperation of Chief Cornelius, continued to act as the primary voice of the Wisconsin Oneidas.[2] On January 13, 1851, Chief Bread appealed to the president for payment of a $650 annuity that was in arrears. In the memorial signed by Chief Cornelius and the chiefs of both parties, he once again pointed out the Oneidas' valuable military service in the Revolutionary War, requesting an American flag for his reservation. Bread and the others reminded the president that the Oneidas "stood without flinching" and "fought, bled and conquered under the same banner with Washington and LaFayette."[3] Two weeks later, the two chiefs sent a petition to Congress asking for annuity payments of $1764.80 for the Oneidas under the provisions of the Treaty of Canandaigua of 1794, insisting that "for nearly twenty years the government has been indebted to them, and has paid no interest on that indebtedness."[4] The following year, he attempted to secure federal military bounty payments from Washington for his people's service at the Battle of Sandy Creek in 1814.[5] A long-time supporter of education and Christianity among his people, Bread supplied one of his houses to serve as the Episcopal school after a fire in 1859 devastated the old educational facility.[6] Yet, by the end of that decade, many things had changed in Bread's family life and in Oneida society as a whole.

A series of family tragedies clearly had a bearing on Bread's inattentiveness to detail and his overall leadership of the Oneidas. Indeed, Bread was to suffer one family setback after another from 1848 to 1856. On June 6, 1848, his wife, Jane, died; he had married her a year after the death of his first wife, Electa, in 1842. In 1851, he married his third wife, a thirty-year-old Mohawk woman named Margaret Fraser. Margaret was to die less than five years later. Besides the loss of his wives, Chief Bread lost three of his children—his son John and two of his daughters, Lucinda and Susannah, in the same period. Thus, at the height of his political achievements, Bread's personal life weighed heavily on him.[7]

In addition to these tragedies, he and the Oneida people were affected by three famines, three major epidemics of smallpox, and the disaster of the American Civil War in the period from 1849 to 1865. In the years 1848-49, 1858-59, and 1863-64, the Oneidas faced severe famines that resulted in near-starvation conditions, leading to the chiefs' appeals for food relief and seeds from the federal government as well as from religious societies.[8]

To make matters worse, by the late spring of 1849 and continuing into the next decade, Bread, Cornelius, and Episcopal missionary Solomon Davis were charged with corruption, having been accused of pocketing annuity moneys and hiding information about annuity payments.[9] None of these accusations made by Bread's white and Indian political enemies were ever proven, and the chief avoided prosecution; nevertheless, the charges undermined Bread's leadership and weakened the relationship between the First Christian and Orchard parties built up in the 1830s and 1840s.

These charges brought into question the role of Solomon D. Davis, the Episcopal missionary and schoolteacher of Oneida children, who was one of the chief's most important allies. Davis, who had been a missionary among members of the First Christian Party since their days in New York in the early 1820s, had built up trust over a quarter-century. Besides serving as a trustee for annuity moneys, he had been put in charge of collecting money on leases made by the nation.[10] Davis was accused of benefiting from the annuity moneys in his capacity as a legal custodian appointed by the chiefs, most importantly Bread, in the early 1840s. The Methodists of the Orchard Party, the "poor cousins" of the First Christian Party, saw this as another instance of treachery by their more powerful tribal rivals. By 1852, two anonymous and disgruntled chiefs within the Orchard Party, reacting to this alleged misappropriation of tribal moneys, suggested allotment as the panacea, believing land-in-severalty, with its fee simple title to each family and promises of future American citizenship, would ensure a better chance for individual families' welfare.[11]

On January 31, 1853, Cornelius and other chiefs of the Orchard Party entered the fray, breaking with Bread and claiming that the First Christian Party chief had broken his agreement with the Orchard Party, by, among other things, going off to Washington without their approval and with an illegal power of attorney in hand. They accused Bread and Chief Elijah Skenandore of denying the warriors and their children annuity moneys under the treaty of 1838.[12] In another sign of a break with Chief Bread, Cornelius, along with the chiefs of the Orchard Party and one from the First Christian Party, wrote the president on December 7, 1853, suggesting that they were willing to exchange lands with the Stockbridge Indians, an Indian nation at the time even more threatened than the Oneidas by white economic development. Chief Cornelius indicated that the Orchard Party was willing to sell the Stockbridges three thousand acres of land at Oneida.[13] This move ran counter to Bread's two-decade-old strategy of separating Oneida Indians from the problems of other New York Indians in Wisconsin and his long opposition to selling any and all of the Oneida Reservation.

Perhaps the greatest threat to Bread's leadership came with the emergence of the city of Green Bay as a major center of the timber industry. Although lumbering operations in nearby DePere dated as far back as 1809, mills began full operation in the 1830s, largely initiated by Ellis and Arndt. By 1846, two mills of considerable size were operating in Green Bay proper, another at the mouth of the Menominee River, and four or five others in the lake shore district to the north of the city. By the 1850s, Green Bay had become the shingle capital of the United States. Millions of board feet of lumber as well as shingles and lesser wood products were shipped out of Green Bay by the beginning of the Civil War.[14] Whites quickly poured into Brown County, seeking the timber resources around Green

Things Fall Apart 131

Bay. They also sought lands in the region ranging between $2.50 and $5.00 per acre by the mid-1850s.[15] Logging companies turned their sights to the rich timber resources of the 65,654-acre Oneida Reservation that lay just southwest of the city.

The first sawmill at Duck Creek had its origins in 1836. John Arndt erected a mill there, concluding a leasing arrangement with Chief Daniel Bread and the Oneida chiefs of the First Christian Party. The mill was later operated by Nathaniel Foster, one of the major lumber barons in Wisconsin history. Foster later hired Oneida boys and girls to pack shingles. By 1844, the Oneidas themselves also had two sawmills operating at Duck Creek, as well as a gristmill and blacksmith shop owned by Chief Bread.[16]

Besides the denuding of the Oneida Indian Reservation in a forty-year period between the late 1830s and mid-1870s, the timber industry had other destructive results. Indian entrepreneurs driven by a source of quick profits became more individually motivated rather than community-directed and then began to ignore tribal leaders such as Chief Bread. These quick but short-run profits also helped foster class divisions. A few Oneidas could afford to muster teams of workhorses and supply logging camps, but a significant number worked as exploited loggers. Many Oneidas abandoned their agricultural pursuits, seduced by this "easy money."

The relentless cutting also created an ecological disaster. These stripped lands had less agricultural potential, and fishing resources became contaminated by mill operations and runoffs, much as had happened on tribal lands around Oneida Lake in central New York. What was left after the Duck Creek Reservation was allotted after 1892 were very small parcels of "sub-marginal lands."[17] The quick profits to be made in lumber had other negative consequences. Oneida alcoholic consumption increased steadily, especially with the expansion of white settlement nearer to the reservation and with the establishment of taverns there.

Oneida problems with alcohol and incidents of alcohol-related violence occurred much more frequently from the 1850s onward.[18]

The result of this catastrophe was a politics of blame at Oneida. Instead of understanding the changing world around them and realizing that history was repeating itself, the Oneidas turned inward on themselves, accusing their leadership of corruption, incompetence, and weakness to cope with the situation. Instead of pulling together as in the 1830s and 1840s, the Oneidas became overly fragmented, repeating some of the same mistakes that had driven them out of New York.

On October 1, 1855, the federal Indian superintendent, Francis Huebschmann, described the worsening situation at Oneida in a letter to the commissioner of Indian Affairs, George Manypenny. Huebschmann called the influence of the local white-owned lumber companies "pernicious" because it was leading Oneidas to neglect their farms. He asked the commissioner to intervene to "put a stop to the trade carried on by the people of Green Bay for the pine logs, lumber, and shingles cut and manufactured by these Indians." Despite the superintendent's effort, he had failed to convince the chiefs of "the importance of dissuading their people" in this detrimental enterprise. Superintendent Huebschmann sadly noted that the Oneidas were tempted because the "price of pine is so high, and the market is so near [Green Bay]." As a result of the weakness of the tribal government, the chiefs did not have "sufficient influence to prevent their younger men from continuing to cut pine and to manufacture shingles." Huebschmann predicted that the Oneidas were on a fast track to ruin unless these tribal resources were protected.[19] The previous year, Bread and the chiefs of the First Christian Party had attempted to control the situation by making a separate tribal mill lease, rather than allow initiatives by individual Oneidas; however, the lease had revealed a growing split in the community. Only the First Christian Party chiefs signed this lease, suggesting the decline of cooperation and mutual respect between the First Christian and Orchard parties.[20]

Other attendant problems resulted from logging. In February, 1858, federal Indian agent A. D. Bonesteel reported to the commissioner of Indian Affairs that the Oneida chiefs were complaining "most bitterly, that their people and *warriors* are getting so that they no longer pay any attention to their laws.... They [the chiefs] cannot govern them at all."[21] In the superintendent's report to the commissioner of Indian affairs in 1858, the situation appeared even to worsen. The report indicated that there were growing "difficulties existing between the chiefs and the people." Whatever authority they had, which was apparent in the 1840s, had largely faded: "There seems to be little or no parental authority in the chiefs. They have lost their influences of domestic government, and are reduced to the level of the common Indian." Although defending the chiefs, the superintendent indicated the increased number of thefts of cattle that were "stolen, driven off and sold to whites," as well as more serious crimes such as murders.[22] Now, because of the growing anarchy at Oneida, Chief Jacob Cornelius and his most loyal followers suggested two solutions, which before had been considered unthinkable to all but a few Oneidas: allotment of the reservation in severalty and the application of federal laws and courts to administer criminal authority on the reservation.[23]

The following year, Agent Bonesteel wrote Commissioner A. B. Greenwood, urging allotment to encourage Oneidas' "ambition to improve and cultivate" their lands. By selling part of the Oneidas' reservation to the Stockbridges, the federal Indian agent maintained that the moneys obtained from the sale of "excess lands" would pay for improvements in the Indian schools. Bonesteel insisted that the present reservation contained "a much larger quantity of land than they [Oneidas] *will ever require for use* [emphasis added]," the moneys obtained from the sales of these so-called "excess" lands will produce the means of "relieving the [Oneidas'] poorer and indigent class, and afford additional means to the able-bodied to make still further improvement." At the same time, he noted that these land sales would benefit white settlers residing in the vicinity, whom he readily admitted were exerting pressures to get at the Oneida land base.[24]

Out of desperation, Bread and Cornelius once again sought to cooperate in early 1859. The previous year's crop failures of wheat and oats had left the Oneidas further weakened. While the council arrangement of twelve chiefs, with the two parties sharing power, was largely dying, the two chiefs joined together in a memorial to secure relief funds from Washington.[25]

By Christmastime of the same year, Chief Bread and the chiefs of the First Christian Party wrote to President James Buchanan, reminding the Great Father of their past military service and hardships in obtaining their new home at Duck Creek; they asked the president to help them provide laws to live under and establish courts to try crimes, insisting at the same time that they were satisfied with their Wisconsin reservation and did not wish to pursue another treaty with the federal government.[26]

A second, more detailed memorial, signed this time by both Chiefs Bread and Cornelius, was sent to the commissioner of Indian Affairs, F. W. Denver. On December 29, 1859, the chiefs documented the lack of visits by the federal Indian agent, but more importantly, the extent of the anarchic conditions at the Oneida Indian community. In a sad commentary, they described how their people had become "lawless, and refuse to yield obedience to their chiefs." They indicated that they feared for their children's and grandchildren's future because, among other things, they were "afraid of our young men."[27]

By this time, a generation gap had developed at Duck Creek. Those Oneidas born in New York who remembered the hardships of removal and resettlement from 1820 to 1838 were dying off. The council of chiefs was still dominated by the "old guard" headed by Bread and Cornelius, but the majority of community members had been born in Wisconsin. Oneidas aged eighteen to thirty-three were no longer listening to the old chiefs lament about the loss of their central New York homeland. Some of these young men had also overindulged in alcohol and, because of drink, had caroused, harassed their neighbors, and become abusive to missionaries. In the same letter of December 29, Chiefs Bread and Cornelius added: "Our young men mostly neglect the cultivation of the soil, and work the pine of our land into shingles and so forth by this means they produce a great deal of strong drink."[28] With taverns springing up nearby at Fort Howard, Green Bay, and DePere, the Oneida consumption of alcohol steadily increased.

This December 29 memorial appears to be partly a reaction to what occurred the previous month when the Episcopal missionary's residence was stoned and his windows broken. One missionary reported that someone had broken into the mission house and stole "a good share" of his poultry.[29] The churches—the glue that held the community together for decades—were now failing to bind, and the consequences amounted to a loss of faith. It could also be argued that these incidents were reprisals against the missionaries of the period, including Episcopal cleric Edward A. Goodnough, who had become involved directly in the politics of the Oneida community and had engendered hostility by interfering in tribal government affairs. Goodnough had drafted letters from the council to Washington and had even suggested that federal officials should reply to him or to the chief. Goodnough saw the old chiefs system as antiquated, suggesting that there would ultimately be a change. In the fall of 1859, the missionary claimed that the "chiefs are year by year more convinced of changing the tribal form of government, and substituting another of more utility."[30] One of those unwilling to see the inevitability of

Goodnough's prediction was Chief Bread, who continued to hold onto power as principal chief of the Oneida Nation of Indians of Wisconsin.[31]

Although Bread and Cornelius had resumed a minimal level of cooperation, Bread had by this time lost support within his own party as a result of the events that had transpired over the previous decade. In March 1860, the Oneidas held a major council at which time some of the eldest and most respected chiefs of the First Christian Party, including Elijah Skenandore and Neddy Archiquette, joined with Orchard Party members to push for a new federal treaty to divide the Oneida lands in severalty. Chief Bread rejected this drastic course of action. Among Bread's supporters were Cornelius Hill, a young chief and Bread's son-in-law, and Chief Henry Powless, Bread's major ally for nearly four decades. The majority of the First Christian Party also apparently opposed the move.[32] With storm clouds of Civil War on the horizon, Washington had little motivation to deal with the Oneida situation. Instead of sending commissioners to negotiate a new treaty, federal officials were soon attempting to recruit Indians into another "war of brothers."[33]

For the Wisconsin Oneidas, the Civil War years were a disaster, ranking next in importance to the Oneida removal to Wisconsin and to allotment under the Dawes General Allotment Act of 1887. Estimates of Oneida enlistment in the Civil War range from 111 to 142 out of approximately 1,100 reservation residents. At least forty-six of these volunteers for the Union were killed, missing in action, or died of disease while at war. Two tribal historians estimate that as many as sixty-five Oneidas were fatalities of the war.[34] Moreover, the Oneida Indian Reservation in Wisconsin was ravaged by major smallpox epidemics, one which raged in 1862 and another from November 1864 through March 1865 (plus one immediately after the conflict in 1866). White communities that suffered in the war were soon replenished with immigrants, but the Wisconsin Oneida Indian community experienced a 4 to 5 percent population decline, which had severe and debilitating repercussions well into the future.

The Oneidas faced a second war, one on the home front. In 1861, Commissioner of Indian Affairs William Dole suggested the consolidation of all the Indians of the Green Bay Agency "onto a single reservation" and the assignment to them of "a proper quantity of land to be held in severalty."[35] In 1863, Dole advocated removal of the Oneidas, in the "best interests of the Indian," to the upper Missouri on lands "obtained from loyal Indians of the Southern Superintendency."[36] Both of these suggestions went counter to the majority thinking of the Oneidas at this time. The federal government did little to help the Oneidas, and by 1863 the Indians at Duck Creek were in desperate shape—impoverished, squabbling over the exploitation of tribal timber resources, divided over allotment, and dealing with the aftereffects of a major smallpox epidemic.

At the conclusion of the Great Sioux Uprising that had spilled over into the state from Minnesota, the Wisconsin adjutant general's office began to recruit Indians in earnest in late 1863; this was after the devastating losses of Union forces in late 1862 and the first half of 1863. Going against the advice of some of the chiefs and missionary Goodnough, Oneida youth were enticed by large monetary payments to become recruits for the Union. By October 1863, the federal government provided a three-hundred-dollar bounty for three-year recruits. By early 1864, it was possible for a volunteer to receive even more money in federal, state, and local bounties. Encouraged by bounty brokers working on commission, the Oneida "dirt farmers" from north-central Wisconsin, like other poor country folk, saw the economics of fighting for the Union. M. M. Davis, the United States Indian agent of the Green Bay Agency, wrote to the commissioner of Indian Affairs on May 31, 1864: "The Oneidas who have enlisted in the military service have done so of their own free will. They have received Government and local bounties and I have no doubt that they are much better provided for in the service than they have ever been heretofore." Davis added that "the families of these enlisted men are also much better off than heretofore. They already received large bounties and they receive $5 per month from the state."[37]

The Oneidas' white neighbors in Brown County began to view these poor Indians as "replacement" soldiers. Although most of them weren't officially substitute soldiers, the Oneidas served to fill the county enlistment quotas required by both Washington and the Wisconsin State adjutant general's office in Madison. The Indians also saw it as their only viable option. From 1860 through 1863, the Oneida economy was in shambles. Agriculture, largely of a subsistence level, had been the basis of the Oneida economy before the Civil War. Oneidas had supplemented their farm income by hunting game, fishing in Duck Creek, and gathering wild berries. Leasing land to whites and selling timber had become increasingly important. During the early 1860s, the Oneidas suffered another drought, severe winters that led to livestock losses, and even experienced a June frost. The *Annual Report* of the commissioner of Indian Affairs for 1864 indicated that many were destitute and that school-age children did not have clothes needed to attend the Indian school.[38] Hence, for the Oneidas, military service, despite the risk, became a way out of their desperate economic condition. War bounties and the substantial relief efforts of the Quakers in early 1864 enabled the Oneidas to survive.[39] Consequently, Oneidas volunteered for service together in the Fourteenth Wisconsin Volunteer Infantry, enlisting in clusters of five on December 31, 1863, and six on both January 4 and 7, 1864, at the recruitment office at Green Bay. In addition, on March 4, 1864, twelve Oneidas volunteered at Fond du Lac.

Because of the labor drain of a large number of young Oneida men at war and deaths caused by a smallpox epidemic in the community, in May 1864, Chief Elijah Skenandore and six other chiefs asked that some of these Indians be discharged from military service.⁴⁰ This action was not to be supported by Bread or Cornelius for fear that their community would be labeled disloyal or having Copperhead leanings. Both of these chiefs' commitment to the Union cause was unswerving—one of Cornelius's sons was killed at war—and they expressed that in their official correspondence. Calling the war an "unholy rebellion," they promised continued loyalty: "We love the flag of our nation and are anxious that it should float over the capital of the nation."⁴¹

During the war, the Oneidas on the home front had to contend with some of the same problems that they had faced in the previous decade. One of those matters included the continued unauthorized stripping of reservation timber resources.⁴² By the end of the Civil War, the federal Indian agent sadly reported to commissioner of Indian Affairs Dennis N. Cooley that "most of the valuable pine has been removed from the reserve."⁴³ The accord between the First Christian Party and the Orchard Party, although patched up in 1859, was clearly not working throughout much of the war. Bread continued to send petitions to the commissioner of Indian Affairs against the push by the Orchard Party to allot reservation lands and sell some of the Oneida lands to the Stockbridge Indians.⁴⁴

The Oneidas in the Fourteenth Wisconsin came marching home on October 26, and the reservation community celebrated their return with a veterans' party six days later.⁴⁵ The war had weakened the already divided community by permanently taking away so many of the youth. The returning veterans were greeted by news of leasing to whites, of a suspicious fire that destroyed a saw and shingle mill in the summer of 1865, of the cutting and sale of timber by individual Oneidas, and by talk of the need to institute a new tribal governmental elected system.⁴⁶ By taking the young warriors, mostly born in Wisconsin, away from the reservation, pressures to overturn the chiefs system of government withered during the war; however, with the return of these hardened veterans, that is, the ones who survived and came back whole with all their faculties intact, some of the same pressures manifested themselves again.

Although still the principal chief of the nation, Bread was slowly being pushed aside.[47] The actions of the Episcopal missionary Goodnough were to undermine his power base and leadership during and after the war. As early as 1863-64, Goodnough, no longer merely acting as a missionary and attending to the spiritual needs of his flock, had become an activist priest, assuming the role as quasi-Indian agent, writing separately to Washington, with his own ideas about the Oneidas and their future.[48] At the same time, in the post-Civil War years, Bread had to contend with an old enemy, Morgan L. Martin, a member of the Green Bay elite who had fallen on hard times and had assumed the lowly position of federal Indian agent in 1866.

Chapter 10
The Fall from Grace

The final years of Daniel Bread's life were hardly peaceful ones for himself, his family, and the Wisconsin Oneida community. Chief Bread had to contend with an internal power struggle that led to the loss of much of his power by 1870, even though he remained a chief and the titular head of the First Christian Party until his death in 1873. In this increasingly fragmented setting, Bread was now seen as a traitor by First Christian Party members because of his new attempts at cooperation with Chief Cornelius and the Orchard Party and his reversal of his position on the allotment of tribal lands. His growing hostility to the actions of missionary Goodnough, who continued to interfere in the politics of the nation, led Bread to become further alienated from others in the Episcopal Church, thus weakening his ability to maintain his leadership.

By March 1870, the federal Indian agent W. R. Bourne notified Commissioner of Indian Affairs Ely S. Parker that Bread had been removed as chief of the First Christian Party the previous fall, singling out two reasons for his loss of power: "desertion of their party and neglecting to attend church."[1] Although his fall from power was clearly the result of these factors, Bread's political demise was also directly related to his loss of influence at the federal Indian agency level and within the hierarchy of the Episcopal Church in Wisconsin. His Oneida opponents at the local level took advantage of the chief's fading influence off the Duck Creek Reservation in the years that followed the American Civil War.

After working with George Boyd to overthrow Eleazer Williams in 1832, Bread built his power base by cooperating with later federal Indian agents at Green Bay and ingratiating himself to Bishop Kemper and the hierarchy of the Episcopal Church in Wisconsin. With the exception of Albert Ellis's tenure as Indian agent in the middle and late 1840s, Bread had understood the benefits that would accrue by currying favor with local federal officials. This strategy would act as a counterweight to local Brown County pressures to get at the Indians' timber resources and lands. His dealings with the agents were not always easy because many of them, even the ones friendly to the Oneidas, were not honest men. Ellen Goodnough, the wife of the missionary, explained the key role of the agent in Oneida community affairs: "These agents have it in their power to do much evil or much good to a tribe."[2] Hence Bread understood this and cultivated a working relationship with numerous federal agents over four decades.

The Episcopal Church had also been a major source of Bread's power. His association and friendship with the highly respected Jackson Kemper led Bread to invite the famous cleric to Oneida on numerous occasions until Kemper's death in 1870. The chief clearly used his friendship with the bishop for his political ends. In her diary, Ellen Goodnough indicated that the bishop had a unique relationship with the Oneidas at Duck Creek and gave his full attention to their needs. She wrote: "The Indians almost idolize him, they are so much attached to him. Whenever he comes they do everything they can to show their respect for him."[3]

Unfortunately, Bread could no longer use his closeness to the bishop to prop up his leadership at Oneida. The revolt against the chief was led by missionary Goodnough, a key adviser to the First Christian Party. Goodnough's relationship with Kemper was a solid one and hence Bread's access to the bishop became limited.

The Episcopal missionary, who first came to Duck Creek in 1853, serving there until his death in 1888, had great influence among certain members of the First Christian Party, especially young chief Cornelius Hill. Besides ministering to the Oneidas' spiritual needs, Goodnough was the teacher at the church school as well as the Duck Creek community's justice of the peace, notary, postmaster, and postman. He acted as the scribe for the First Christian Party's memorials to Washington, was involved in their council meetings, and freely offered his advice to Chief Hill. He frequently wrote his own letters to both Washington officials and local Brown County newspapers, presenting his own views about situations affecting the Oneidas.[4] His determined opposition to Bread and to the allotment of the Oneida reservation and his interference in internal tribal politics was clearly evident in the post-Civil War setting. Importantly, the Episcopal missionary, the spiritual adviser to the First Christian Party, and his Methodist counterpart, the spiritual adviser to the Orchard Party, were both guilty of meddling. According to the federal Indian agent in 1870: "It appears to me that the trouble as well as many others existing among the peoples is caused by the ministers of the two churches." He added: "Mr Arbison, the Methodist minister, advocates the division of the lands while Mr. Goodnough, the Episcopalian, is very well satisfied with his home arrangements and wants the lands owned at present."[5]

To defend the overbearing Goodnough, the missionary clearly saw that his Oneida charges were totally impoverished and desperate peoples. In famine times, the only way for Oneida men to survive was by cutting the forest, making shingles, cutting firewood, squaring timber and railroad ties, and, for the women, by making and selling baskets and brooms. Goodnough disliked, as Chief Bread did, the arbitrary power of Morgan L. Martin, the new Indian agent whom he accused of dispensing bribes; however, the clergyman disagreed with Bread about the Oneidas' future. To Goodnough, the only way for the poverty-stricken Oneidas to feed themselves, after being weakened by war, smallpox, and famine, was to allow individual tribesmen free rein to exploit the tribe's rich forest lands.[6] Goodnough's view fed into the increasing discontent with the chiefs over control of treaty annuities and the belief that these funds were being used solely to benefit certain tribal leaders and their families.

In contrast, Bread and Cornelius saw these timber resources as the tribal estate, properly controlled by the chiefs who had to be respected as the traditional leaders of the nation. No outside white clergyman or upstart young chief, who had not suffered the travail of removal from New York, could speak for the entire Oneida Nation. After all, he and Cornelius were proud leaders who had earned respect by serving the collective interest of the Oneidas since the 1820s.

Ironically, Bread's obsession with preventing another Oneida removal, the modus operandi of his leadership since 1830, resulted in his ultimate fall from power in the last eight years of his life. He would do anything to prevent another removal, including changing his position on allotment. This reversal, one that led him once again to ally himself with Chief Cornelius and the Orchard Party, provided his rivals with ammunition to usurp his authority.

On the surface, Bread's fall appears simply to be related to his change of heart in favor of allotment of tribal lands, the position favored by Chief Jacob Cornelius and the Orchard Party. Bread's support of allotment was especially affected by the growing anarchy and the desperate economic conditions the Oneidas faced. Individual Oneida timber-stripping of the community's natural resources continued to be a problem during and after the Civil War while another epidemic of smallpox raged in the community as Oneida veterans returned home.

Because of the level of poverty among the Oneidas and the loss of young men in the prime of their lives, Bread frequently supported Civil War pension applications, helping numerous downtrodden Indian families cope with their losses. He aided widows and orphans who had no place to turn. In the spring of 1867, Bread himself became the guardian of Sallie Anthony, the teenage daughter of Thomas Anthony of the Fourteenth Wisconsin who had died in military service. He attempted to secure for Sallie her father's back pay and military pension as well.[7]

Chief Bread, perhaps realizing his own mortality, dealt with other issues that he felt needed to be resolved, namely the relationship of the Oneidas at Duck Creek with the Stockbridge Indians and with his Oneida kin in Canada and New York; he also began to wrestle with the question of the status of "Homeless Party" within the Wisconsin Oneida Nation. It seems clear that, while he was losing faith in Episcopalianism and was rarely in attendance at the Hobart Church, he was becoming more ecumenical in his thinking, working closer with the Orchard Party at the expense of his leadership of the First Christian Party. For a hard-boiled politician with a vindictive streak, this was a sign of emotional growth and humanity; however, to his enemies, the tight-to-the vest master of Oneida politics had shown weakness and was now susceptible to a political challenge from within.

On October 12, 1865, Bread and First Christian Party Chief Adam Swamp went over to the Orchard Party's position on allotment. Joining in with Cornelius, Bread wrote Washington complaining about Goodnough. They asked for the missionary's dismissal, charging the cleric with telling his flock to disobey federal Indian agent Davis's order to stop cutting and selling tribally owned lumber. Bread and the others pointed out that a certain number of chiefs of the First Christian Party believed missionary Goodnough "in all what he says." The clergyman, according to Bread, told these Indians to disobey the order, claiming it did not forbid cutting and selling lumber off the reservation, and urged them to sell as much as they could. Then Bread pleaded for federal government intervention to remedy the evil and better the conditions for the Oneidas by establishing federal criminal laws on the reservation. Despite this plea, Bread had a larger purpose in mind, one that revealed his commitment to his community and to Oneida existence in Wisconsin. He suggested that the federal government help relocate "a certain number of our people who are now living in Canada" to the Duck Creek Reservation. They "desire to come back to the American side. We lived together once in the state of New York."[8]

In the same memorial, Bread also promoted the idea of selling Oneida lands to the Stockbridge Indians, a position favored for more than a decade by all of the chiefs of the Orchard Party and some chiefs of the First Christian Party. Joining in with a majority of the chiefs' council as well as the Woodman Party, Bread pushed for land-in-severalty, as well as for the extension of federal criminal law to the Oneida Reservation. Bread's lament was the result of frustrations about his inability to guard tribal resources such as timber and about the overall breakdown of the chiefs' authority over daily life on the reservation.[9]

Bread, the Oneida nationalist, articulated his long-held dream, one that he had clung to, namely the reunification of the Oneida Nation in Wisconsin. In 1849 he had expressed the same idea to Alfred Cope and to visiting Oneidas of the Thames from Canada. Ironically, while he was being challenged for power internally, he reached out to his kin in Canada as well as to the Homeless Oneidas.[10]

In a turnabout, Bread attempted to deal with their problems, winning support for his efforts within the nation. He recommended, with Chief Cornelius's support, that these "Homeless" Oneida Indians should not be left out in any division of the reservation into fee simple title. In effect, Bread's promotion of fee simple title of the reservation was his way to attempt to help some of his most poverty-stricken tribesmen and solve a vexing problem that had persisted for three decades; however, the move could benefit Bread too. Realizing that the "Homeless Party" (Woodman Party) had grown substantially at Duck Creek and represented 382 Indians, approximately one-third of the Oneidas, Bread understood that officially incorporating these Indians into the community would bring political support to him and his leadership. Bread's attempts failed and the Homeless Oneidas were not allowed in the door of tribal politics until two decades after the chief's death.[11]

Besides Goodnough's criticism of tribal leadership, the last eight years of Bread's life were affected by the actions of Morgan L. Martin and Cornelius Hill. To Bread, Martin's reappearance in Oneida tribal affairs in 1866 must have seemed as if it were a recurrent nightmare. Martin, one of the most important figures in the territorial movement for Wisconsin statehood, had a long history and association with the Oneida Indians dating back to New York State in the early years of the nineteenth century. The son of Gen. Walter Martin who had settled on five thousand acres on formerly owned Oneida Territory in Lewis County, New York, Martin, at the advice and encouragement of his first cousin James Duane Doty, settled in Green Bay in 1827 and remained there until his death six decades later.[12]

From the time of Colonel Stambaugh in 1830, Martin became a major antagonist of Chief Bread and the interests of the Oneida Nation at Duck Creek. As a promoter of Green Bay's development, Martin promoted the idea of making the city the great center of the upper Midwest. From 1838 to 1844, he was on the territorial council of Wisconsin and, between 1845 and 1847, represented the territory in the United States Congress. Martin served as president of the constitutional convention of 1847-48, which framed Wisconsin's state charter. Later, in the 1850s, he served in the Wisconsin State Assembly and Senate.[13]

Martin's interest in Indians was conditioned not by promoting their welfare but by various schemes to get at their lands. He was heavily involved in land speculation in the Fox River Valley and in other areas of the territory. His varied interests also included the promotion of the dairy industry in Wisconsin and the founding of the city of Milwaukee.[14] Much like Stambaugh before him, Martin promoted the improvement and further development of the transportation network from Green Bay to the Mississippi River. Along with Daniel Whitney, he was active in establishing the Fox River Portage Company, which planned to bridge the Fox River at Green Bay, dam the river at DePere, and cut various canals, especially the one-mile-long Fox River-Wisconsin River portage, to the Mississippi. By 1846, as the territorial representative in Washington, he promoted this idea further, receiving federal moneys for what became the Fox-Wisconsin River Improvement Company.[15]

The 1846 act allowed Wisconsin to profit from federal land sales so that the state could then use the moneys for internal improvements in transportation. The promotion of the project also put pressure on the Indians in and around Lake Winnebago, lands that had been assigned to the Brothertown and Stockbridge Indians. If some of these lands could be opened up by treaty cessions, Wisconsin speculators could do a "land office business" by buying up these lands quickly and selling the timber and the land itself for a vast profit. These fertile lands would also be considered prime real estate if and when the Indians would sell their allotments and become citizens of the United States.

The Brothertown and Stockbridge Indians had faced a harsher fate than the Oneidas. In the 1830s, the Brothertown Indians agreed to allot their lands, take fee simple title, and become United States citizens; however, some tribal members instead opted to join in with the Stockbridges. By 1848, the Stockbridge themselves were divided into a pro-allotment "citizens party" and an "Indian party," those opposed to allotment. The Indian party also opposed land sales and supported the continued leadership of their chiefs and headmen led by Bread's former allies, John W.

Quinney and John Metoxen. In 1856, threatened with removal out of Wisconsin, the Stockbridges, along with some Brothertown Indians, were removed from the environs of Lake Winnebago, which was rapidly being settled by whites at that time, to lands approximately one hundred miles to the north that had formerly been Menominee territory.[16] Would the same fate happen to the Oneidas after the Civil War? Would tribal divisions aggravated by the push for fee simple title and United States citizenship, the pressures of white settlement, and the demand for timber resources lead the Oneidas down the path taken by the Brothertown and Stockbridge Indians?

Drawing from the incredible success of the Erie Canal, Martin, for a four-decade period, promoted the idea of a Fox River–Lake Winnebago–Wisconsin River–Mississippi River passage, formerly the canoe route of French voyageurs. He advocated improving the navigational channels and building canals. By achieving these feats, Martin would accomplish several objectives: land values would dramatically rise in the Fox River Valley because the region would be accessible by transportation and be seen as attractive to easterners, especially dairymen whom he wanted to bring west; Green Bay would become the center of a vast transportation nexus that stretched from New York City to New Orleans; and significant population increases would result, leading to Wisconsin statehood and personal fame and fortune for its promoters.

Oneidas, in part, had been driven out of New York State by canal pressures and rapid settlement that followed. Now Martin's Fox-Wisconsin River Improvement Company had the potential to do the same in Wisconsin. Importantly, many of the backers of the project were individuals originally from New York. Aside from Doty and Martin, they included the Seymour family—Horatio and Horatio's brother John; Wisconsin State Senator Orson Head; Salmon P. Chase, later secretary of the treasury under Abraham Lincoln; and Erastus Corning, governor of New York. Moreover, Whitney,

Baird, and Arndt were all involved in Morgan's transportation push.[17] Importantly, these entrepreneurs also had designs on the rich timber resources in and around Wisconsin Indian reservations.

Martin had been a strong proponent of Indian removal from Wisconsin since the 1830s. In the 1840s, he, along with the territorial governor, Henry Dodge, had pushed this idea at treaty councils. Both men were federal commissioners at treaty negotiations, focusing on the possibility of Oneida removal from Wisconsin, which the tribe overwhelmingly rejected in 1845.[18] After the Civil War, Chief Bread's worst nightmare was realized when, in 1866, Martin replaced M. M. Davis as the federal Indian agent in Green Bay. Next to Ellis and Stambaugh, Martin was perhaps the most hated white in nineteenth-century Wisconsin Oneida history. Now he was in charge of the major communications link to the "Great Father" and to the Commissioner of Indian Affairs. A crisis of immense proportions was now at hand, just at the time many Oneidas were questioning the viability of the old chiefs system and the leadership of Chief Daniel Bread.

The financial bubble of the speculative Fox-Wisconsin River Improvement Company burst in the late 1850s and 1860s, although the idea was revived periodically. With the rapid replacement of canals by the railroad interests, many of the leading families became investors in this new technology, promoting the Green Bay and Lake Pepin Railroad Company; however, some of the original investors in the Fox-Wisconsin River Improvement Company had suffered major financial setbacks, the most prominent loser economically and politically being Morgan L. Martin.[19] To overcome his financial difficulties, Martin sought political sinecures, including the positions of Civil War paymaster in Green Bay and later federal Indian agent in 1866.

For his first six months in office as Indian agent, Martin mostly concentrated on dealing with Oneida tribal requests for unpaid annuities under the treaty of 1794, and pensions for Union Indian soldiers and their widows and families.[20] Taking advantage of the internal squabbling within the Oneidas' ranks, the agent pushed for allotment of the Oneida Indian Reservation and the extension of United States citizenship, much as in the earlier Stockbridge and Brothertown cases. In his letter of June 25, 1867, to the Commissioner of Indian Affairs, Martin described the intratribal conflict occurring at the time among the Oneidas: "About one half of them, headed by Breads, Powlesses, Williams and other old chiefs are in favor of disposing of their surplus lands and having the remainder allotted in small quantities among the individual members of the tribe." Martin added that the "other half headed by the young chiefs and warriors oppose both the sale and allotments."[21] Two weeks later, Martin insisted that Bread and Cornelius represent a "large portion of the Oneida tribe" and favor allotment and land sales.[22] The missionary's wife, Ellen Goodnough, noted in her diary that the Indian agent was making trouble and that he was a "very harsh and arbitrary man and determined to get at these lands from the Indians and drive them West."[23]

In September 1867, in his annual report, the federal Indian agent showed his racial bias. He claimed that the Oneidas were so acculturated that they had lost their Indian manners and customs. In a backhanded compliment, he suggested that they were "almost equal" to those whites in a "state of advancement" and "better qualified to enjoy political rights than the freedman, or even the poorer of the white race who mingle with them." The report went on to justify allotment as a "cure" for the Oneidas, claiming that it would instill individual initiative, encourage the respect for private property, and allow for the proceeds of land sales to be applied to an increase in the school fund for these Indians. After all, Martin argued, it would take centuries for the Oneidas to put all of their land into cultivation, a goal that he saw as a requirement of civilization, since "only" four thousand out of over sixty thousand acres were being cultivated. "Even if you cut the reservation to 20 percent of its size," the agent continued, "there would still be abundant room for the coming generations of this tribe, until they shall have entirely disappeared or become incorporated with the white race which now surrounds them." In a most revealing statement, Martin noted that the Oneidas did not want to be removed to Indian Territory; however, he pointed out that many believed that allotment was inevitable and could not be resisted.[24]

Well into 1868, agent Martin promoted his agenda. According to Goodnough's diary, Martin actually told the Oneidas "that if they cut their timber and refuse to sell" their lands, the federal government would "send soldiers to drive them away."[25] It should be pointed out that at this time when Indians were being removed from Kansas to Indian Territory, Navajos were still being incarcerated at the Bosque Redondo to force cooperation and acculturation, and the Lakotas in the Black Hills and in the Great Plains were faced with the full wrath of the United States Army.

In 1868 the federal Indian agent insisted that the Oneidas had "much more lands than can ever be required by members of the tribe." He reported that intratribal politics had become nasty, with threats of reprisals against the chiefs if they agreed to a new treaty.[26] In his annual report dated September 25, 1868, Martin repeated the same arguments for allotment and observed that the Oneidas were slowly becoming degraded by the whiskey traffic in the Green Bay region. He lamented the continued timber stripping of the reservation's land.[27]

Martin made it seem to appear that he was committed to protecting tribal timber resources after he received specific orders from the Commissioner of Indian Affairs. His primary intention, however, was to gain control of the 65,654-acre Duck Creek Reservation. If Oneida lands were allotted, the agent knew that they could be taxed and then would be subject to foreclosure. By claiming that the Indians did not need such a large land base and hadn't cultivated their lands to their fullest potential, he was also implying that they had "excess" lands which they might sell off, if and when the reservation was allotted.

Right through the end of his tenure as federal Indian agent, Martin continued to portray the Oneidas in a most unfavorable light, suggesting that allotment would be a workable formula to solve all of their problems. The irony was that he was actually using his former enemy and Bread's name to endorse his own schemes. Calling Bread's supporters of allotment the nation's "most intelligent and influential" group, Martin pushed ahead.[28]

Both Chiefs Bread and Cornelius saw no hope in the late 1860s, since their historic enemy Martin controlled the channels of communication with Washington. Only a younger generation of idealistic chiefs led by Cornelius Hill hoped for a brighter day, which seemed to Bread as "pie in the sky tomorrow." For the "realists," the older chiefs such as Bread, who understood that his tribesmen had been weakened by fights of control of tribal timber resources as well as by epidemics, famines, and the devastation of the Civil War, the best hope was for the Oneidas to accept what was presented to them as a fait accompli, namely allotment. After all, what could they expect from Washington if all the federal government could do for the Oneidas was to send a long-time enemy to "help" them. For Bread and Cornelius, pessimism was the order of the day. The apocalypse was at hand and the four horsemen—famine, pestilence, war, and conquest—reigned supreme.

Martin was later accused of being part of a "ring" whose aim was to appropriate for himself the proceeds of the sales of timber from the Oneida Reservation. That, however, does not appear to have been the main reason for his actions. "Besides frightening them into selling their lands," Ellen Goodnough suggested, Martin had bribed some Oneidas to win influence and lied in his correspondence to Washington. The missionary's wife also added that by presenting himself as a defender of tribal timber resources, the agent was actually trying to force the impoverished Indians to choose allotments and carry out the agenda of those in Green Bay who coveted the Indians' lands once the reservation was opened up.[29]

In 1869, Martin was finally replaced as federal Indian agent by John Manley. Delighted to get rid of Martin, Chiefs Bread and Cornelius supported Manley and immediately defended his actions.[30] Manley was fully aware that four million feet of pine logs had been carried away from the Oneida Reservation in 1867-68 and sold well below market value, all without the authorization of Oneida chiefs Bread and Cornelius.[31] Deferential to the chiefs, Manley was also complimentary to the Oneidas. He described the Oneidas as "the most civilized and self supporting tribe of this agency."[32] When the agent initiated suits against whites for trespassing on the Oneida, Menominee, and Stockbridge reservations, he was soon replaced by agent W. R. Bourne.[33] By the time the federal government concerned itself with this issue and brought suit to protect Indian tribal forestry resources in *U.S. v. Cook*, decided by the U.S. Supreme Court in 1873, the delay had resulted in further theft of tribally owned timber by the relentless stripping of trees.[34] Moreover, the proceeds of these illegal actions were going into individual pockets, not benefiting the Indian nation as a whole.[35]

Despite Martin's challenge to Oneida existence and Manley's dismissal as federal Indian agent, the real threat to Bread's maintenance of power came from within the community at Duck Creek. In 1869 and 1870, insurgents within the ranks of the First Christian Party led by Cornelius Hill, a young chief born at Duck Creek who had married Bread's granddaughter, successfully challenged the principal chief's power. Chief Hill, known by the Oneidas as "Onuhkwas tkó" or "Big Medicine," was, like Bread, one of the great leaders in the history of the Wisconsin Oneidas. As early as 1860, Hill's name appears on memorials as one of the Oneidas on the council of chiefs. After Bread's demise and until Hill's death just prior to World War I, Hill was the leading voice of the community, frequently referred to as the last of the Oneida chiefs.[36]

Hill, a pinetree chief, was to employ two of Bread's routes to power: oratory and the Hobart Church. Indeed, besides being a notable chief, Hill, a devout Episcopalian, was later ordained as the first Oneida Indian priest. Much like Bread, the Wisconsin-born young chief was to dominate Oneida political affairs for four decades. Also much like Bread, Hill was educated by missionaries. Hill went to school at the Nashotah Episcopal Seminary, the same institution that had trained missionary Goodnough, who served as his friend and mentor.[37]

Hill's emergence from Bread's shadow occurred immediately after the Civil War. On March 5, 1866, Hill wrote President Andrew Johnson, pointing out the Oneida military sacrifice in the Civil War. He expressed the fear that the president had "forgotten the promises you gave us." Big Medicine then insisted that tribal members respect each other and that his Wisconsin community live by one abiding rule, namely that they refuse to sell tribal "land to white men."[38] Despite Hill's points, tribal resources continued to be appropriated by individual Oneidas and sold off to white entrepreneurs in the areas surrounding Duck Creek.

As early as 1867, Hill was pushing for a drastic change in the structure of the Oneida tribal government. On March 29, 1867, he sent a draft copy of a new "Constitution and Laws of the Oneida Nation in Wisconsin" to the Office of Indian Affairs, hoping to gain acceptance.[39] Three months later, Hill and six other chiefs, excluding Bread, wrote President Andrew Johnson, insisting that they had the firm intention to live in Wisconsin forever and that they opposed selling any land to the Stockbridge Indians or to anyone else. In a veiled threat, they suggested that these actions could lead to trouble and violence. They adamantly opposed the allotment of tribal lands into fee simple parcels. The chiefs insisted that, although there were always some Oneidas willing to dispose of their lands, the community was "unable to agree" about selling "any of their lands for any purposes." These chiefs asserted that not one individual or group of Oneidas had the right to sell tribal lands.[40] Over the next three years, Hill's role became even more visible as the major voice of the First Christian Party battling outwardly with Martin over the agent's racist statements, or internally with Bread in a power struggle for leadership within the Oneida Nation, which Hill clearly won in 1870.

The debate over allotment reached crisis proportions by the fall of 1869 and into the first three months of 1870. Tribal opponents attempted to overthrow Bread's control of the council of chiefs by holding an election.[41] According to the federal Indian agent, this "election" allegedly led to the rejection of Bread's rule as principal chief. This action was followed by a council meeting on February 28, 1870, at which time the council of chiefs, going against tribal custom that required at least an outward expression of consensus, voted 8 to 5 (twelve chiefs and Bread as the principal chief) in favor of allotment. By this time. Chief Henry Powless, Bread's most loyal political ally, had turned against the principal chief and joined with Chief Hill to fight allotment. After hearing arguments rationalizing allotment, Bread's opponents, many of whom were members of the chief's First Christian Party, "tried to put him [Bread] down as chief." They insisted that they would never consent to have their "land surveyed and allotted and would have nothing to do with the laws of the United States." Before the "council of the whole nation," they threatened "to kill Daniel Bread the oldest chief of the tribe" and said that they would do so in case he persisted in his endeavor to push allotment.[42]

After the February 28 council, Bread and his allies—First Christian Party chiefs Elijah Skenandore and Adam Swamp and Orchard Party chiefs Jacob and John Cornelius—wrote to the commissioner of Indian Affairs explaining their position. They maintained that the Oneidas were a split nation and that two divisions existed within the community. The chief claimed that the pro-allotment group

The Fall from Grace

he led represented the majority of chiefs, and the 8 to 5 vote was done "legally that is according to the custom of the tribe."[43]

Their memorial to the commissioner contained a full explanation of the pro-allotment position entitled "A Special Homestead Act":

> We wish to have our land surveyed and allotted to each individual owner of the Reserve, each one taking land in the shape of a Homestead as is hereby provided, and each one to take as much land as is duly his share, and those who have made improvements upon the land where they are now living may be allowed to keep the same if they choose to after the survey is made.[44]

Bread and his large family, it should be noted, had substantial landholdings and had made many improvements on these lands. Therefore, they would have benefited economically, more than most Oneidas, from allotment.

"A Special Homestead Act" proposed by Bread and his supporters made other points that clarified their position on allotment. They insisted on protections for those Oneidas who agreed to fee simple title. These allotted lands should be "exempted from taxation so long as we shall remain under the Homestead law." They added that no Oneidas could "sell, convey, mortgage, or in any way convey" these individually owned parcels. In a revealing part of this policy statement, this proposal insisted that heads of families had the right to sell the timber on these lands if they chose to do so, thus apparently conceding to the individual pressures that Bread had fought so passionately against for nearly two decades. In order to ensure order, the proposal advocated that federal laws of the United States be applied "for all criminal cases" and that the state laws of Wisconsin be employed to prevent trespassers on these newly allotted lands. They insisted that after the passage of this "special homestead act," any Oneida Indian, if he desired, could become a United States citizen, but only after a five-year waiting period during which he was shown to be an "orderly and industrious man," capable of managing his own affairs and supporting his family.⁴⁵

Bread's opponents were not satisfied with his public humiliation in council. On March 7, Hill and five other chiefs including Chief Powless, sent a memorial, notarized by missionary Goodnough, to the commissioner of Indian Affairs, formally rebuking and removing their principal chief: "the said party [First Christian Party] will no longer recognize any acts of said Bread as at all officially binding or in any way valid." They reiterated their opposition to allotment: "we do not wish to be troubled any more about dividing or selling our land here." They accused their opponents of selfishness for wanting "to sell and divide" tribal lands, suggesting that they were few in number and only out for "personal advantage." Hill and the others insisted that they did not want to lose "our tribal connection" by becoming United States citizens and appealed to the "Great Father" for protection.⁴⁶

Even though Bread's name continued to be on correspondence, leases, memorials, and petitions as an Oneida chief right up to the time of his death in 1873, his power and influence evaporated after the 1870 showdown.⁴⁷ His political opponents, using Chief Hill's model constitution developed after the Civil War, replaced the discredited council of chiefs and established an elected system, one that operated much like town governments in other Wisconsin communities. Although the old council of chiefs continued to meet, the real governmental authority of the nation was transferred to an elected council. Despite this upheaval, the new political order, beset with continued pressures for allotment, fared little better than the older council of chiefs.⁴⁸

While Bread's long career was going up in flames, the Oneidas were soon faced with dealing with the consequences of two incredibly destructive fires in 1871—the Great Chicago Fire and the Great Peshtigo Fire. The two fires created even more demand for Oneida timber. The Peshtigo fire, one of

The Fall from Grace 159

the largest in American history, produced an autumn in which the air was "thick and oppressive with smoke." Ellen Goodnough commented in her diary that the "flames reached the Oneida forests and destroyed much of their valuable timber."[49] By October 1872, the price of hardwoods had shot up, bringing six hundred to one thousand dollars' profit per individual, and the federal Indian agent predicted that there would be no more trees at Duck Creek within a few years because of the continued uncontrolled stripping.[50]

Daniel Bread died of bilious fever on July 23, 1873. Joseph Powless, an Oneida, made reference to the chief's death in his diary. To Powless, Chief Bread was "the greatest and most important man of all Oneidas as well as among the white people."[51] Thomas Chase, the new federal Indian agent, noted in his annual report that Daniel Bread had died and that "for many years" he was "the leading chief of the tribe."[52] Despite his tragic fall, even his political enemies understood to some degree what the old chief's leadership had meant to his party and to the Oneida Nation at Duck Creek. On September 18, 1873, Chief Hill requested $176 from federal funding to pay for Bread's medicines while he was ill, his burial, and a monument to his memory. The chief's request was never acted on, and no monument, except for Bread's family tombstone, was ever erected in his memory.[53]

An obituary in the *Green Bay Advocate* of August 7, 1873, provided some insightful comments about the chief's leadership. The writer praised the chief's intelligence and physical vigor. He observed: "On a wider stage he would have been one of the greatest of men; with better opportunities and surroundings he would have been one of the best of men." The obituary writer described the late chief as a man of "straightforward and sensible" religious values; however, he also viewed Bread as a man with human foibles—having a temper, being jealous, and seeking retribution against his enemies: "His disposition when not crossed was very kind and peaceable." Yet, Bread could also be "harsh and implacable." Although Bread was a loyal and earnest friend, if one was his enemy "he left no means of injury untried."[54]

Bread engendered much criticism during the last two decades of his life and was a calculating, opportunistic tribal politician who feathered his own nest, but he had no peer of equal abilities, either among the Oneidas or in any other community in Iroquoia during his lengthy career. He spoke fluent Mohawk, Oneida, and English and his ability to read and write English gave him "a step up." A brilliant mind allowed him to balance and deal with many issues at the same time. This mental breadth was reflected in his administration of grand projects, especially the sizable Oneida evacuations from New York in the 1820s and 1830s; his level of cooperation with most Indian agents and religious leaders at Green Bay, the center of forces opposed to Oneida interests; his unique relationship with Chief Jacob Cornelius; his courageous defense of Oneida interests in parlays with the likes of President Jackson as well as with Dodge, Ellis, Martin, and Stambaugh.

Bread understood that the allotment policy would eventually occur at Duck Creek. As a political realist, he looked back to the Oneida experience in New York to gain insights into what to do in Wisconsin. Although his generation of leadership, the council of chiefs, was replaced, the new electoral innovation proved just as weak as the previous structure, and allotment came to Oneida two decades after the chief's death.

The chief recognized that the forces at work in Green Bay and environs were exactly the same ones he and the Oneidas had faced during his first twenty-eight years in New York. In the Empire State, he had seen the future in the form of the Erie Canal, the major engineering feat of America in the nineteenth century. He knew that new transportation routes and methods of transportation would open up land for settlement and result in a rush for Oneida lands and

American Indian communities in Wisconsin today. Sources: Oneida Nation of Indians of Wisconsin.

natural resources in Wisconsin. The Indians, whether native to the area or relocated there, like the Oneidas at Duck Creek, would ultimately suffer.

Bread knew well that it was tough to be Indian, especially in nineteenth-century frontier America. His extraordinary coalition-building efforts to achieve internal cohesion were noble but short-lived in the face of overwhelming odds. Although no stone monument stands at Duck Creek honoring him, he would take pride that his work helped produce a nation of fifteen thousand Indians who have survived and flourished into the next millennium.

Despite his loss of power and influence, Bread was truly the founding father of his Iroquois nation, ranking in importance with the Oneida chiefs of the past, most notably Good Peter who had fought so courageously attempting to lead the nation in New York after the American Revolution. Bread was not a devout preacher in the manner of Good Peter, and Bread used religion in a calculating fashion to further his political ambitions; nevertheless, Bread deserves immense credit for his careful stewardship of the Oneidas in the great transition from Oneida Castle to Duck Creek, no simple achievement.

Abbreviations

ARCIA	Annual Reports of the Commissioner of Indian Affairs
Coll	Collection
DHI	Francis Jennings et al., eds., *Iroquois Indians—A Documentary History of the Six Nations and Their League.* 50 microfilm reels. Woodbridge, Conn.: Research Publications, 1985.
GBAR	Green Bay Agency Records
HC	Hamilton College, Clinton, N.Y.
HL	Huntington Library, San Marino, Calif.
ICC	Indian Claims Commission
M	Microcopy
MR	Microfilm Reel
MSS	Manuscript Collection
NA	National Archives, Washington, D.C.
NYSA	New York State Archives, Albany, N.Y.
NYSL	New York State Library, Manuscript Division, Albany, N.Y.
OIA	Office of Indian Affairs
OLFP	Oneida Language and Folklore Project

RG	Record Group
SHSW	State Historical Society of Wisconsin, Madison
Stat.	*United States Statutes at Large*
SU	Syracuse University, George Arents Research Library, Bird Library, Syracuse, N.Y.
TPUS	Clarence E. Carter and John Porter Bloom, eds. *The Territorial Papers of the United States.* 28 vols. Washington, D.C.: U.S.G.P.O. and National Archives, 1934–1975.
USGPO	United States Government Printing Office
UWGBARC	University of Wisconsin Green Bay Area Research Center
WHC	*Wisconsin Historical Collections,* State Historical Society of Wisconsin, Madison, Wis.
WMH	*Wisconsin Magazine of History*
Whipple Report	New York State Legislature. Assembly. *Report of the Special Committee to Investigate the Indian Problem of the State of New York.* Albany, N.Y., 1889.
WPA	Works Progress Administration

Notes

Preface

1. A Friend, "Daniel Bread," *Green Bay Advocate*, August 7, 1873.
2. The exceptions are: Clinton Rickard, *Fighting Tuscarora: The Autobiography of Chief Clinton Rickard*, ed. Barbara Graymont, (Syracuse: Syracuse University Press, 1973); Christopher Densmore, *Red Jacket: Iroquois Diplomat and Orator* (Syracuse, N.Y.: Syracuse University Press, 1999); William A. Armstrong, *Warrior in Two Camps: Ely S. Parker, Union General and Seneca Chief* (Syracuse University Press, 1978); and Thomas S. Abler, ed., *Chainbreaker: The Revolutionary War Memoirs of Governor Blacksnake as Told to Benjamin Williams* (Lincoln: University of Nebraska Press, 1989). Although there are biographies of Cornplanter and Joseph Brant, they are inadequate. Sadly, there is no biography of Handsome Lake.
3. Jack Campisi and Laurence M. Hauptman, "Talking Back: The Oneida Language and Folklore Project, 1938-1941," *Proceedings of the American Philosophical Society* 125 (December 1981): 441-48.

Chapter 1

1. The treatment of the Battle of Big Sandy (Sandy Creek) is derived from the following: J. Mackay Hitsman, *The Incredible War of 1812: A Military History* (Toronto: University of Toronto Press, 1998), pp. 155, 172; Douglas R. Hickey, *The War of 1812: A Forgotten Conflict* (Urbana: University of Illinois Press, 1989), p. 185; Greg Chester, *The Battle of Big Sandy*, (Adams, N.Y.: Historical Association of South Jefferson County, 1981); and Hauptman's fieldnotes among the Wisconsin Oneidas, who still talk about the battle.
2. See Barbara Graymont, "The Oneidas in the American Revolution," in *The Oneida Indian Experience: Two Perspectives*, eds. Jack Campisi and

Laurence M. Hauptman, (Syracuse, N.Y.: Syracuse University Press, 1988), pp. 31-42; Barbara Graymont, *The Iroquois in the American Revolution* (Syracuse University Press, 1972), pp. 132-41; Karim Tiro, "The People of the Standing Stone: The Oneida Indian Nation from Revolution through Removal, 1765-1840" (Ph.D. diss., University of Pennsylvania, 1998), pp. 99-146. Joseph Glaathaar, the noted military historian, is completing a work on the Oneidas' military role in the American Revolution, which will be published by Harvard University Press.

3. I have learned much about the Cornelius family and its genealogy from Todd Larkin. For Henry Cornelius, see Graymont, *The Iroquois in the American Revolution*, pp. 132-33; and Abstract of Pension Application No. 10002, Henry Cornelius, Records of the New York State Adjutant-General's Office, Claims, Applications and Awards for Service in the War of 1812, Division of Military and Naval Affairs, NYSA. Clifford Abbott to Laurence M. Hauptman, Dec. 16, 1999, letter in author's possession. Dr. Abbott of the University of Wisconsin at Green Bay is the leading academic scholar on the Oneida Indian language.

4. Laurence M. Hauptman, Oneida fieldnotes, 1986-2001.

5. Lyman C. Draper, "Report on Picture Gallery," *WHC* 3 (1856), pp. 56-58.

6. "Daniel Bread," *Green Bay Advocate*, August 7, 1873.

7. Joseph Powless Diary, UWGBARC. See the image of Bread's sister in Catlin's painting in this book.

8. Graymont, "The Oneidas and the American Revolution," p. 37, and *The Iroquois in the American Revolution*, pp. 149, 155; Walter Pilkington, ed., *Journals of Samuel Kirkland* (Clinton, N.Y.: Hamilton College, 1980), pp. 360-65; *Whipple Report*, pp. 244-66. "Peter Bread," item 24, William M. Beauchamp MSS, SC17369, box 15, vol. 3, NYSL.

9. Stadler King story, WPA, OLFP, Series II, Oneida Nation of Indians, Oneida, Wis.

10. Ibid.

11. Jack Campisi, "Wisconsin Oneidas between Disasters," in *The Oneida Indian Journey*, eds. Laurence M. Hauptman and L. Gordon McLester. (Madison: University of Wisconsin Press, 1999), pp. 76-81.

12. Stadler King story, WPA, OLFP.

13. Campisi, "Wisconsin Oneidas between Disasters," 77.

14. Ibid.

15. There is a dire need to write a corrective biography of Eleazer Williams since myth has replaced the facts of his life and influence. An example of these inadequate articles is found in the *American National Biography* [20: 452] written by Kenny A. Franks. Another example is Geoffrey Buerger's "Eleazer Williams: Elitism and Multiple Identity on Two Frontiers," in *Being and Becoming Indian: Biographical Studies of North American Frontiers*, ed. James A. Clifton (Chicago: Dorsey Press, 1989), pp. 112-36. The older accounts are even more inadequate: Albert G. Ellis, "Advent of the New York Indians into Wisconsin," *WHC* 2 (1856): 415-45; Ellis, "Recollections of Eleazer Williams," *WHC* 8 (1879), 325-52; and Ellis, "Fifty-four Years' Recollections of Men and Events in Wisconsin," *WHC* 7 (1876): 207; William Wight, "Eleazer Williams," in Parkman Club *Papers* (Milwaukee, 1896), 1:133-203; Lyman C. Draper, "Additional Notes on Eleazer Williams," *WHC* 8 (1879): 353-69; John N. Davidson, "The Coming

of the New York Indians to Wisconsin," in *Proceedings of the Wisconsin State Historical Society* (Madison: SHSW, 1900), pp. 176-77. For a reappraisal, see Reginald Horsman, "The Origins of Oneida Removal to Wisconsin, 1815-1822," reprinted in *The Oneida Indian Journey*, pp. 53-69. The best analysis of Williams so far is Tiro, "The People of the Standing Stone," pp. 219-30.

16. See *New York Times*, April 20, 2000, p. 1. In 1999 an opera on the life of Eleazer Williams, much too favorable to the clergyman, was performed in Green Bay and caused a strong negative reaction from the Wisconsin Oneida Indian community. Hauptman, Oneida fieldnotes, 1999-2001.

17. Ellis, "Advent of the New York Indians into Wisconsin," 415-45; Ellis, "Fifty-four Years of Recollections of Men and Events in Wisconsin," 207; and Ellis, "Recollections of Rev. Eleazer Williams," 344.

18. George Catlin, *Letters and Notes on the Manners, Customs and Condition of the North American Indians* (London, 1841), 2:311.

19. Solomon Davis letter of reference, March 13, 1851, OIA, MC234, MR321, GBAR, RG75, NA.

20. James Duane Doty letter of reference, Feb. 28, 1851, OIA, MC234, MR321, GBAR, RG75, NA.

21. Mrs. Mark Powless to Ida Blackhawk, I-41, WPA, OLFP.
22. Sarah Summers to Tillie Baird, T-1, WPA, OLFP.
23. Sarah Summers to Ida Blackhawk, I-34, WPA, OLFP.
24. Ida Blackhawk I-76, WPA, OLFP.
25. Levi Elm to Ida Blackhawk, I-11, WPA, OLFP.
26. Stadler King story, WPA, OLPF.
27. Ibid.
28. John Skenandore, WPA, OLFP, Series II.
29. Ibid.
30. For the relationship of Bread to Cornelius Hill, We relied on the excellent work of Todd Larkin, who is the foremost authority on Oneida genealogy.

Chapter 2

1. A. D. Gridley, *History of the Town of Kirkland* (New York: Hurd & Houghton, 1874), pp. 7-8; Jeremy Belknap, *Journal of a Tour from Boston to Oneida, June 1796*, ed. George Dexter (Cambridge, Mass.: John Wilson, 1882), 21-24; Timothy Dwight, *Travels in New England and New York* (1822; reprint, ed. Barbara Miller Solomon Cambridge, Mass.: Belknap Press of Harvard University, 1969), p. 149.

2. Belknap, *Journal*, p. 21.
3. Laurence M. Hauptman, Oneida fieldnotes.
4. "Daniel Bread," *Green Bay Advocate*, August 7, 1873; Draper, "Report on the Indian Portrait Gallery," 56-58.

5. Oneida Memorial to Lewis Cass, Territorial Governor of Michigan, August 12, 1820; Oneida Memorial to Secretary of the Territory of Michigan, August 12, 1820, *DHI*, eds. Francis Jennings et al., MR 46. Bread also made his mark on annuity receipts as "chief" of the First Christian Party, beginning in 1821 and continuing through the 1820s. See, for example, Daniel Bread et al. receipt, January 26, 1821, Records of the Indian Commissioners, A0832B4F5, Oneida Petitions and Receipts, NYSA.

6. See his signature on Memorial to the Legislature of the State of New York, January 21, 1828, *DHI,* MR46. Although he continued to make his mark on documents into the 1830s, he signed most of the Oneida petitions and memorials after 1830. See, for example, Bread to Silas Wright, August 16, 1830, A0832B4F8, Records of the New York State Comptroller, Oneida Petitions and Receipts, NYSA.

7. For a fuller treatment of Samuel Kirkland, see Laurence M. Hauptman, *Conspiracy of Interests: Iroquois Dispossession and the Rise of the Empire State* (Syracuse, N.Y.: Syracuse University Press, 1999), pp. 37-45.

8. Ibid., pp. 39-48.

9. Julian Ursyn Niemcewicz, "Journey to Niagara, 1805," ed. Metchie J. E. Budka, *New-York Historical Society Quarterly* 74 (January 1960): 95; Belknap, *Journal,* pp. 21-22; William W. Campbell, ed., *The Life and Writings of De Witt Clinton* (New York: Baker & Scribner, 1849), pp. 187-88.

10. See endnote 9.

11. For evidence of epidemics, see the Quaker missionary account of Joseph Clark, *Travels among the Indians: 1797* (Doylestown, Pa.: Charles Ingerman at the Quixott Press, 1968), pp. 3, 5.

12. See *An Address Delivered to the Oneida Indians, September 24, 1810, By Samuel Blatchford, D. D. Together With the Reply, By Christian, A Chief of Said Nation* (Albany: Northern Missionary Society/Webster & Skinner Printers, 1810), pp. 10-11.

13. Ibid.

14. Skenandoah speech reprinted in pamphlet form in *Instances of Indian Genius, 1816,* SHSW (an article from the *Commercial Advertiser*). This speech can also be found in William W. Campbell, *The Annals of Tryon County* (Cherry Valley, N.Y.: Cherry Valley Gazette Printers, 1880), Appendix, pp. 233-36.

15. Samuel Kirkland to Alexander Miller, May 24, 1800, Samuel Kirkland MSS, no. 211C, HC; Pilkington, *Journals of Samuel Kirkland,* pp. 360-65; Elisabeth Tooker, "The Iroquois White Dog Sacrifice in the Later Part of the Eighteenth Century," *Ethnohistory* 12 (1965): 129-40.

16. Anthony F. C. Wallace, *The Death and Rebirth of the Seneca* (New York: Random House, 1969), pp. 308-9; Elisabeth Tooker, "On the New Religion of Handsome Lake," *Anthropological Quarterly* 41 (1968): 187-200; and Tooker, "On the Development of the Handsome Lake Religion," *Proceedings of the American Philosophical Society* 133 (1989): 35-50.

17. Niemcewicz, "Journey to Niagara, 1805," 95-100.

18. John Maude, "Visit to the Falls of Niagara, 1800," in *In Mohawk Country: Early Narratives about a Native People,* eds. Dean Snow, Charles T. Gehring, and William A. Starna (Syracuse: Syracuse University Press, 1996), p. 360.

19. Friedrich Rohde, "Journal of Trip from New Jersey to Oneida Lake, 1802," in *In Mohawk Country,* p. 376.

20. For further descriptions of the Oneida world in this period, see Timothy Dwight, *Travels in New England and New York* (Cambridge, Mass.: Harvard University Press, 1969), 3:125; 4:128-49.

Chapter 3

1. For Bread's oratorical skills, see Draper, "Report on Picture Gallery," 56-58; Levi Konapot, Jr., letter to Reverend Cutting Marsh, March 6, 1857, reprinted in "The Last of the Mohicans," *WHC* 4 (1859): 304; William M. Beauchamp, "Daniel Bread," item no. 450, William M. Beauchamp MSS, SC17369, box 15, vol. 3, NYSL.
2. Lewis Henry Morgan, *League of the Ho-de-no-sau-nee, or Iroquois* (1851; reprint, New York: Corinth Books, 1962), p. 107. For the form and importance of Iroquois oratory, see Densmore, *Red Jacket*, pp. 60-75.
3. Morgan, *League of the Iroquois*, p. 441; Laurence M. Hauptman, "Samuel George (1795-1873): A Study of Onondaga Indian Conservatism," *New York History* 70 (January 1989): 9-10, 10 n. 14.
4. Quoted in Henry J. Cookinham, *History of Oneida County, New York from 1700 to the Present Time* (Chicago: S. J. Clarke Publishing Co., 1912), pp. 19-20.
5. New York State Legislature, Assembly, Document no. 260: *Report of the Committee on Indian Affairs, on the petition of certain members of the First Christian Party of Oneida Indians*, March 7, 1835, p. 2. *Laws of New York*, 58th sess., chap. 285 (May 11, 1835).
6. Petition of 1st Christian Party to New York State Legislature, January 28, 1835, Records of the New York State Surveyor-General's Office, Land Records, Series II, A4016-11.74, NYSA.
7. Solomon Davis Affidavit, February 19, 1835, Records of the Office of the New York State Surveyor-General, Land Records, Series II, A4016-11.74, NYSA. Davis was the Episcopal missionary to the Oneidas in New York beginning in 1822, succeeding Eleazer Williams. He later (in the 1830s) became the Oneidas' missionary at Duck Creek, succeeding Williams again. See James H. Smith, *History of Chenango and Madison Counties, New York* (Syracuse: D. Mason & Co., 1880), p. 64; Bloomfield, *The Oneidas*, 2d ed. (New York: Alden Bros., 1907), pp. 178-85.
8. Robert Sutcliff, *Travels in Some Parts of North America in the Years 1804, 1805 and 1806*, 2d ed. (London: Longman, Hurst & Co., 1815), pp. 155-56.
9. This calculation is based on the Records of the Indian Claims Commission, Oneida Nation, Docket no. 301 (Claims 3-8). Findings of Fact, August 18, 1971—Map no. 1 (March 1967/Revised August 1973); Map no. 2 (April 1973), RG279, NA.
10. Thurlow Weed, *Memoir of Thurlow Weed* [by his grandson, Thurlow Weed Barnes] (Boston: Houghton, Mifflin & Co., 1884), 1:6.
11. Ibid., 2:148.
12. Jack Campisi, "Ethnic Identity and Boundary Maintenance in Three Oneida Communities" (Ph.D. diss., Albany: SUNY at Albany, 1974), pp. 74-107, 500-502; Hauptman, *Conspiracy of Interests*, chaps. 2-5.
13. Quoted in Tiro, "People of the Standing Stone," pp. 206-7.
14. For Denny and his family, see Campbell, *Life and Writings of De Witt Clinton*, pp. 190-91; Sutcliff, *Travels*, pp. 152-55. See also Hauptman, *Conspiracy of Interests*, pp. 18, 55-56, 85.

15. Alexander Dallas to Daniel D. Tompkins, January 22, 1816, M15, Letters Sent by the Secretary of War, Indian Affairs, 1800, MR3, NA.
16. W. Edwin Hemphill, ed., *The Papers of John C. Calhoun* (Columbia, S.C.: University of South Carolina Press, 1963-1975), 2:lxxix; 3:667-70; 5:105-6, 160, 331-33, 631; 6:49, 438, 543-44, 564, 632-33; 8:196-98, 253, 330; 9:15. See also Horsman, "Origins of Oneida Removal to Wisconsin, 1815-1822," 53-70. For information on Calhoun as secretary of war, see Merrill D. Peterson, *The Great Triumvirate: Webster, Clay and Calhoun* (New York: Oxford University Press, 1987), pp. 84-95; John Niven, *John C. Calhoun and the Price of Union: A Biography* (Baton Rouge: Louisiana State University Press, 1988), pp. 58-101; Roger J. Spiller, "John C. Calhoun as Secretary of War, 1817-1825" (Ph.D. diss., Louisiana State University, 1977), especially on Indian policy, pp. 178-243; John C. Barsness, "John C. Calhoun and the Military Establishment, 1817-1825," *WMH* 50 (Autumn 1966): 43-53.
17. *TPUS: Territory of Illinois*, 17:478-79. See also Francis Paul Prucha and Dennis F. Carmony, "A Memorandum of Lewis Cass: Concerning a System for the Regulation of Indian Affairs," *WMH* 52 (Autumn 1968): 35-50.
18. *TPUS: Territory of Michigan*, 11:69-70.
19. Petition to Governor De Witt Clinton by Sachems and Warriors of the 1st and 2nd Party of the Oneida Indians, November 11, 1818, reprinted in New York State, *Assembly Journal*, 42nd sess. (1819): pp. 39-40.
20. Receipts (with Daniel Bread's name and mark) of Annuities Received by First Christian Party, January 26, 1821, June 1, 1822, June 1, 1825, June 1, 1826, etc. Records of the Indian Commissioners, A0832B4F8, NYSA.
21. *Whipple Report*, pp. 280-87.
22. Ibid., pp. 287-97. *Laws of New York*, 47th sess., chap. 305 (November 24, 1824), pp. 359-60.
23. Tiro, "People of the Standing Stone," pp. 219-21.
24. Hemphill, *The Papers of John C. Calhoun*, 6:438.
25. Campisi, "Ethnic Identity and Boundary Maintenance in Three Oneida Communities," 104-6.
26. Ibid.; also see Ellis, "Recollections of Eleazer Williams," p. 333. Ogden had frequent praise for Williams's efforts and encouraged him. See Hemphill, *The Papers of John C. Calhoun*, 5:631.
27. Daniel Tegawiatiron et al. to Lewis Cass [Territorial Governor of Michigan], August 12, 1820; Daniel Tegawiatiron to Willaim Woodbridge [Secretary of Michigan Territory], August 12, 1820, DHI, MR46.
28. See preceding note and also Hemphill, *The Papers of John C. Calhoun*, 5:331-33; 6:49. For Morse's investigative report on Indian affairs, see *A Report to the Secretary of War of the United States on Indian Affairs, Comprising a Narrative of a Tour Performed in the Summer of 1820 for the Purpose of Ascertaining, for the Use of the Government, the Actual State of the Indian Tribes in Our Country* (New Haven, Conn.: S. Converse, 1822), pp. 16, 24-27, apps. A, 1-6; I, 62-64; M, 75-89.
29. Tegawiatiron et al. to Lewis Cass, August 12, 1820.
30. Tegawiatiron et al. to William Woodbridge, August 12, 1820.
31. See chap. 4.
32. Hemphill, *The Papers of John C. Calhoun*, 9:15.

33. Broadside from Oneida chiefs, July 18, 1826, *DHI*, MR46.
34. *Whipple Report*, pp. 287-90.
35. David A. Ogden to Lewis Cass, July 1, 1820, *DHI*, MR46; Hemphill, *The Papers of John C. Calhoun*, 5:631; Campisi, "Ethnic Identity and Boundary Maintenance," p. 106.
36. Albert G. Ellis informed Secretary Calhoun of Williams's marriage and increased support among the Menominees for his mission. Hemphill, *The Papers of John C. Calhoun*, 8:196-98.
37. Ellis, "Recollections of Rev. Eleazer Williams," 322-69.
38. See note 9 above; *Whipple Report*, pp. 287-91. Henry Powless Affidavit, 1839, Re: Daniel Bread, Claim no. 3 of First Christian Party Under Treaty of Buffalo Creek, OIA, MC234, GBAR, MR317, RG75, NA.
39. Henry Powless affidavit.
40. ICC Findings of Fact cited in note 9; *Whipple Report*, pp. 291-98.
41. ICC Findings of Fact cited in note 9; *Whipple Report*, pp. 287-91.
42. ICC Findings of Fact cited in note 9; *Whipple Report*, p. 292.
43. New York State Legislature. Assembly. Doc. 260 (March 7, 1835).
44. Daniel Bread et al. [Oneida chiefs] protest against Northern Missionary Society, February 15, 1828, *DHI*, MR46.
45. Petition of chiefs [Daniel Bread et al.] and warriors of the First Christian Party of the Oneida Indians to New York State Legislature, December 30, 1829, *DHI*, MR46; Daniel Bread et al. to Silas Wright, August 16, 1830, NYSL.
46. See note 43 above.
47. Ibid.
48. Petition of First Christian Party, January 28, 1835, New York State Surveyor General's Office, Ser. 2, A4016-11: 75a, NYSA; New York State Legislature. Senate Doc. 46 (February 27, 1849); New York State Legislature. Assembly Doc. 198 (March 12, 1865).

Chapter 4

1. Joseph Powless Diary, UWGBARC; Records of the Holy Apostles Church, MR1&2, UGBARC. Todd Larkin's research suggests that Daniel and Electa Bread had eight children, five of whom were born in New York before removal, including Thomas Bread. According to Larkin, in his three confirmed marriages, Bread had fifteen children.
2. New York State. Assembly Doc. no. 315 (April 17, 1833).
3. Henry Powless affidavit.
4. Smith, *History of Wisconsin*, vol. 1 (Madison: SHSW, 1973), pp. 192-93.
5. Kerry A. Trask, "Settlement in a 'Half-Savage' Land: Life and Loss in the Métis Community of La Baye," *Michigan Historical Review* 15 (Spring 1989): 4-6.
6. See especially Smith, *History of Wisconsin*, 1: 434-46; Ella Neville et al., *Historic Green Bay, 1834-1840* (Green Bay: privately printed, 1893), p. 250.
7. Bloomfield, *The Oneidas*, 2d ed., pp. 173-77.
8. Patricia K. Ourada, *The Menominees: A History* (Norman: University of Oklahoma Press, 1979), chaps. 1-3.
9. Ibid., p. 75.

10. John D. Haeger, "A Time of Change: Green Bay, 1815-1834," *WMH* 54 (Summer 1971): 285-98; Jeanne Kay, "John Lawe: Green Bay Trader," *WHH* 64 (1980): 3-7; and Kay, "The Land of La Baye: The Ecological Impact of the Green Bay Fur Trade, 1634-1836" (Ph.D. diss., Madison: University of Wisconsin, 1977), p. 224; Trask, "Settlement in a Half-Savage Land," 1-27; David R. M. Beck, "Siege and Survival: Menominee Responses to an Encroaching World" (Ph.D. diss., Chicago: University of Illinois, 1994), pp. 101-40, 322-89; Mark Wyman, *The Wisconsin Frontier* (Bloomington: University of Indiana Press, 1998), pp. 38-65, 101-2, 134-35, 170-84; Brian C. Hosmer, *American Indians in the Marketplace: Persistence and Innovation among the Menominees and Metlakatlans, 1870-1920* (Lawrence: University Press of Kansas, 1999), pp. 19-27.

11. See the discussion of Colonel Samuel C. Stambaugh and his plans for Green Bay in chapter 5.

12. Hauptman, *Conspiracy of Interests*, chaps. 3-5. See also Stuart Mitchell, *Horatio Seymour of New York* (Cambridge, Mass.: Harvard University Press, 1938; reprint, New York: Da Capo Press, 1970), pp. 193-201. The family of John Seymour, the founder of Seymour, Wisconsin, which is adjacent to the Oneida Indian Reservation, illustrates this point. He was one of the founders of the Fox-Wisconsin River Improvement Company, a promoter of Wisconsin canals. His grandfather, Henry, was from Utica and was a major promoter of the Erie Canal. His brother Horatio was the governor of New York and promoter of canals. His nephew Horatio, Jr. was chief canal engineer of New York State. For more on John Seymour, see Fox River Improvement Prospectus, John Seymour MSS, box 1, SHSW.

13. Reuben Thwaites, "Documents Relating to the Episcopal Church and Mission in Green Bay," *WHC* 14 (1898): 450-515, especially 452.

14. Horsman, "Origins of Oneida Removal," pp. 63-65; Campisi, "Ethnic Identity and Boundary Maintenance," pp. 106-7; Ourada, *The Menominees*, pp. 71-79; Ellis, "Advent of the New York Indians into Wisconsin," pp. 423-30; Ellis, "Fifty-four Years' Recollections of Men and Events in Wisconsin," pp. 223-26.

15. Beck, "Siege and Survival," p. 360.

16. *TPUS: Michigan Territory*, 11:335-39.

17. Hemphill, *The Papers of John C. Calhoun*, 7:311; 8:253, 330; Horsman, "The Origins of Oneida Removal," pp. 64-65, 69 n. 39.

18. Ourada, *The Menominees*, pp. 76-98.

19. Calvin Colton, *Tour of the American Lakes and Among the Indians of the North-West Territory in 1830* (London, 1833; reprint: Port Washington, N.Y.: Kennikat Press, 1972), 2:176-77. Minister Colton saw it as a vast conspiracy: "The wild tribes [the Menominees and Winnebagos], therefore,. . . are to be regarded, as mere tools. They were *brought* to Washington, to protest against the claims of the New York Indians, and to force them to the acceptance of a small tract of land, which would not interfere with the design of erecting a new State in that quarter; and where they would soon be surrounded and hemmed in by a white population, as they were ten years ago, in the State of New York, before they removed."

20. Bloomfield, *The Oneidas*, 2d ed., pp. 176-77.

21. Petition of New York Tribes [Daniel Bread et al.] to Governor Enos Troop [of New York State], August 13, 1831, Thomas Dean MSS, SHSW; Daniel Bread to Silas Wright, August 16, 1830, Records of the New York State Comptroller's

Office, box 4, A0832, NYSA; New York State Legislature, Assembly, Document no. 315 (April 17, 1833): 1-3; *Laws of New York,* 58th sess., chap. 294 (May 11, 1835): 334; Petition of Chiefs [including Daniel Bread] and Warriors of the First Christian Party of the Oneida Indians to New York State Legislature, December 30, 1829, *DHI,* MR46.

22. Charles J. Kappler, comp., *Indian Treaties: Laws and Affairs,* 5 vols. (Washington, D.C.: U.S.G.P.O., 1903-1941; reprinted as vol. 2: *Indian Treaties, 1778-1883,* Mattituck, N.Y.: Amereon House, 1972), pp. 281-83.

23. Ellis, "Advent of New York Indians into Wisconsin" 431-32.

24. *Journal of the Board of Commissioners Appointed by the President of the United States under date of 7th June 1830,* to locate a District or Country at Green Bay, and establish the boundaries thereof for the accommodation and settlement of the New York Indians. OIA, MC234, GBAR, MR315, RG75, NA.

25. John Eaton to U.S. Commissioners, June 9, 1830, found as preface to *Journal of the Board of Commissioners Appointed by the President of the United States under date of 7th June 1830....*

26. *Journal of the Board of Commissioners Appointed by the President of the United States under date of 7th June 1830....*

27. Ibid.
28. Ibid.
29. Ibid.
30. Ibid.

31. Ibid. For Doty's involvement, see Alice E. Smith, *James Duane Doty: Frontier Promoter* (Madison, Wis.: SHSW, 1954), pp. 34-49, 64-73, 79-121, 135-38. Doty "was one of the most remarkable men in the early history of Wisconsin.... He was also a consummate politician and land promoter-speculator whose schemes often exceeded his means, but his ethics were questionable. Some of his devious maneuvers have defied unraveling for nearly 150 years." From Jack Rudolph, *Birthplace of a Commonwealth: A Short History of Brown County, Wisconsin* (Green Bay: Brown County Historical Society, 1976), p. 10.

32. Smith, *James Duane Doty,* p. 110.

33. For more on Martin, see chapter 10.

34. James Duane Doty to John H. Eaton (Secretary of War), April 1, 1830, October 26, 1830; Doty to Silas Wright (Comptroller of New York State), September 3, 1830, March 26, 1831, December 25, 1831); Doty to J. T. Mason (federal commissioner), September 12, 1830; Doty to C. E. Dudley, October 30, 1830; Doty to Governor Lewis Cass, November 10, 1830; July 23, 1831; Doty to Van Buren, February 8, 1831, James Duane Doty MSS, Letterbook, HL, San Marino, Calif. (microfilm in SHSW).

35. James Duane Doty to President Andrew Jackson, Sept. 18, 1830, HL.

36. James Duane Doty to J. T. Mason, February 1, 1831, HL.

37. James Duane Doty to Martin Van Buren, September 22, 1830, Morgan L. Martin MSS, box 2, folder 1, Neville Museum of Brown County, Green Bay, Wis.

38. "[James] McCall's Journal of a Visit to Wisconsin in 1830," *WHC* 12 (1892):170-215; Colton, *Tour of the American Lakes,* 2 vols.

39. "McCall's Journal": pp. 170-215.

40. Ourada, *The Menominees*, pp. 86-87; James McCall, "McCall's Journal": 170-215.
41. Colton, *Tour of the American Lakes*, 2:260-63.
42. Ibid.
43. Ibid.

Chapter 5

1. Still the best work on Jackson's Indian policies is Ronald Satz, *American Indian Policy in the Jacksonian Era*, first published in 1975 and reissued in a reprint edition (Norman: University of Oklahoma Press, 2002).
2. *TPUS: Michigan Territory* 12:14-15.
3. William Hoyt, ed., "Zachary Taylor on Jackson and the Military Establishment, 1835," *American Historical Review*, 51 (April 1946): 480-84; Ourada, *The Menominee Indians*, pp. 87-94; *WHC* 11 (1892): 392.
4. Ellis, "Advent of New York Indians into Wisconsin" 432-33.
5. Ibid. For Stambaugh's views, see Col. Samuel Stambaugh to Andrew Jackson, September 8, 1830; Stambaugh to John Eaton (Secretary of War), September 8, 1830, March 8, 1831, April 14, 1831, MC234, GBAR, MR315, RG75, NA.
6. Proceedings of a treaty at Green Bay, August, 1831 [sent to Secretary of War John Eaton], OIA, MC234, GBAR, MR315, RG75, NA.
7. Smith, *James Duane Doty*, pp. 103-10, 117-19; Ourada, *The Menominee Indians*, pp. 87-94; Ellis, "Advent of New York Indians into Wisconsin" 435-38.
8. Petition of the New York Indians to the President of the United States [including Daniel Bread as one of signatories], January 30, 1831, OIA, MC234, GBAR, MR315, RG75, NA.
9. Kappler, *Indian Treaties*, pp. 319-23 (February 8, 1831).
10. Ibid., pp. 323-25 (February 17, 1831).
11. *Cherokee Nation v. Georgia*, 5 Peters 15 (March 5, 1831).
12. Herman J. Viola, *Diplomats in Buckskin: A History of Indian Delegations to Washington City* (Washington, D.C.: Smithsonian Institution Press, 1981), p. 141. See Colton, *Tour of the Lakes*, 2:163-212. See also Catlin's portrait of Bread on the cover of this book.
13. See note 11.
14. Viola, *Diplomats in Buckskin*, p. 11.
15. Quoted in Ibid., p. 141.
16. Stambaugh report of November 8, 1831, to Secretary of War John Eaton can be found in OIA, MC234, GBAR, MR315, RG75, NA. The report reads as an economic prospectus for the future development of Green Bay and environs, including the Oneidas' Duck Creek Reservation. This report has been reprinted: see Samuel Stambaugh, "Report on the Condition and Quality of Wisconsin Territory, 1831," *WHC* 15 (1900): 399-438, especially pp. 430-37. See also Stambaugh to John Eaton [Secretary of War], March 8, April 14, November 8, 1831, OIA, MC234, GBAR, MR315, RG75, NA.
17. Stambaugh report, pp. 432-33. See also Smith, *James Duane Doty*, pp. 108-19.
18. See preceding note.

19. Daniel Bread et. al. to Enos Troop, April 13, 1831 [Petition of New York Tribes], Thomas Dean MSS, SHSW.
20. Later, Bread attempted to be reimbursed for expenses incurred in 1830-31 on his delegation to Washington. Memorial of Daniel Bread to Commissioner Luke Lea [Commissioner of Indian Affairs], January 23, 1850, OIA, MC234, GBAR, MR321, RG75, NA.
21. George B. Porter Report to Lewis Cass, Feb. 8, 1832, OIA, MC234, GBAR, MR315, RG75, NA.
22. Ibid.
23. Ibid.
24. Ibid.
25. Ibid.
26. *Petition to the Senate of the United States. The New York Indians having, by renewed application to the Executive, ineffectually sought to obtain through its interposition such modifications of the treaty lately concluded with the Menominee Tribe* (1832), Pamphlet, Madison, Wis.: State Historical Society Library.
27. Ibid., pp. 12-13.
28. Kappler, *Indian Treaties*, pp. 377-82.
29. Diary of George B. Porter, October 19-December 10, 1832 kept by his secretary, Joshua Boyer, Joshua Boyer MSS, SHSW.
30. Ibid.
31. Ibid.
32. Ibid.

Chapter 6

1. Daniel Bread to Henry Dodge [Territorial Governor], August 29, 1836, OIA, MC234, GBAR, MR316, MR316, RG75, NA.
2. Ellis, "Recollections of Rev. Eleazer Williams," pp. 343-346; Bloomfield, *The Oneidas*, 2d ed., pp. 177-79.
3. See the apparent forged letter of recommendation for Williams. Memorial of the New York Indians, November 4, 1828, *DHI*, MR46. The handwriting of Bread's name is distinctly different here.
4. Letter of Daniel Bread et al. to the Editor of *Gospel Messenger*, January 20, 1833, Records of the Church of the Holy Apostles, UWGBARC.
5. John Nelson Davidson, "The Coming of the New York Indians to Wisconsin." *Proceedings* of the State Historical Society of Wisconsin 47 (1899): 153-85.
6. Proceedings of an Oneida Treaty Council held by Governor Dodge and Other Federal Commissioners at Duck Creek, November 19-21, 1845, OIA, M234, GBAR, MR319, RG75, NA.
7. The report found discrepancies in some items, receipts, and expenditures. New York State Legislature, *Assembly Document no. 315* (April 17, 1833).
8. Memorial of sixty Oneidas designating Daniel Bread, Jacob Cornelius, Henry Powless, Elijah Skenandore to operate for them [in negotiations with John C. Schermerhorn], October 6, 1837, OIA, MC234, GBAR, MR316, RG75, NA.

9. The best analysis of Schermerhorn's career is James W. Van Hoeven, "Salvation and Indian Removal: The Career Biography of Rev. John Freeman Schermerhorn, Indian Commissioner" (Ph.D. diss., Nashville, Tenn.: Vanderbilt University, 1972), pp. 8-9, 104-9.

10. Gary Moulton, ed., *The Papers of Chief John Ross* (Norman: University of Oklahoma Press, 1985), 1, 573-74.

11. Van Hoeven, "Salvation and Indian Removal," pp. 98-123, 239, 262-64; Kappler, Comp., *Indian Affairs: Laws and Treaties*, pp. 502-12.

12. Memorial of sixty Oneidas designating Daniel Bread . . ., October 6, 1827.

13. Lyman Draper, ed., "Some Wisconsin Indian Conveyances," *WHC*, 15 (1900): 20-24.

14. Ibid.
15. Ibid.
16. Ibid.

17. For more on Gillet and his role in the Buffalo Creek Treaty, see Laurence M. Hauptman, "Four Eastern New Yorkers and Seneca Lands: A Study in Treaty-Making," *Hudson River Regional Review*, 13 (March 1996): 1-19.

18. Kappler, *Indian Affairs: Laws and Treaties*, pp. 502-12.

19. Hauptman, *Conspiracy of Interests*, chaps. 10-12. See also Henry S. Manley, "Buying Buffalo from the Indians," *New York History*, 28 (July 1947): 313-29; Jack Campisi, "Consequences of the Kansas Claims to Oneida Tribal Identity," in *Proceedings of the First Congress, Canadian Ethnology Society*, Jerome H. Barkow, ed. [Canada] National Museum of Man Ethnology Division, *Mercury Series Paper 17* (Ottawa, 1974), pp. 35-47.

20. Kappler, *Indian Affairs: Laws and Treaties*, pp. 517-18.

Chapter 7

1. Fenton, *The Great Law and the Longhouse*, p. 31.
2. Powless affidavit; see chaps. 3 and 5.
3. Receipt of payment, Detroit Party of Oneidas, June 1, 1830 (signed by "chiefs of the First Christian Party of the Oneida Indians"—William Hill, Jacob Anthony, Jacob Doxtator, and Henry Anthony), Oneida Petitions and Receipts, A0832B4F8, NYSA; Eleazer Williams Journal, 1821-1830, Eleazer Williams MSS, MR1, SHSW.
4. Reginald Horsman, "The Wisconsin Oneidas in the Preallotment Years," in *The Oneida Indian Experience*, p. 70.
5. For the Orchard Party settlement in Wisconsin, see Henry Colman, "Recollections of the Oneida Indians," in State Historical Society of Wisconsin *Proceedings* for 1911 (Madison, Wis.: SHSW, 1912), pp. 40-45.
6. Memorial of First Christian Party (Neddy Archiquette, Elijah Skenandore, et al.), August 31, 1836, OIA, M234, GBAR, MR316, RG75, NA.
7. Daniel Bread, Jacob Cornelius, et al. to Henry Dodge, September 2, 1836, OIA, M234, GBAR, MR316, RG75, NA.
8. Powless affidavit. For the desperate condition of these refugees, see Clayton Mau, ed., *The Development of Central and Western New York* (Rochester: DuBois Press, 1944), p. 336.
9. New York State Legislature. *Assembly Doc. no. 260* (March 7, 1835).

10. Campisi, "The Wisconsin Oneidas between Disasters," in *The Oneida Indian Journey*, pp. 75-76.
11. Censuses of the First Christian Party and Orchard Party, June 15 and November 15, 1838, OIA, M234, GBAR, MR317, RG75, NA.
12. Campisi, "The Wisconsin Oneidas between Disasters," pp. 75-76.
13. Malcolm Rohrbough, *The Land Office Business: The Settlement and Administration of American Public Lands, 1789-1837* (New York: Oxford University Press, 1968), pp. 234-35.
14. Robert E. Bieder, *Native American Communities in Wisconsin, 1600-1960: A Study of Tradition and Change* (Madison, Wis.: University of Wisconsin Press, 1995), pp. 153-54.
15. *ARCIA 1838/1839*, pp. 162-66.
16. *ARCIA 1839/1840*, pp. 106-10.
17. James Duane Doty to T. Hartley Crawford, October 19, 1843, OIA, M234, GBAR, MR318, RG75, NA.
18. Daniel Bread et al. affidavit relating to church, September 2, 1839, Records of the Church of the Holy Apostles, UWGBARC, Green Bay.
19. Diary of Bishop Jackson Kemper, September 2, 1839, Jackson Kemper MSS., SHSW. For more about the bishop, see Jackson Kemper, "Journal of an Episcopalian Missionary's Tour to Green Bay, 1834," WHC 14 (1898): 394-449.
20. Bloomfield, *The Oneidas*, 2d ed., pp. 226-27, 232-33, 252, 276.
21. Campisi, "The Wisconsin Oneidas between Disasters," p. 79.
22. [Henry Dodge] Proceedings of a treaty council with the Oneida Indians at Duck Creek, November 19-21, 1845, OIA, M234, GBAR, MR319, RG75, NA.
23. *TPUS: Wisconsin Territory*, 27: 1078-87.
24. Ibid., 27: 1211-213.
25. John Anthony, Hanyost Smith, et al. to Joel R. Poinsett [Secretary of War], March 18, 1839, OIA, M234, GBAR, MR317, RG75, NA.
26. Beck, "Siege and Survival," pp. 133-34, 133 n. 105, 560.
27. George Boyd to Governor George P. Porter, January 1, 1833, George Boyd MSS, SHSW. In the letter, Boyd referred to Bread as "our friend" and called Eleazer Williams "anything but an honest man."
28. Boyd to Secretary of War, August 13, 1832; Boyd to Oneida chiefs, July 26, 1837; Boyd to John Schermerhorn, October 7, 1837; Boyd to John Bell, April 20, 1841; Boyd to Carey A. Harris [Commissioner of Indian Affairs], September 30, 1837, January 2, 1839; Boyd to Elbert Herring, April 25, 1835, George Boyd MSS, SHSW. Boyd was critical of Oshkosh, Augustus Grignon, and Morgan L. Martin and his "half-breed friends." Boyd to Lewis Cass, August 25, 1834 [calling Oshkosh a "bad man, by the way, and totally unworthy of his rank"]; Boyd to L. Hartley Crawford [Commissioner of Indian Affairs], March 4, 1840, George Boyd MSS., SHSW. Boyd to Commissioner of Indian Affairs, March 12, 1838, OIA, M234, GBAR, MR317, RG75, NA. Boyd was undercut by Martin, who attempted with success to get rid of him. See *TPUS: Wisconsin Territory*, 28: 131-35, 137-39, 154-57. For Bread and the Oneidas' support of Boyd, see *TPUS: Wisconsin Territory*, 28: 155-57. Daniel Bread to Crawford, February 24, 1840, OIA, MC234, MR318, GBAR, RG75, NA. For more on Boyd, see his "Papers of Indian Agent Boyd—1832 with Sketch of George and James M. Boyd by Herbert B. Tanner," WHC 12 (1892): 266-98.

29. *TPUS: Wisconsin Territory,* 27: 941.
30. *ARCIA* 1837/1838: pp. 62-63.
31. Daniel Bread, Jacob Cornelius, et al. to Commissioner T. Hartley Crawford, February 14, 1840, OIA, M234, GBAR, MR318, RG75, NA.
32. *ARCIA* 1844/1845: p. 48.
33. Oneida Memorial (Daniel Bread et al.) to David Jones, February 26, 1844, OIA, M234, GBAR, MR319, RG75, NA.
34. David Jones to Commissioner T. Hartley Crawford, February 28, 1844, OIA, M234, GBAR, MR319, RG75, NA.
35. Daniel Bread, Jacob Cornelius, et al. to Commissioner of Indian Affairs, July 14, 1845, OIA, M234, GBAR, MR319, RG75, NA.
36. Albert G. Ellis Report, September 24, 1845, OIA, M234, GBAR, MR319, RG75, NA.
37. Proceedings of a treaty council, November 19-21, 1845.
38. Ibid.
39. Ibid.
40. Ibid.
41. Ibid.
42. Ibid.
43. The Missouri Emigrating Party continued to be involved in Oneida politics to the time of Daniel Bread's death in the 1870s. Memorial [Thomas Comminck] to President Zachary Taylor, June 19, 1849; John T. Sundown to Our Great Father, January 21, 1850, OIA, M234, GBAR, MR320, RG75, NA; Oneida Memorial to President of the United States, June 28, 1860, OIA, M234, GBAR, MR323, RG75, NA. Later, this party split into two groups; see Petition of Peter Denny to Commissioner of Indian Affairs, August 1, 1871, OIA, MC234, MR327, GBAR, MR327, RG75, NA. Denny and his group of homeless Oneidas decided that it was best not to push to go to Indian Territory.
44. Henry Dodge to William Medill, December 1, 1845, OIA, M234, GBAR, MR319, RG75, NA.
45. Albert G. Ellis and Henry Dodge, April 2, 1846, OIA, M234, GBAR, MR319, RG75, NA.

Chapter 8

1. Cope, "Mission to the Menominees," pp. 120-44.
2. Ibid., pp. 135-44.
3. Ibid.
4. Ibid., p. 137.
5. Ibid., pp. 136-38.
6. Ibid., pp. 136-41.
7. Ibid., pp. 135-44.
8. Campisi, "The Oneidas between Disasters," pp. 76-77.
9. For the best treatment of the Iroquois Condolence Council, see Fenton, *The Great Law and the Longhouse,* pp. 3-18, 135-242. For its importance in Iroquoian diplomacy, see William N. Fenton, "Structure, Continuity and Change in the Process of Iroquois Treaty-making," in *The History and Culture of Iroquois Diplomacy: An Interdisciplinary Guide to the Treaties of the Six*

Nations and Their League. Francis Jennings et al., eds. (Syracuse, N.Y.: Syracuse University Press, 1985), pp. 3-36.
10. Fenton, *The Great Law and the Longhouse,* p. 8.
11. Ibid., p. 6.
12. Ibid., pp. 99, 209; Fenton, "Structure, Continuity and Change," pp. 16-18.
13. Fenton, "Structure, Continuity and Change," pp. 21-27.
14. Fenton, *The Great Law and the Longhouse,* p. 6.
15. Ibid., p. 27, 130, 618. On July 4, 2001, the Wisconsin Oneidas reintroduced lacrosse at their annual pow-wow.
16. "Celebration of the Fourth at Oneida Settlement: Speech of Daniel Bread," *Green Bay Advocate,* July 4, 1854.
17. Ibid.
18. Ibid.
19. Draper, "Report on the Picture Gallery," *WHC,* 3 (1856), 56-58.
20. Quoted in ibid., p. 57.
21. Ibid., pp. 56-58.

Chapter 9

1. Campisi, "Ethnic Identity and Boundary Maintenance," p. 141.
2. Daniel Bread, Jacob Cornelius, et al., Oneida Memorials to the President of the United States, October 23, December 3, 1850, January 13, 1851, OIA, M234, GBAR, MR321, RG75, NA.
3. Bread, Cornelius, et al. to President of the United States, January 13, 1851.
4. Petition of Daniel Bread and Jacob Cornelius, Chiefs and Delegates of the First Christian and Orchard Parties of the Oneida Indians of Wisconsin, 31st Cong., 2d sess., H. Rep. no. 18, January 29, 1851, Serial Set 606.
5. U.S. Congress, Senate, Committee of Claims Report Regarding Compensation for the Capture of Three Gun Boats [in the War of 1812—petition of Oneida Indians], 32nd Cong., 1st sess., Sen. Rep. 286, July 6, 1852, Serial Set 631. For later efforts to seek compensation for War of 1812 military service by the chiefs, including Daniel Bread, see A. D. Bonesteel to A. B. Greenwood [Commissioner of Indian Affairs], July 8, 1859, OIA, M234, GBAR, M323, RG75, NA. Approximately twelve Oneidas received pension moneys for their War of 1812 service.
6. *ARCIA,* 1858/1859, pp. 42-43. For Bread's early support of schools among the Oneidas—"our children should be educated as white children"; "we are poor and unable to bear the expense of paying a teacher—see Daniel Bread et al., Petition of the Chiefs of the First Christian Party, undated [probably 1833 or 1834], OIA, M234, GBAR, MR316, RG75, NA.
7. Records of the Church of the Holy Apostles, MR1&2, UWGBARC; Joseph Powless Diary.
8. The deaths from the smallpox epidemic during the Civil War are cited in the Joseph Powless Diary. For an earlier epidemic, see Daniel Bread et al. to William Medill [Commissioner of Indian Affairs], June 1, 1849, OIA, M234, GBAR, MR320, RG75, NA. For evidence of crop failures, see Bloomfield, *The Oneidas,* 2d ed., p. 247; Daniel Bread's petition of June 1, 1849, as well as Jacob

Cornelius et al., Memorial of Chiefs of Oneida Nation, March 15, 1859, OIA, M234, GBAR, MR323; and *ARCIA*, 1864, pp. 43, 443-44; M. M. Davis to William Dole, May 10, 1864, OIA, M234, GBAR, MR324, RG75, NA.

9. For these charges, see Albert G. Ellis to William Medill, December 24, 1848, OIA, M234, GBAR, MR320, RG75, NA. Report of New York State Attorney General [A. L. Jordan et al.] on the Petition of the First Christian Party of Oneida Indians, New York State Legislature, Senate Doc. no. 35 (February 26, 1848).

10. Solomon Davis to William Bruce [federal Indian agent], June 11, 1849, OIA, M234, GBAR, MR320, RG75, NA.

11. Elijah Skenandore [Scanonedon/Skenandoah] to Indian Agent, March 24, 1852, OIA, M234, GBAR, MR321, RG75, NA.

12. Jacob Cornelius and the Chiefs of the Orchard Party to the President of the United States, January 31, 1853, OIA, M234, GBAR, MR322, RG75, NA.

13. Jacob Cornelius et al. Chiefs of the Orchard Party to the President of the United States, December 7, 1853, OIA, M234, GBAR, MR322, RG75, NA.

14. Robert F. Fries, *Empire in Pine: The Story of Lumbering in Wisconsin, 1830-1900* (Madison, Wis.: SHSW, 1951), pp. 18, 70, 87. 202; Anthony Godfrey, *A Forestry History of Ten Wisconsin Indian Reservations under the Great Lakes Agency* (Salt Lake City, Utah: U.S. West Research, Inc. for BIA Branch of Forestry, 1996), 13-22; Deborah Martin Brown, *History of Brown County, Wisconsin: Past and Present* (Chicago: S. J. Clarke, 1913), 1: 173-84; Frederick Merk, *Economic History of Wisconsin During the Civil War* (Madison, Wis.: SHSW, 1916), pp. 57-110; Richard N. Current, *The History of Wisconsin*, vol. 2: *The Civil War Era, 1848-1873*, pp. 100-102, 468.

15. Calvin Davis to Brother and Sister, March 10, 1856, Calvin Davis MSS, SHSW.

16. Daniel Bread et al., Assignment of Mill Property Lease to John Arndt, January 4, 1836, Nathaniel Foster MSS, University of Wisconsin, Eau Claire.

17. Hauptman, *The Iroquois and the New Deal*, pp. 70-87.

18. For the increasing problem of alcohol abuse and the impact of the alcohol trade, see George Eastman to Charles Mix, November 6, 1857, OIA, M234, GBAR, MR323, RG75, NA.

19. *ARCIA*, 1854/1855, pp. 40-42.

20. Elijah Skenandore [Skenandoah] to L. Huebschmann, March 24, 1854; Daniel Bread et al. to Secretary of Interior, undated 1854, lease to Alexander Douglass and Iona S. Hale, OIA, M234, GBAR, M322, RG75, NA.

21. A. D. Bonesteel to Charles Mix [Acting Commissioner of Indian Affairs], February 18, 1858, OIA, M234, GBAR, M322, RG75, NA.

22. *ARCIA*, 1857/1858, pp. 30-31.

23. Jacob Cornelius et al. (includes a few members of the First Christian Party), Orchard Party Petition to A. D. Bonesteel, July 6, 1858, OIA, M234, GBAR, M323, RG75, NA.

24. *ARCIA*, 1858/1859, pp. 38-42.

25. A. D. Bonesteel to Charles Mix, March 23, 1859, OIA, M234, GBAR, M323, RG75, NA; Daniel Bread, Jacob Cornelius, et al., March 15, 1859, Ibid.

26. Daniel Bread et al., Chiefs of the First Christian Party to President of the United States, December 27, 1859, OIA, M234, GBAR, M323, RG75, NA.

27. Daniel Bread, Jacob Cornelius, et al., Memorial of Oneida Chiefs to F. W. Denver [Commissioner of Indian Affairs], December 29, 1859, OIA, M234, GBAR, M323, RG75, NA.
28. Ibid.
29. David Lewis [Methodist Episcopal Missionary] to Commissioner of Indian Affairs, November 8, 1859, OIA, M234, GBAR, M323, RG75, NA. Missionary Lewis, employing former Methodist minister Henry Colman, pushed for land in severalty for the Oneidas, suggesting as early as 1860 that a majority of Oneidas favored allotment, which would be a "great good" and "promote ambition" among the Indians. H. R. Colman to Commissioner of Indian Affairs, January 10, 1860, OIA, M234, GBAR, M323, RG75, NA.
30. For Goodnough's views on the future of the chiefs' council and for his other views, see his school report of September 3, 1859, to agent A. D. Bonesteel in *ARCIA*, 1858/1859, pp. 42-43. Instead of focusing on educational reform, Goodnough pushed for the creation of a legal system on the reservation, the institution of a new political system, and federal restrictions on whiskey traders at Fort Howard, Green Bay, and DePere.
31. See chapter 10. For a positive portrayal of Goodnough, see Bloomfield, *The Oneidas*, 2d ed., pp. 235-40, 246, 248, 281.
32. A. D. Bonesteel to A. B. Greenwood, March 12, 1860, OIA, M234, GBAR, M323, RG75, NA.
33. For the Oneidas in the war, see Laurence M. Hauptman, *The Iroquois in the Civil War* (Syracuse: Syracuse University Press, 1993), pp. 67-83, 132-33, 150.
34. Robert Smith and Loretta Metoxen, "Oneida Traditions," in Campisi and Hauptman, eds., *Oneida Indian Experience*, pp. 150-51. See also Reginald Horsman, "The Wisconsin Oneidas in the Preallotment Years," pp. 74-75; Frank L. Klement, *Wisconsin and the Civil War* (Madison, Wis.: SHSW, 1963), p. 42; *ARCIA*, 1865, p. 52.
35. *ARCIA*, 1861, p. 42.
36. *ARCIA*, 1863, p. 34.
37. M. M. Davis to William Dole, May 31, 1864, OIA, M234, GBAR, M324, RG75, NA.
38. *ARCIA*, 1864, pp. 43, 443-44.
39. Joseph Powless Diary, SHSW; *ARCIA* 1864: pp. 43, 443-444.
40. Hauptman, *Iroquois in the Civil War*, pp. 67-83.
41. Daniel Bread, Jacob Cornelius, et al., Indians and Chiefs of the Oneida Tribe of Indians, to M. M. Davis, May 25, 1864, OIA, M234, GBAR, M324, RG75, NA.
42. M. M. Davis to William Dole, October 12, 1861, August 25, September 9, December 12, 1863, OIA, M234, GBAR, M324, RG75, NA.
43. M. M. Davis to Dennis N. Cooley [Commissioner of Indian Affairs], August 11, October 3, 1865, OIA, M234, GBAR, M325, RG75, NA.
44. Daniel Bread, Cornelius Hill, et al., Oneida Memorial to William Dole, December 24, 1863, OIA, M234, GBAR, M324, RG75, NA. For these allotment pressures, see M. M. Davis to William Dole, December 12, 17, 1863.
45. Powless Diary, SHSW.
46. Horsman, "Wisconsin Oneidas in the Preallotment Years," pp. 74-75.

47. M. M. Davis, the federal Indian agent, continued to refer to Bread and Cornelius as the principal chiefs of the Wisconsin Oneidas. Davis to Dennis N. Cooley, August 11, 1865, OIA, M234, GBAR, M325, RG75, NA.
48. See, for example, E. A. Goodnough to William Dole, December 10, 1863, OIA, M234, GBAR, M324, RG75, NA.

Chapter 10

1. W. R. Bourne [federal Indian agent] to Ely S. Parker [Commissioner of Indian Affairs], March 24, 1870, OIA, M234, GBAR, MR327, RG75, NA.
2. Quoted in Bloomfield, *The Oneidas*, 2d ed., p. 274.
3. Ibid., p. 276.
4. Ibid., pp. 246-49, 280-81. On February 6, 1868, Goodnough was accused of standing in the way of the good of the tribe and of sabotaging the best interests of the United States by his active stand against allotment of tribal lands and sales of these lands, through a new treaty, to the Stockbridge Indians. Darius Charles to N. A. Taylor [Commissioner of Indian Affairs], February 6, 1868, OIA, M234, GBAR, MR326, RG75, NA. For evidence of Goodnough's lobbying against the actions of federal Indian agent Morgan L. Martin, see O. H. Browning [Secretary of the Interior] to Commissioner N. A. Taylor, February 3, 1868, Ibid.
5. Bourne to Parker, March 24, 1870.
6. Bloomfield, *The Oneidas*, 2d ed., pp. 235-36, 246-49, 280-81.
7. Morgan L. Martin to Commissioner of Indian Affairs, April 1, 1867, OIA, M234, GBAR, MR325, RG75, NA. For more on the Anthony case, see Hauptman, *The Iroquois and the Civil War*, p. 133.
8. Daniel Bread, Jacob Cornelius, et al., to M. M. Davis, October 12, 1865, OIA, M234, GBAR, MR325, RG75, NA.
9. Ibid.
10. For Bread's and Cornelius' appeal in regard to resettling Oneidas in Canada at Duck Creek, see Daniel Bread, Jacob Cornelius, et al. to M. M. Davis, October 12, 1865, OIA, M234, GBAR, MR325, RG75, NA. For the 1849 offer by Chief Bread to his Canadian Oneida kin, see chapter 7.
11. See Oneida Petition to Commissioner of Indian Affairs, March 15, 1866, OIA, M234, GBAR, MR325, RG75, NA. By this time, Bread and two other First Christian Party chiefs, as well as representatives of the Woodman's Party, supported fee simple title for *all* Oneidas at Duck Creek. William Woodman to N. A. Taylor, November 4, 1868, OIA, M234, GBAR, MR326, RG75, NA; Horsman, "The Wisconsin Oneidas in the Preallotment Years," pp. 74-78.
12. For more on Martin, see Smith, *History of Wisconsin*, 1: 194-95, 232-33, 278-90, 365-66, 419-22, 455-63, 661-62; Deborah Brown Martin [Morgan L. Martin's daughter], *History of Brown County*, 1:100, 174-76, 200; 2:28-31. Mitchell, *Horatio Seymour of New York*, pp. 189-201; Thwaites, "Reminiscences of Morgan L. Martin," pp. 380-84; Horsman, "The Wisconsin Oneidas in the Preallotment Years," pp. 75-78.
13. Thwaites, "Reminiscences of Morgan L. Martin," pp. 380-84.
14. According to Alice Smith, Martin was the first to breed full-blood Durham shorthorns with cows, whose offspring proved to be excellent milking cows. Smith, *History of Wisconsin*, 1:526.

15. For a fuller treatment of Martin's major role in early Wisconsin history, see Smith, *History of Wisconsin*, 1:351-52, 448-62. For a prospectus of the Fox-Wisconsin River Improvement Company, see John Seymour MSS, box 1, SHSW.

16. See Bieder, *Native American Communities in Wisconsin*, pp. 164-66; Joseph Schafer, *The Winnebago-Horicon Basin: A Type Study in Western History* (Madison, Wis.: SHSW, 1937), pp. 58-74.

17. See notes 12 and 15 above. For the overwhelming pressures that the Oneidas faced in New York from canal development, see Hauptman, *Conspiracy of Interests*, chap. 1.

18. Thwaites, "Reminiscences of Morgan L. Martin," pp. 380-84.

19. Ibid.; see Martin, *History of Brown County*, 1:100, 174-76, 200; 2:28-31; Current, *History of Wisconsin*, 2:19-23, 448, 581-84.

20. Morgan L. Martin to Dennis N. Cooley, July 27, 28, August 8, 1866; Martin to N. A. Taylor, May 10, 18, 1867, OIA, M234, GBAR, MR325, RG75, NA.

21. Morgan L. Martin to N. A. Taylor, June 25, 1867, OIA, M234, GBAR, MR325, RG75, NA.

22. Morgan L. Martin to N. A. Taylor, July 9, 1867, OIA, M234, GBAR, MR325, RG75, NA.

23. Quoted in Bloomfield, *The Oneidas*, 2d ed., p. 274.

24. *ARCIA*, 1866/1867, pp. 331-33.

25. Bloomfield, *The Oneidas*, 2d ed., pp. 280-81.

26. Morgan L. Martin to N. A. Taylor, January 28, 1868, OIA, M234, GBAR, MR326, RG75, NA.

27. *ARCIA*, 1867/1868, pp. 294-95.

28. Morgan L. Martin to Ely S. Parker, June 5, 1869, OIA, M234, GBAR, MR326, RG75, NA.

29. Bloomfield, *The Oneidas*, 2d ed., pp. 246-47.

30. For the Oneidas' defense of federal agent Manley, see Memorial of Chiefs [including Daniel Bread and Jacob Cornelius] of the Oneidas to Indian Department, January 31, 1870, OIA, M234, GBAR, MR327, RG75, NA. Later, Manley was accused of being associated in a "ring" with Morgan L. Martin to control timber sales and proceeds of these sales on the Oneida Reservation. John Manley to Commissioner Ely S. Parker, January 22, 1870, OIA, M234, GBAR, MR327, RG75, NA.

31. Daniel Bread et al., Memorial of Oneida Chiefs to Great Father et al., November 18, 1868, John Manley to Ely S. Parker, September 20, 1869, OIA, M234, GBAR, MR326, RG75, NA.

32. John Manley Report to Ely S. Parker, December 1, 1869, OIA, M234, GBAR, MR326, RG75, NA.

33. Bourne to Parker, March 7, 1870.

34. *ARCIA*, 1870/1871, pp. 511-14; *ARCIA*, 1871/1872, pp. 205-8; *ARCIA*, 1872/1873, pp. 176-78; *ARCIA*, 1873/1874, pp. 185-87. W. T. Richardson [federal Indian agent] report, January 28, 1873; Richardson to Ely S. Parker, January 27, 1871, OIA, M234, GBAR, MR327, RG75, NA.

35. W. T. Richardson to Ely S. Parker, January 13, 1871, OIA, M234, GBAR, MR327, RG75, NA.

36. Horsman, "The Wisconsin Oneidas in the Preallotment Years," pp. 75-78. For an excellent discussion of Cornelius Hill and agent Martin, see

Campisi, "Ethnic Identity and Boundary Maintenance," pp. 143-48. See also Bloomfield, *The Oneidas,* 2d ed., pp. 246-49.
37. See footnote 36, above.
38. Cornelius Hill et al. Oneida Petition to President of the United States, March 5, 1866, OIA, M234, GBAR, MR325, RG75, NA.
39. Cornelius Hill to Charles Mix, March 29, 1867, OIA, M234, GBAR, MR325, RG75, NA.
40. Cornelius Hill et al. to President of the United States, June 28, 1867, OIA, M234, GBAR, MR325, RG75, NA.
41. Bourne to Parker, March 24, 1870.
42. Daniel Bread, Jacob Cornelius, et al. to Commissioner of Indian Affairs, no date, Petition received March 12, 1870, OIA, M234, GBAR, MR327, RG75, NA.
43. Ibid.
44. "A Special Homestead Act," undated, OIA, M234, GBAR, MR327, RG75, NA.
45. Ibid.
46. Cornelius Hill, Henry Powless, et al. to President of the United States, March 7, 1870, OIA, M234, GBAR, MR327, RG75, NA.
47. Even after his fall from power, Bread continued to be viewed as a "chief." William Richardson to Ely S. Parker, January 3, 1871; W. R. Bourne to Ely S. Parker, May 23, 1870, OIA, M234, GBAR, MR327, RG75, NA.
48. Campisi, "Ethnic Identity and Boundary Maintenance," pp. 143-48; Horsman, "The Wisconsin Oneidas in the Preallotment Years," pp. 75-78. For Hill's "war" with Chief Bread, see Memorial of First Christian Party [Cornelius Hill et al.], March 7, 1870, OIA, M234, GBAR, MR327, RG75, NA.
49. Quoted in Bloomfield, *The Oneidas,* 2d ed., pp. 252-53. For the Peshtigo fire, see Peter Pernin, "The Great Peshtigo Fire: An Eyewitness Account," *WMH* 54 (September 1971): 246-272.
50. *ARCIA,* 1871/1872, pp. 205-8. See also W. T. Richardson Report, January 28, 1873, OIA, M234, GBAR, MR329, RG75, NA.
51. Joseph Powless Diary, UWGBARC.
52. *ARCIA,* 1872/1873, pp. 176-78.
53. Thomas Chase [federal Indian agent] to E. P. Smith [Commissioner of Indian Affairs], September 18, 1873, with attached Memorial of Oneida Chiefs [Cornelius Hill et al.], September 6, 1873, OIA, M234, GBAR, MR329, RG75, NA.
54. "Daniel Bread," *Green Bay Advocate,* August 7, 1873.

Bibliography

Archives and Manuscript Collections

Hamilton College, Clinton, N.Y.
  Kirkland, Samuel MSS.
Huntington Library, San Marino, Calif.
  Doty, James Duane Letterbook and Journal
Library of Congress, Washington, D.C.
  Jackson, Andrew MSS.
  Van Buren, Martin MSS.
Madison County (N.Y.) Historical Society
  Vertical Files on Oneida Indians
  Photographic Collection
National Archives, Washington, D.C.
  Cartographic Records
  Correspondence of the Office of Indian Affairs. Letters Received, 1824-1881. M234. RG75
    Green Bay Agency, 1824-1880
    Michigan Superintendency, 1824-1836
    New York Agency Emigration, 1829-1851
    New York Agency, 1829-1880
    Seneca Agency in New York, 1824-1832
    Six Nations Agency, 1824-1832
  Records of the Indian Claims Commission. RG279
  Records Relating to Indian Treaties
    Documents Relating to the Negotiation of Ratified and Unratified Treaties, 1801-1869. T494

Ratified Indian Treaties, 1722-1869. M668
Records of the War Department
    Letters Received by the Secretary of War Relating to Indian Affairs, 1800-1823. M271
    Civil War Pension Records of the Fourteenth Wisconsin Volunteer Infantry Companies F and G
    Records of the Adjutant General's Office, RG94
        Appointment, Commission, and Personnel Records
        Compiled Service Records
        Regimental Books
    Special Case File 29—Kansas Claims
Neville Museum of Brown County, Wis. Green Bay, Wis.
    Martin, Morgan L. MSS
    Williams, Eleazer MSS
New York Public Library, New York, N.Y.
    Schuyler, Philip MSS.
New York State Archives, Albany, N.Y.
    Records of the Division of Military and Naval Affairs
        Adjutant General's Office. Claims, Applications, and Awards for Service in the War of 1812
    Office of the New York State Surveyor-General. Land Office Records, ser. 1 and 2
    Records of the Indian Commissioners
    Records of Indian Deeds and Treaties, 1748-1847
    Records of the New York State Legislature. Assembly Papers: Petitions, Correspondence, and Reports Related to Indians.
    Records of the State Comptroller's Office. Indian Annuity Claims, Receipts and Related Documents, 1796-1925
    Records of the State Treasurer (Comptroller's Office)
New York State Library, Manuscript Division, Albany, N.Y.
    Beauchamp, William MSS
    Gillet, Ransom MSS
    Holland Land Company MSS
    Hough, Franklin Benjamin MSS
    Hutchinson, Holmes MSS
    Jennings, Francis et al., eds. *Iroquois Indians: A Documentary History of the Six Nations and Their League.* 50 microfilm reels. Newberry Library, Woodbridge, Conn.: Research Publications, 1985.
    Ogden Land Company MSS
    Schuyler Family MSS
    Scriba, George MSS
    Seymour, Horatio MSS
    Van Buren, Martin MSS
    Van Rensselaer Family MSS
    Watson, Elkanah MSS
    Wright, Benjamin MSS
Oneida Nation of Indians of Wisconsin, Oneida, Wis.
    WPA Oneida Folklore and Language Project: Stories

Bibliography

Memories of the Old Days—Elders stories.
A Collection of Oneida Stories. Translated by Maria Hinton.
Jan Malcolm, ed. "The Oneida Veterans Pentagon Project."
Onondaga Historical Association, Syracuse, N.Y.
    Beauchamp, William MSS
    New York State Comptroller Records (Albany Papers)
    Vertical Files
St. John Fisher College, Rochester, N.Y.
    Decker, George P. MSS
State Historical Society of Wisconsin, Madison, Wis.
    Boyd, George MSS
    Boyer, Joshua MSS
    Colman, Henry R. MSS
    Davis, Calvin MSS
    Dean, Thomas MSS
    Doane, Gilbert MSS
    Doty, James Duane MSS
    Draper, Lyman MSS—Frontier Wars Papers, Series 11U
    Green Bay and Prairie du Chien MSS
    Grignon, Charles A. MSS
    Grignon, Lawe and Porlier MSS
    Kemper, Jackson MSS
    Martin, Morgan MSS
    Seymour, John F. MSS
    Williams, Eleazer MSS
Syracuse University, Bird Library, Arents Research Library, Syracuse, N.Y.
    De Witt Family MSS
    Smith, Peter MSS
University of Rochester, Rush Rhees Library, Rochester, N.Y.
    Morgan, Lewis Henry MSS
    Parker, Arthur C. MSS
    Seward, William H. MSS
    Skivington, George J. Collection
University of Wisconsin
    Eau Claire, Wis.
    Foster, Nathaniel MSS
    Green Bay, Wis.
        Archiquette, John Diary
        Christ Episcopal Church (Green Bay) Records
        Holy Apostles Episcopal Church (Oneida) Records
        Powless, Joseph Diary
        Martin, Morgan L. MSS
        Williams, Eleazer MSS

Government Publications

American State Papers: Documents, Legislative and Executive of the Congress of the United States. 38 vols. [Class 2: Indian Affairs. 2 vols.] Washington, D.C.: Gales & Seaton, 1832-1861.

The Balloting Book and Other Documents Relating to Military Bounty Lands in the State of New York. Albany: Packard & Van Benthuysen, 1825.

Brannon, John, comp. *Official Letters of the Military and Naval Officers of the United States During the War with Great Britain in the Years 1812, 13, 14, 15....* Washington, D.C.: Way & Gideon, 1823.

Carter, Clarence E., and John Porter Bloom, eds. *The Territorial Papers of the United States.* 28 vols. Washington, D.C.: U.S. Government Printing Office and National Archives, 1934-1975.

Donaldson, Thomas, comp. *The Six Nations of New York.* Extra Census Bulletin of the 11th Census [1890] of the United States. Washington, D.C.: U.S. Census Printing Office, 1892.

Godfrey, Anthony. *A Forestry History of Ten Wisconsin Indian Reservations under the Great Lakes Agency.* Salt Lake City: U.S. West Research, Inc. for BIA Branch of Forestry, 1996.

Hastings, Hugh, ed. *The Public Papers of George Clinton.* 8 vols. Albany: Oliver Quayle, 1904.

Hastings, Hugh, ed. *Public Papers of Daniel D. Tompkins, Governor of New York, 1807-1817.* 3 vols. New York: Wynkoop, Hallenback & Crawford, 1898.

Hough, Franklin Benjamin, comp. *Proceedings of the Commissioners of Indian Affairs Appointed by Law for the Extinguishment of Indian Titles in the State of New York.* 2 vols. Albany: Joel Munsell, 1861.

Kappler, Charles J., comp. *Indian Affairs: Laws and Treaties.* 5 vols. Washington, D.C.: U.S. Government Printing Office, 1903-1941.

Morse, Jedidiah. *A Report to the Secretary of War of the United States on Indian Affairs, Comprising a Narrative of a Tour Performed in the Summer of 1820....* New Haven, Conn.: S. Converse, 1822.

New York State Adjutant General's Office. *Index of Awards: Soldiers of the War of 1812.* Baltimore: Genealogical Publishing Co., 1969.

New York State Legislature, Assembly. Document no. 51: *Report of the Special Committee to Investigate the Indian Problem of the State of New York.* Appointed by the Assembly of 1888. 2 vols. Albany: Troy Press, 1889. [Popularly known as the *Whipple Report.*]

New York State Legislature, *Assembly Journal.*

New York State Legislature, *Senate Journal.*

New York Secretary of State. *Census of the State of New York for 1825.* Albany, 1826.

New York Secretary of State. *Census of the State of New York for 1835.* Albany, 1836.

New York Secretary of State. *Census of the State of New York for 1845.* Albany, 1846.

New York Secretary of State. *Census of the State of New York for 1855.* Albany, 1857.

O'Callaghan, Edmund B., and Berthold Fernows, eds. *Documents Relative to the Colonial History of the State of New York.* 15 vols. Albany: Weed, Parsons, 1853-1887.

O'Callaghan, Edmund B., ed. *Documentary History of the State of New York.* 4 vols. Albany: Weed, Parsons, 1849-1851.

Bibliography

Richardson, James D., comp. *A Compilation of the Messages & Papers of the Presidents, 1789-1897.* 10 vols. Washington, D.C.: U.S. Government Printing Office, 1896-1899.

Royce, Charles C., comp. *Indian Land Cessions in the United States.* 18th Annual Report of the Bureau of American Ethnology, 1896-1897. Part 2. Washington, D.C.: U.S. Government Printing Office, 1899.

State of Wisconsin. *Journal of the Assembly, 1848-1873.* Madison, Wis., 1849-1874.

State of Wisconsin. *Journal of the Senate, 1848-1873.* Madison, Wis., 1849-1874.

Territory of Wisconsin. *Journal of the Council, 1836-1847.* Madison, Wis., 1837-1848.

Territory of Wisconsin. *Journal of the House, 1836-1848.* Madison, Wis., 1837-1849.

U.S. Bureau of the Census. 1st (1790)-10th (1870) Censuses.

U.S. Congress. *Annals of Congress, 1789-1824.*

U.S. Congress. *Congressional Globe, 1833-1851.*

U.S. Congress. *Congressional Serial Set,* 16th Congress-43rd Congress, 1821-1873.

U.S. Congress, House of Representatives. *Journal of the House of Representatives* [1789-1815]. Washington, D.C.: Gales & Seaton, 1826.

U.S. Indian Claims Commission. *Decisions of the Indian Claims Commission.* Microfiche edition. New York: Clearwater Publishing Co., 1973-1978.

U.S. Interior Department, Secretary of the Interior. *Annual Report* [1849-1874].

U.S. Interior Department, Commissioner of Indian Affairs. *Annual Report* [1849-1874].

U.S. War Department, Commissioner of Indian Affairs. *Annual Report* [1829-1848].

Whitford, Noble E., *History of the Canal System of the State of New York....* 2 vols. Albany: Brandow Printing [Supplement to the Annual Report of the State Engineer and Surveyor of the State of New York], 1906.

Books, Booklets, and Pamphlets

Abernathy, Byron R., ed. *Private Elisha Stockwell, Jr., Sees the Civil War.* Norman: Univ. of Oklahoma Press, 1958.

Abler, Thomas S., ed. *Chainbreaker: The Revolutionary War Memoirs of Governor Blacksnake as Told to Benjamin Williams.* Lincoln: Univ. of Nebraska Press, 1989.

Ambrose, Stephen, ed. *A Wisconsin Boy in Dixie: The Selected Letters of James K. Newton.* Madison: SHSW, 1968.

Anderson, Theodore A. *A Century of Banking in Wisconsin.* Madison, Wis.: SHSW, 1954.

Beauchamp, William M., *A History of the New York Iroquois.* New York State Museum *Bulletin* 78. Albany, 1905.

Belknap, Jeremy. *Journal of a Tour from Boston to Oneida, June 1796.* Edited by George Dexter. Cambridge, Mass.: John Wilson & Co., 1882.

Benn, Carl. *The Iroquois in the War of 1812.* Toronto: Univ. of Toronto Press, 1998.
Bieder, Robert E. *Native American Communities in Wisconsin, 1600-1960: A Study of Tradition and Change.* Madison: Univ. of Wisconsin Press, 1995.
Blatchford, Samuel. See Christian.
Bloomfield, Julia. *The Oneidas.* 2d ed. New York: Alden Bros., 1907.
Calloway, Colin G. *Crowns and Calumet: British-Indian Relations, 1783-1815.* Norman: Univ. of Oklahoma Press, 1987.
——. *The American Revolution in Indian Country: Crisis and Diversity in Native American Communities.* New York: Cambridge Univ. Press, 1995.
Campbell, William W. *Annals of Tryon County.* Cherry Valley, N.Y.: Cherry Valley Gazette Printers, 1880.
——, ed. *The Life and Writings of De Witt Clinton.* New York: Baker & Scribner, 1849.
Campisi, Jack, Michael Foster, and Marianne Mithun, eds. *Extending the Rafters: Interdisciplinary Approaches to Iroquoian Studies.* Albany: SUNY Press, 1984.
Campisi, Jack, and Laurence M. Hauptman, eds. *The Oneida Indian Experience: Two Perspectives.* Syracuse: Syracuse Univ. Press, 1988.
Catlin, George. *Letters and Notes on the North American Indians.* Michael M. Mooney, ed. 1825. Reprint, New York: Clarkson N. Potter, 1975.
Chester, Gregory. *Battle of Big Sandy.* Adams, N.Y.: Historical Association of South Jefferson County, 1981.
Christian (Chrisjohn/Christjohn). *An Address Delivered to the Oneida Indians, September 24, 1810, By Samuel Blatchford, D.D., Together with the Reply, By Christian, a Chief of Said Nation.* Albany, N.Y.: Northern Missionary Society, Websters and Skinner, 1810.
Christjohn, Amos, and Marie Hinton. *An Oneida Dictionary,* Clifford Abbott, Ed. Oneida, Wis.: Oneida Nation of Indians of Wisconsin, 1998.
Clark, John G. *The Grain Trade in the Old Northwest.* Urbana: Univ. of Illinois Press, 1966.
Clark, Joshua V. H. *Onondaga; or, Reminiscences of Early and Later Times.* ... 2 vols. Syracuse: Stoddard & Babcock, 1849.
Clark, Joseph. *Travels among the Indians, 1797.* Doylestown, Pa.: Charles Ingerman, Quixott Press, 1968.
Clarke, T. Wood. *Utica: For a Century and a Half.* Utica: Widtman Press, 1952.
Cohen, Felix S. *Handbook of Federal Indian Law.* Washington, D.C.: U.S. Department of the Interior, 1942; Albuquerque: Univ. of New Mexico Press, 1972.
Colton, Calvin. *Tour of the American Lakes and Among the Indians of the Northwest Territory in 1830.* 2 vols. 1833, reprint, Port Washington, N.Y.: 1972.
Cookinham, Henry J. *History of Oneida County, New York.* Vol. 1. Chicago: S. J. Clarke Publishing Co., 1912.
Current, Richard. *Wisconsin: A Bicentennial History.* New York: W. W. Norton, 1977.
Current, Richard N. *Pine Logs and Politics: A Life of Philetus Sawyer, 1816-1900.* Madison, Wis.: SHSW, 1960.

Bibliography

———. *The History of Wisconsin.* vol. 2: *The Civil War Era, 1848-1873.* Madison: SHSW, 1976.
Cusick, David, *Sketches of Ancient History of the Six Nations... 1827.* 2d ed. Lockport, N.Y.: Cooley & Lothrop, 1828.
Dearborn, Henry A. S. *Journals of Henry A. S. Dearborn.* Edited by Frank H. Severance. Buffalo Historical Society *Publications* 7, Buffalo: Buffalo Historical Society, 1904.
Durant, Samuel W. *History of Oneida County, New York.* Philadelphia: Everts & Fariss, 1878.
Dwight, Timothy. *Travels in New England and New York.* 3 vols. 1822. Edited by Barbara Miller Solomon. Reprint, Cambridge, Mass.: Belknap Press of Harvard University Press, 1969.
Evans, Paul D. *The Holland Land Company.* Buffalo, N.Y.: Buffalo Historical Society, 1924.
Fenton, William N. *The Great Law and the Longhouse: A Political History of the Iroquois Confederacy.* Norman: Univ. of Oklahoma Press, 1998.
———, ed. *Symposium on Local Diversity.* Bureau of American Ethnology *Bulletin* 149. Washington, D.C., 1951.
Fitzpatrick, John C., ed. *The Autobiography of Martin Van Buren.* Reprint of 1920 edition, New York: Da Capo Press, 1973.
Foreman, Grant. *The Last Trek of the Indians.* Chicago: Univ. of Chicago Press, 1946; New York: Russell & Russell, 1972.
Fowler, John. *Journal of a Tour in the State of New York, in the Year 1830....* London: Whittaker, Treacher & Arnot, 1831.
Frazier, Patrick. *The Mohicans of Stockbridge.* Lincoln: Univ. of Nebraska Press, 1992.
French, J. H., comp. *Gazetteer of the State of New York.* Syracuse: R. Pearsall Smith, 1860.
Fries, Robert F. *Empire in Pine: The Study of Lumbering in Wisconsin, 1830-1900.* Madison, Wis.: SHSW, 1951.
Garraty, John. *Silas Wright.* New York: Columbia Univ. Press, 1949.
Gerlach, Don R. *Proud Patriot: Philip Schuyler and the War of Independence, 1775-1783.* Syracuse: Syracuse Univ. Press, 1987.
Gottschalk, Louis R. *Lafayette between the American and the French Revolutions, 1783-1789.* Chicago: Univ. of Chicago Press, 1950.
Graymont, Barbara. *The Iroquois in the American Revolution.* Syracuse: Syracuse Univ. Press, 1972.
Gridley, Amos D. *History of the Town of Kirkland.* New York: Hurd & Houghton, 1874.
Grumet, Robert S. *Historic Contact: Indian People and Colonists in Today's Northeastern United States in the Sixteenth through Eighteenth Centuries.* Norman,: Univ. of Oklahoma Press, 1995.
Hagan, William T. *American Indians.* 3d ed. Chicago: Univ. of Chicago Press, 1993.
———. *The Sac and Fox Indians.* Norman: Univ. of Oklahoma Press, 1958.
Hale, Horatio E. *The Iroquois Book of Rites.* 2 vols. Philadelphia: D. G. Brinton, 1883.
Hammond, Jabez D. *The History of Political Parties in the State of New York.* 2 vols. Albany: Charles Van Benthuysen, 1842.

Hauptman, Laurence M. *Between Two Fires: American Indians in the Civil War.* New York: The Free Press, 1995.
———. *Conspiracy of Interests: Iroquois Dispossession and the Rise of New York State.* Syracuse, N.Y.: Syracuse Univ. Press, 1999.
———. *The Iroquois and the New Deal.* Syracuse, N.Y.: Syracuse Univ. Press, 1981.
———. *The Iroquois in the Civil War: From Battlefield to Reservation.* Syracuse: Syracuse Univ. Press, 1993.
———. *The Iroquois Struggle for Survival: World War II to Red Power.* Syracuse: Syracuse Univ. Press, 1986.
Hauptman, Laurence M. and L. Gordon McLester III. *The Oneida Indian Journey: From New York to Wisconsin, 1784-1860.* Madison, Wis.: Univ. of Wisconsin Press, 1999.
Haydon, Roger, ed. *Upstate Travels: British Views of Nineteenth-Century New York.* Syracuse: Syracuse Univ. Press, 1982.
Hemphill, W. Edwin, et al., eds. *The Papers of John C. Calhoun.* 16 vols. Columbia: Univ. of South Carolina Press, 1959-1984.
Hewitt, J. N. B. *Iroquois Cosmology.* Part I. Bureau of American Ethnology, 21st Annual Report. Washington, D.C.: U.S. Government Printing Office, 1899-1900.
———. *Iroquoian Cosmology.* Part II. Bureau of American Ethnology, *Annual Report.* Washington, D.C.: Bureau of American Ethnology, 1928.
Hitsman, J. Mackay. *The Incredible War of 1812.* Toronto: Univ. of Toronto Press, 1965.
Horsman, Reginald. *Expansion and American Indian Policy, 1783-1812.* East Lansing: Michigan State Univ. Press, 1967.
———. *The Frontier in the Formative Years, 1783-1815.* New York: Holt, Rinehart & Winston, 1970.
Hosmer, Brian C. *American Indians in the Marketplace: Persistence and Innovation among the Menominees and Metlakatlans, 1870-1920.* Lawrence: University Press of Kansas, 1999.
Hough, Franklin B. *Notices of Peter Penet and His Operations Among the Oneida Indians.* Lowville, N.Y.: Albany Institute, 1866.
Houghton, Frederick. *The History of the Buffalo Creek Reservation.* Buffalo Historical Society *Publication* 24. Buffalo, N.Y.: Buffalo Historical Society, 1920.
Hurst, James Willard. *Law and Economic Growth: The Legal History of the Lumber Industry in Wisconsin, 1836-1915.* Cambridge, Mass.: Harvard Univ. Press, 1964.
Hurt, R. Douglas. *Indian Agriculture: Prehistory to the Present.* Lawrence: Univ. Press of Kansas, 1987.
Idzerda, Stanley J., ed. *Lafayette in the Age of the American Revolution: Selected Letters and Papers, 1776-1790.* 2 vols. Ithaca, N.Y.: Cornell Univ. Press, 1977.
Jennings, Francis, William N. Fenton, et al., eds. *The History and Culture of Iroquois Diplomacy: An Interdisciplinary Guide to the Treaties of the Six Nations and Their League.* Syracuse: Syracuse Univ. Press, 1985.
Johnston, Charles M., ed. *The Valley of the Six Nations....* Toronto, Ont.: Univ. of Toronto, 1964.

Bibliography

Jones, Pomroy. *Annals and Recollections of Oneida County.* Rome, N.Y.: privately published, 1851.
Kelsey, Isabel Thompson. *Joseph Brant, 1743-1807: Man of Two Worlds.* Syracuse: Syracuse Univ. Press, 1984.
Kent, James, *Commentaries on American Law.* 3 vols. 1826. Reprint, New York: Da Capo Press, 1971.
Klement, Frank L. *Wisconsin and the Civil War.* Madison, Wis.: SHSW, 1963.
Kvasnicka, Robert, and Herman Viola, eds. *The Commissioners of Indian Affairs, 1824-1977.* Lincoln: Univ. of Nebraska Press, 1979.
Lafitau, Joseph François. *Customs of the American Indians.* 1724. Reprint (2 vols.) Edited by William N. Fenton. Translated by Elizabeth Moore. Toronto, Ont.: Champlain Society, 1974.
Lampard, Eric E. *The Rise of the Dairy Industry in Wisconsin: A Study in Agricultural Change, 1820-1920.* Madison, Wis.: SHSW, 1963.
Lennox, H. J. *Samuel Kirkland's Mission to the Iroquois.* Chicago: Univ. of Chicago Libraries, 1935.
Linklaen, Jan [John]. *Travels in the Years 1791 and 1792 in Pennsylvania, New York and Vermont: Journals of John Linklaen, Agent of the Holland Land Company.* New York: G. P. Putnam's Sons, 1897.
Love, William De Loss. *Wisconsin in the War of the Rebellion....* New York: Love Publishing, 1866.
Lurie, Nancy O. *Wisconsin Indians.* Madison: SHSW, 1987.
Mancall, Peter C. *Deadly Medicine: Indians and Alcohol in Early America.* Ithaca, N. Y.: Cornell Univ. Press, 1995.
Manley, Henry S. *The Treaty of Fort Stanwix, 1784.* Rome, N.Y.: Sentinel Co., 1932.
Martin, Deborah B. *History of Brown County, Wisconsin: Past and Present.* 2 vols. Chicago: S. J. Clarke, 1913.
Martineau, Harriet. *Retrospect of Western Travel.* 3 vols. London: Saunders & Otley, 1838.
Mason, Carol I. *Introduction to Wisconsin Indians: Prehistory to Statehood.* Salem, Wis.: Sheffield Publishing Co., 1987.
Mau, Clayton, ed. *The Development of Central and Western New York.* New York: DuBois Press, 1944.
Maximilian, Prince of Wied. *Travels in the Interior of North America.* Translated by H. Evans Lloyd. London: Ackerman & Co., 1843.
McKenney, Thomas L. *Sketches of a Tour to the Lakes.* 1826. Reprint. Barre, Mass.: Imprint Society, 1972.
Meinig, D. W. *The Shaping of America: A Geographical Perspective on 500 Years of History.* 2 vols. New Haven, Conn.: Yale Univ. Press, 1986, and 1993.
Merk, Frederick. *Economic History of Wisconsin During the Civil War Decade.* Madison, Wis.: SHSW, 1916.
Miller, Nathan. *The Enterprise of a Free People: Aspects of Economic Development in New York State during the Canal Era, 1792-1838.* Ithaca, N.Y.: Cornell Univ. Press, 1962.
Mitchell, Stewart. *Horatio Seymour of New York.* Cambridge, Mass.: Harvard Univ. Press, 1938.

Morgan, Lewis Henry. *League of the Ho-de-no-sau-nee, or Iroquois*. Rochester: Sage & Bros., 1851. Paperback reprint, edited by William N. Fenton, New York: Corinth Books, 1962.

Moss, Richard J. *The Life of Jedidiah Morse: A Station of Peculiar Exposure.* Knoxville: Univ. of Tennessee Press, 1995.

Moulton, Gary E. *The Papers of Chief John Ross*. 2 vols. Norman: Univ. of Oklahoma Press, 1985.

Nesbit, Robert C. *Wisconsin: A History.* Madison, Wis.: SHSW, 1973.

Neville, Ella, et al. *Historic Green Bay, 1834-1840.* Green Bay, Wis.: privately published, 1893.

New York Indians. Petition to United States Senate. *The New York Indians having, by renewed application to the Executive, ineffectually sought to obtain through its interposition such modifications of the treaty lately concluded with the Menomonie [sic] tribe.* 1832[?]. Pamphlet in SHSW, Madison.

Niven, John. *John C. Calhoun and the Price of Union: A Biography.* Baton Rouge: Louisiana State Univ. Press, 1988.

Ourada, Patricia K. *The Menominee Indians: A History.* Norman: Univ. of Oklahoma Press, 1979.

Parker, Arthur C. *Parker on the Iroquois.* Edited by William N. Fenton. Syracuse: Syracuse Univ. Press, 1968.

Pernin, Peter, *The Great Peshtigo Fire*, 2d ed. Madison, Wis.: SHSW, 1999.

Phillips, Joseph W. *Jedidiah Morse and New England Congregationalism.* New Brunswick, N.J.: Rutgers Univ. Press, 1983.

Pilkington, Walter, ed. *The Journals of Samuel Kirkland.* Clinton, N.Y.: Hamilton College, 1980.

Prucha, Francis Paul. *American Indian Policy in the Formative Years: The Indian Trade and Intercourse Acts, 1790-1834.* Cambridge, Mass.: Harvard Univ. Press, 1962.

———. *American Indian Treaties: The History of a Political Anomaly.* Berkeley and Los Angeles: Univ. of California Press, 1994.

———. *The Great Father: The United States Government and the American Indians.* 2 vols. Lincoln: Univ. of Nebraska Press, 1984.

Quiner, Edwin B. *Military History of Wisconsin; a Record of the Civil and Military Patriotism of the State, in the War for the Union.* Chicago: Clarke Publishing, 1866.

Remini, Robert V. *Andrew Jackson and the Course of American Empire.* 3 vols. New York: Harper & Row, 1977-1984.

———. *Henry Clay: Statesman for the Union.* New York: W. W. Norton & Company, 1991.

———. *Martin Van Buren and the Making of the Democratic Party.* New York: Columbia Univ. Press, 1959.

Richards, Cara E. *The Oneida People.* Phoenix: Indian Tribal Series, 1974.

Richter, Daniel K. *The Ordeal of the Longhouse: The Peoples of the Iroquois League in the Era of European Colonization.* Chapel Hill: Univ. of North Carolina Press, 1992.

Richter, Daniel K., and James H. Merrell, eds. *Beyond the Covenant Chain: The Iroquois and Their Neighbors in Indian North America, 1600-1800.* Syracuse: Syracuse Univ. Press, 1987.

Bibliography

Ritzenthaler, Robert E. *The Oneida Indians of Wisconsin.* Public Museum of the City of Milwaukee *Bulletin* 19 (November, 1950).
Rohrbough, Malcolm J. *The Land Office Business: The Settlement and Administration of American Public Lands, 1789-1837.* New York: Oxford University Press, 1968.
Rudolph, Jack. *Birthplace of a Commonwealth: A Short History of Brown County, Wisconsin.* Green Bay, Wis.: Brown County Historical Society, 1976.
Russo, David J. *The Major Political Issues of the Jacksonian Period and the Development of Party Loyalty in Congress, 1830-1840.* Transactions of the American Philosophical Society, 62, pt. 5. Philadelphia, Pa.: American Philosophical Society, 1972.
Ryan, Mary P. *Cradle of the Middle Class: The Family in Oneida County, New York, 1790-1865.* Cambridge, U.K.: Cambridge Univ. Press, 1981.
Satz, Ronald. *American Indian Policy in the Jacksonian Era.* Norman: University of Oklahoma Press, 2002.
Schafer, Joseph. *A History of Agriculture in Wisconsin.* Madison: SHSW, 1922.
———. *The Winnebago-Horicon Basin: A Type Study in Western History.* Madison, Wis.: SHSW, 1937.
Schoolcraft, Henry R. *Narrative Journal of Travels Through the Northwestern Regions of the United States ... in the Year 1820,* Albany, N.Y.: E. E. Horsford, 1821. Reprint, edited by Mentor L. Williams, East Lansing: Michigan State Univ. Press, 1953.
———. *Notes on the Iroquois, or Contributions to American History, Antiquities and General Ethnology.* Albany: Erastus H. Pense, 1847.
———. *Schoolcraft's Expedition to Lake Itasca, the Discovery of the Source of the Mississippi.* Edited by Philip P. Mason. East Lansing: Michigan State Univ. Press, 1958.
Shattuck, George C. *The Oneida Indians Land Claims: A Legal History.* Syracuse: Syracuse Univ. Press, 1991.
Shaw, Ronald E. *Canals for a Nation: The Canal Era in the United States, 1790-1860.* Lexington: Univ. Press of Kentucky, 1990.
———. *Erie Water West: A History of the Erie Canal, 1792-1854.* Lexington: Univ. Press of Kentucky, 1966.
Sheriff, Carol. *The Artificial River: The Erie Canal and the Paradox of Progress.* New York: Hill & Wang, 1996.
Smith, Alice E. *The History of Wisconsin.* Vol. 1: *From Exploration to Statehood.* Madison: SHSW, 1973.
———. *James Duane Doty, Frontier Promoter.* Madison, Wis.: SHSW, 1954.
Smith, James H., *History of Chenango and Madison Counties, New York.* Syracuse, N.Y.: D. Mason & Co., 1880.
Smith, John E., ed. *Our Country and Its People: Descriptive and Biographical Records of Madison County, N.Y.* Boston: Boston History Co., 1899.
Snow, Dean, Charles Gehring, and William A. Starna, eds. *In Mohawk Country: Early Narratives about a Native People.* Syracuse: Syracuse Univ. Press, 1996.
Snyder, Charles M., ed. *Red and White on the New York Frontier ... From the Papers of Erastus Granger, 1807-1819.* Harrison, N.Y.: Harbor Hill Books, 1978.

Soltow, Lee. *Patterns of Wealthholding in Wisconsin Since 1850.* Madison: Univ. of Wisconsin Press, 1971.
Spafford, Horatio Gates. *A Gazetteer of the State of New-York....* Albany: B. D. Packard, 1824.
Stagg, J. C. A., *Mr. Madison's War.* Princeton, N.J.: Princeton Univ. Press, 1983.
Sutcliff, Robert. *Travels in Some Parts of North America in the Years 1804, 1805 and 1806.* 2d ed. London: Longman, Hurst & Co., 1815.
Tanner, Helen Hornbeck et al. eds. *Atlas of Great Lakes Indian History.* Norman: Univ. of Oklahoma Press, 1987.
Taylor, George Rogers. *The Transportation Revolution, 1815-1860.* New York: Rinehart & Co., 1951.
Tenney, H. A., and David Atwood, comps. *Memorial Record of the Fathers of Wisconsin....* Madison, Wis.: David Atwood, 1880.
Tocqueville, Alexis de. *Democracy in America.* 2d ed. Translated by Henry Reeve. Preface and notes by John C. Spencer. New York: Adlard, 1838.
Tooker, Elisabeth. *The Iroquois Ceremonial of Midwinter.* Syracuse: Syracuse Univ. Press, 1970.
Trennert, Robert A., Jr. *Indian Traders on the Middle Border: The House of Ewing, 1827-1854.* Lincoln: Univ. of Nebraska Press, 1981.
Trigger, Bruce G., ed. *Handbook of North American Indians.* Vol. 15: *The Northeast.* Washington, D.C.: Smithsonian Institution, 1978.
Trigger, Bruce G., and Wilcomb E. Washburn. *The Cambridge History of the Native Peoples of the Americas: North America.* 2 vols. Cambridge, U.K.: Cambridge Univ. Press, 1996.
Trollope, Frances Milton. *Domestic Manners of the Americans.* 1832. Reprint, edited by Donald Smalley. Gloucester, Mass.: Peter Smith, 1974.
Truettner, William H. *The Natural Man Observed: A Study of Catlin's Indian Gallery.* Washington, D.C.: Smithsonian Press, 1979.
Tuttle, Charles R. *An Illustrated History of the State of Wisconsin.* Madison, Wis.: B. B. Russell & Co., 1875.
Upton, Helen M. *The Everett Report in Historical Perspective: The Indians of New York.* Albany: New York State American Revolution Bicentennial Commission, 1980.
Vandewater, Robert J. *The Tourist Pocket Manual for Travelers on the Hudson River, the Western Canal and Stage Road to Niagara Falls....* 3rd ed. New York: Harper & Bros., 1834.
Vecsey, Christopher, and William A. Starna, eds. *Iroquois Land Claims.* Syracuse: Syracuse Univ. Press, 1988.
Viola, Herman, J. *Diplomats in Buckskin: A History of Indian Delegations in Washington City.* Washington, D.C.: Smithsonian Institution Press, 1981.
Viola, Herman. *Thomas L. McKenney: Architect of America's Early Indian Policy, 1816-1830.* Chicago: Swallow Press, 1974.
Wager, Daniel E., ed. *Our County and Its People: A Descriptive Work on Oneida County, New York.* Boston: Boston History Co., 1896.
Wallace, Anthony F. C. *The Death and Rebirth of the Seneca.* New York: Alfred A. Knopf, 1969.
Walsh, Margaret. *The Manufacturing Frontier: Pioneer Industry in Antebellum Wisconsin, 1830-1860.* Madison, Wis.: SHSW, 1972.

Washburn, Wilcomb E., ed. *The American Indian and the United States: A Documentary History.* 4 vols. Westport, Conn.: Greenwood, 1973.
Waugh, Frederick W. *Iroquois Foods and Food Preparation.* Anthropological Series 12, Memoirs of the Canadian Geological Survey 86. Ottawa, Ont., 1916.
Weed, Thurlow. *Autobiography of Thurlow Weed.* Edited by Harriet Weed. Boston: Houghton, Mifflin & Company, 1883.
———. *Memoir of Thurlow Weed.* Edited by Thurlow Weed Barnes. Boston: Houghton, Mifflin & Company, 1884.
White, Richard. *The Middle Ground: Indians, Empires, and Republics in the Great Lakes Region, 1650-1815.* New York: Cambridge Univ. Press, 1991.
Wright, Frances. *Views of Society and Manners in America.* Edited by Paul R. Baker. Cambridge, Mass.: Belknap Press of Harvard University Press, 1963.
Wyman, Mark. *The Wisconsin Frontier.* Bloomington: University of Indiana Press, 1998.

Articles

Baird, Henry S. "Population of Brown County, June 1830." *WHC* 13 (1895): 468-72.
Barsness, John C. "John C. Calhoun and the Military Establishment, 1817-1825." *WMH* 50 (Autumn 1966): 43-53.
Biddle, James W. "Recollections of Green Bay in 1816-1817." *WHC* 1 (1855): 49-63.
Billington, Ray Allen. "The Fort Stanwix Treaty of 1768." *New York History* 25 (1944): 182-94.
Boyd, George. "Papers of Indian Agent Boyd [George]—1832 [with sketch of George & James Boyd by Herbert B. Tanner]." *WHC* 12 (1892): 266-98.
Burke, Joseph C. "The Cherokee Cases: A Study in Law, Politics, and Morality." *Stanford Law Review* 21 (February 1969): 501-31.
Campisi, Jack. "Consequences of the Kansas Claims to Oneida Tribal Identity." In *Proceedings* of the First Congress, Canadian Ethnology Society. Edited by Jerome H. Barkow. Ottawa, Ont.: Canada National Museum of Man, Ethnology Division. Mercury Series 17 (1974), pp. 35-47.
———. "New York-Oneida Treaty of 1795: A Finding of Fact." *American Indian Law Review* 4 (Summer 1976): 71-82.
———. "Oneida." In *Handbook of North American Indians.* Vol. 15, *The Northeast,* edited by Bruce G. Trigger. Washington, D.C.: Smithsonian Institution, 1978, 481-90.
———. "The Oneida Treaty Period, 1783-1838." In *The Oneida Indian Experience: Two Perspectives.* Edited by Jack Campisi and Laurence M. Hauptman. Syracuse, N.Y.: Syracuse University Press, 1988.
———. "The Wisconsin Oneidas between Disasters." In Laurence M. Hauptman and L. Gordon McLester III, eds., *The Oneida Indian Journey: From New York to Wisconsin, 1784-1860.* Madison, Wis.: University of Wisconsin Press, 1999, pp. 70-84.
Campisi, Jack, and Laurence M. Hauptman. "Talking Back: The Oneida Language and Folklore Project, 1938-1941." *Proceedings* of the American Philosophical Society 125 (Dec. 1981): 441-48.

Colman, Henry. "Recollections of Oneida Indians, 1840-1845." *Proceedings* of the State Historical Society at its Fifty-Ninth Annual Meeting. Madison: State Historical Society, 1912, pp. 152-59.
Cope, Alfred. "Mission to the Menominee: A Quaker's Green Bay Diary." *Wisconsin Magazine of History* 50 (Winter 1967): 120-44.
Davidson, John Nelson. "The Coming of the New York Indians to Wisconsin." *Proceedings* of the SHSW 47. Madison: Democrat Printing Co., 1899, pp. 153-85.
——. "Mission on Chequamegon Bay." *WHC* 12 (1892): 434-52.
Densmore, Christopher. "New York Quakers among the Brotherton, Stockbridge, Oneida, and Onondaga." *Man in the Northeast* no. 44 (Fall 1992): 83-93.
Doty, James Duane. "Northern Wisconsin in 1820." *WHC* 7 (1876): 195-206.
Draper, Lyman C. "Additional Notes on Eleazer Williams." In *WHC* 8 (1879): 353-69; reprint, Madison: SHSW, 1908.
——. "Report on the Indian Portrait Picture Gallery," *WHC* 3 (1857): 56-58.
——. "Some Wisconsin Indian Conveyances," *WHC* 15 (1900): 1-24.
——. "Wisconsin and Her Internal Navigation." *WHC* 3 (1857): 466-69.
Ellis, Albert G. "Fifty-four Years' Recollections of Men and Events in Wisconsin." *WHC* 7 (1876): 207-68. Reprint, Madison: SHSW, 1908.
——. "Recollections of Rev. Eleazer Williams." In *WHC* 8 (1879): 322-52. Reprint, Madison: SHSW, 1908.
——. "Some Accounts of the Advent of the New York Indians into Wisconsin." *WHC* 2 (1856): 415-49.
Fenton, William N. "The Iroquois in History." In *North American Indians in Historical Perspective*. Edited by Nancy O. Lurie and Eleanor Leacock. New York: Random House, 1971.
——. "Locality as a Basic Factor in the Development of Iroquois Social Structure." Bureau of American Ethnology *Bulletin* 149 (1951): 35-54.
——. "Northern Iroquoian Culture Patterns." In *Handbook of North American Indians*. Vol. 15, *The Northeast*, edited by Bruce G. Trigger. Washington, D.C.: Smithsonian Institution, 1978, 296-321.
Gilman, Rhoda R. "The Fur Trade in the Upper Mississippi, 1630-1850." *WMH* 58 (Autumn 1974-1975): 3-18.
Graymont, Barbara. "New York State Indian Policy after the Revolution." *New York History* 58 (October 1976): 438-74.
Grignon, Augustin. "Seventy-two Years Recollections of Wisconsin." *WHC* 3 (1857): 195-295.
Haeger, John D. "A Time of Change: Green Bay, 1815-1834." *WMH* 54 (1970-1971): 285-98.
Hauptman, Laurence M. "Designing Woman: Minnie Kellogg, Iroquois Leader." In *Indian Lives: Essays on Nineteenth and Twentieth Century Native American Leaders*. Edited by L. G. Moses and Raymond Wilson. Albuquerque, N.M.: University of New Mexico Press, 1985, pp. 159-88.
——. "Four Eastern New Yorkers and Seneca Lands: A Study in Treaty-Making." *Hudson Valley Regional Review* 13 (March 1996): 1-19.
——. "Governor Blacksnake and the Seneca Indian Struggle to Save the Oil Spring Reservation." *Mid-America* 81 (Winter 1999): 51-73.

———. "The Iroquois Indians and the Rise of the Empire State: Ditches, Defense and Dispossession." *New York History* 79 (October 1998): 325-58.
———. "Samuel George (1795-1873): A Study of Onondaga Conservatism," *New York History* 70 (January 1989): 5-22.
Horsman, Reginald. "The Origins of Oneida Removal to Wisconsin, 1815-1822." In *An Anthology of Western Great Lakes Indian History*. Edited by Donald Fixico. Milwaukee: American Indian Studies Program of the Univ. of Wisconsin, Milwaukee, 1987, pp. 203-32.
———. "Wisconsin and the War of 1812." *WMH* 46 (Autumn 1962): 3-15.
———. "The Wisconsin Oneidas in the Preallotment Years." In *The Oneida Indian Experience*, Edited by Jack Campisi and Laurence M. Hauptman. Syracuse, N.Y.: Syracuse University Press, 1988, pp. 65-82.
Hoyt, William, ed. "Zachary Taylor on Jackson and the Military Establishment, 1835." *American Historical Review* 51 (April 1946): 480-84.
Kay, Jeanne. "John Lawe: Green Bay Trader." *WMH* 64 (Autumn 1980): 3-27.
———. "Wisconsin Indian Hunting Patterns, 1634-1836." *Annals* of the Association of American Geographers 69 (September 1979): 402-18.
Kemper, Jackson. "Journal of an Episcopalian Missionary's Tour to Green Bay, 1834." *WHC* 14 (1898): 394-49.
Konapot, Levi, Jr. "Letter to Reverend Cutting Marsh, March 6, 1857." *WHC* 4 (1859).
Lehman, J. David. "The End of the Iroquois Mystique: The Oneida Land Cession Treaties of the 1780s." *William and Mary Quarterly* 47 (October 1990): 523-47.
Locklear, Arlinda. "The Allotment of the Oneida Reservation and Its Legal Ramifications." In *The Oneida Indian Experience*, edited by Jack Campisi and Laurence M. Hauptman. Syracuse, N.Y.: Syracuse University Press, 1988, pp. 83-100.
McCall, James. "McCall's Journal of a Visit to Wisconsin in 1830 [with a sketch of James McCall by Ansel J. McCall]." *WHC* 12 (1892): 170-215.
Marryat, Frederick. "An English Officer's Description of Wisconsin in 1837." *WHC* 14 (1898): 137-54.
Meinig, D. W. "Geography of Expansion, 1785-1855." In *Geography of New York State*, edited by John H. Thompson. Revised edition in paperback, Syracuse: Syracuse Univ. Press, 1977.
Miller, Nathan. "Private Enterprise in Inland Navigation: The Mohawk Route Prior to the Erie Canal." *New York History* 31 (October 1950): 398-413.
Niemcewicz, Julian Ursyn. "Journey to Niagara, 1805." Edited by Metchie J. E. Budka. *New-York Historical Society Quarterly* (1961): 72-113.
Pound, Cuthbert W. "Nationals without a Nation: The New York State Tribal Indians." *Columbia Law Review* 22 (February 1922): 97-102.
Prucha, Francis Paul. "Thomas L. McKenney and the New York Indian Board." *Mississippi Valley Historical Review* 48 (March 1962): 635-55.
Prucha, Francis Paul, and Donald F. Carmony, eds. "A Memorandum of Lewis Cass Concerning a System for the Regulation of Indian Affairs." *WMH* 52 (Autumn 1968): 35-50.
Remini, Robert V. "The Albany Regency." *New York History* 39 (October 1958): 341-55.

Ricciardelli, Alex F. "The Adoption of White Agriculture by the Oneida Indians." *Ethnohistory* 10 (Fall 1963): 309-28.
Richter, Daniel K. "War and Culture: The Iroquois Experience." *William and Mary Quarterly* 40 (1983): 528-59.
Ronda, James P. "Reverend Samuel Kirkland and the Oneida Indians." In *The Oneida Indian Experience: Two Perspectives*, edited by Jack Campisi and Laurence M. Hauptman. Syracuse, N.Y.: Syracuse University Press, 1988, pp. 23-30.
Smith, Alice E. "Daniel Whitney: Pioneer Businessman." *WMH* 24 (March 1941): 283-304.
Smith, Robert, and Loretta Metoxen. "Oneida Traditions." In *The Oneida Indian Experience*, edited by Jack Campisi and Laurence M. Hauptman. Syracuse, N.Y.: Syracuse University Press, 1988, pp. 50-51.
Synderman, George S. "Behind the Tree of Peace: A Sociological Analysis of Iroquois Warfare." *Pennsylvania Archaeologist* 38 (Fall 1948): 3-93.
Stambaugh, Samuel. "Report on the Quality and Condition of Wisconsin Territory, 1831." *WHC* 15 (1900): 399-438.
Starna, William A. "The Oneida Homeland in the Seventeenth Century." In *The Oneida Indian Experience: Two Perspectives*, edited by Jack Campisi and Laurence M. Hauptman. Syracuse, N.Y.: Syracuse University Press, 1988, pp. 9-22.
Taylor, Alan. "The Art of 'Hook & Snivey': Political Culture in Upstate New York During the 1790s." *Journal of American History* 80 (March 1993): 1371-96.
Thwaites, Reuben, ed. "Documents Relating to the Episcopal Church and Mission in Green Bay, 1825-1841." *WHC* 14 (1898): 450-515.
Thwaites, Reuben Gold, ed. "Papers of James Duane Doty." In *WHC* 13 (1895): 163-246.
Thwaites, Reuben Gold, ed. "Sketch and Narrative of Morgan L. Martin," *WHC* 11 (1888): 380-415.
Thwaites, Reuben Gold, ed. "The Territorial Census for 1836," *WHC* 13 (1895): 247-70.
Tiro, Karim M. "James Dean in Iroquoia." *New York History* 80 (October 1999): 391-422.
Tooker, Elisabeth. "Iroquois Since 1820." In *Handbook of North American Indians*. Vol. 15, *The Northeast*, edited by Bruce G. Trigger. Washington, D.C.: Smithsonian Institution, 1978, 449-65.
Tooker, Elisabeth. "The Iroquois White Dog Sacrifice in the Latter Part of the Eighteenth Century." *Ethnohistory* 12 (1965): 129-40.
———. "The League of the Iroquois: Its History, Politics and Ritual. In *Handbook of North American Indians*. Vol. 15, *The Northeast*, edited by Bruce G. Trigger. Washington, D.C.: Smithsonian Institution, 1978.
———. "On the New Religion of Handsome Lake." *Anthropological Quarterly* 41 (1968): 187-200.
Trask, Kerry A. "Settlement in a Half-Savage Land: Life and Loss in the Métis Community of La Baye." *Michigan Historical Review* 15 (Spring 1989): 1-27.
Wallace, Michael. "Changing Concepts of Party in the United States: New York, 1815-1828." *American Historical Review* 74 (December 1968): 453-71.

Bibliography

Newspapers and Magazines

Albany Argus
Appleton Crescent
The Friend
Green Bay Advocate
Green Bay Press
Green Bay Intelligencer
Milwaukee Sentinel
New York Herald
New York Times
New York Tribune
Niles Register
Utica Patriot and Patrol

Dissertations and Theses

Basehart, Harry S. "Historical Changes in the Kinship System of the Oneida Indians." Ph.D. diss., Harvard University, 1952.
Beck, David R. M. "Siege and Survival: Menominee Responses to an Encroaching World." Ph.D. diss., University of Illinois at Chicago, 1994.
Campisi, Jack. "Ethnic Identity and Boundary Maintenance in Three Oneida Communities." Ph.D. diss., SUNY at Albany, 1974.
Conable, Mary. "A Steady Enemy: The Ogden Land Company and the Seneca Indians." Ph.D. diss., Univ. of Rochester, 1995.
Geier, Philip Otto. "A Peculiar Status: A History of the Oneida Indian Treaties and Claims: Jurisdictional Conflict within the American Government, 1775-1920." Ph.D. diss., Syracuse University, 1980.
Kay, Jeanne. "The Land of La Baye: The Ecological Impact of the Green Bay Fur Trade, 1634-1836." Ph.D. diss., University of Wisconsin, 1977.
Patrick, Christine. "Samuel Kirkland: Missionary to the Oneida Indians." Ph.D. diss., Buffalo: SUNY at Buffalo, 1992.
Schein, Richard H. "A Historical Geography of Central New York: Patterns and Processes of Colonization on the New Military Tract, 1782-1820." Ph.D. diss., Syracuse University, 1989.
Spiller, Roger J. "John C. Calhoun as Secretary of War." Ph.D. diss., Louisiana State University, 1977.
Tiro, Karim. "The People of the Standing Stone: The Oneida Indian Nation From Revolution through Removal, 1765-1840." Ph.D. diss., University of Pennsylvania, 1998.
Van Hoeven, James W. "Salvation and Indian Removal: The Career Biography of Rev. John Freeman Schermerhorn, Indian Commissioner." Ph.D. diss., Vanderbilt University., 1972.

Index

Adams, John Quincy, 109
Agriculture, Oneida, 22-23, 29, 54, 57, 61, 100, 110-11, 117-19, 131, 134, 138, 152-53
Agwelondongwas (Agwrondongwas). See Good Peter
Albany Regency, 38-39
Albany Register, 28
Alcohol abuse, 8, 14, 19-22, 29, 32, 119, 131-32, 135, 152
Allegany Indian Reservation, 31
Allotment pressures, 129-31, 133, 136-38, 141, 143-44, 146-49, 151-57, 160, 181n.29, 182n.14
Amended Treaty of Buffalo Creek (Feb. 3, 1838), 95-96, 98, 101-102, 106-108
American Fur Company, 10, 34-35, 43-44, 46-47, 57-58, 65
American Revolution, 3, 4, 6, 8, 12, 19, 32, 35, 45, 77, 113, 121, 124-25, 128, 162
Annuities, Oneida tribal, 8, 11, 20, 37-39, 64, 96, 101, 108-109, 128-30, 144, 150, 167n.5
Anthony, John, 36, 56, 60, 65, 70, 74, 76, 90-91, 108, 115

Anthony, Sallie, 145
Anthony, Thomas, 145
Archiquette (Otsiquette), Neddy, 36, 52, 56, 60, 136
Arndt, John, 47-48, 55, 130-31, 150
Astor, John Jacob, 46-47, 57
Augustine, Peter, 38
A-yah-manta (Menominee Indian), 75

Baird, Cornelius, 36
Baird, Henry, 47-48, 55, 104, 109, 111-13, 149-50
Baird, Tillie, 12
Battles. See Oriskany, Battle of; Sandy Creek, Battle of; Saratoga, Battle of
Bear, Henry, 114
Bear Grease (Menominee Indian), 56
Beck, David R. M., 48
Beechtree (Oneida Indian), 25
Belknap, Jeremy, 16
Big Sandy, Battle of. See Sandy Creek, Battle of
Blatcop (Oneida Indian), 4
Black Hawk, 75
Black Hawk War, 75, 94, 104

Index

Blackhawk, Ida, 11-12
Bonesteel, A. D., 133-34
Boundary Commission (1830), U.S., 54-62
Bourne, W. R., 141, 154
Bowyer, John, 34-35
Boyd, George, 15, 89, 109-10, 142, 177n.28
Bread, Daniel: attempts to win support from New York politicians, 69; becomes pinetree chief, 33; Bishop Jackson Kemper and, 15, 107, 126, 142-43; boyhood at Oneida Castle, 17-19, 21-24, 30; Christianity and, 17; confronts President Jackson, 70-73, 175n.20; cooperation with federal Indian agents, 109-12; death of, 158; decline of Bread's influence and chiefs council authority, 132-33, 135, 156-58; delegate on exploring party to Michigan Territory, 35-36; education of, 17; efforts to replace Bread as chief, 141, 156-57; emerging political power, 37-40; establishes cooperation with Chief Jacob Cornelius and the Orchard Party, 99-103, 119; faces generation gap, 134-35; faces insurgency by Chief Cornelius Hill within First Christian Party, 154-55; family of, 128, 171n.1; favors allotment of Oneida lands after the Civil War, 141, 144; genealogy of, 5-6; Green Bay power elite and, 47-48, 57-62, 147-54; influence of Eleazer Williams on, 33-34; July 4th celebration and, 121-26; leads Oneidas to Wisconsin, 11-12, 27-28, 37, 43, 100-102, 110, 160; made principal chief, 102; meets with American Indian leaders in Washington, D.C., 67; Oneida lobbyist against Stambaugh treaties, 63-66, 68; Oneida opinions of Chief Bread, 11-14, 159; opposes Albert Ellis as federal Indian agent, 112-14; opposes removal of Oneidas from Wisconsin 92-94, 99, 104-107, 111-15; oratory of, 26, 44, 121, 123-26; outspoken advocate of Oneidas' position relative to Treaties of 1821 and 1822, 55; overthrows Eleazer Williams, 88-90; quarrels with Reverend Edward A. Goodnough, 143-47; rejects scheme to reduce Oneida landholdings, 57-62; resettles Oneidas in Wisconsin, 27-28, 37, 43, 100-102, 110, 160; seeks to bring Canadian Oneidas to Wisconsin, 119, 126, 145-46, 182n.10; split with Eleazer Williams, 36-37; support of Oneida schools, 15, 17, 109, 118, 133, 179n.6; John C. Schermerhorn and, 90-94; Treaties of 1821 and 1822 and, 48, 50, 54; Treaty of Buffalo Creek (and Amended Treaty of Buffalo Creek) and, 94-97; turns on Chief John Anthony, 90; woos Woodman Party, 107-108; works with federal Indian agent John Manley, 154; U.S.-Menominee Treaty of 1832 and, 74-77; wealth of, xiv, 11-14, 100-101, 118-19, 131
Bread, Dinah (Daniel Bread's mother), 6
Bread, Electa (Daniel Bread's first wife), 43, 128
Bread, Jane (Daniel Bread's second wife), 128
Bread, John (Daniel Bread's son), 43, 128
Bread, Margaret Fraser (Daniel Bread's third wife), 128
Bread, Peter, 4, 6
Bread, Susanah (Daniel Bread's daughter), 128
Brothertown Indians, 3, 9, 46, 60, 70, 73, 100, 112-13, 118, 148-51
Brown County, Wis., 37, 121, 125, 130-31, 138, 142-43. *See also* Green Bay, Wis.; Fox River Valley
Buchanan, James, 134
Buffalo Creek Reservation, 94-95

Index

Buffalo Creek Treaty (1838), 92-99, 101-102, 106-108, 130. *See also* Amended Treaty of Buffalo Creek (1838)
Butte Des Morts, Treaty of (1827), 53-54, 60

Calhoun, John C., 31, 35-36
Campisi, Jack, 8, 103, 120, 127
Canadian Oneidas. *See* Oneidas of the Thames; Six Nations Reserve
Canals. *See* Erie Canal; Fox-Wisconsin River Improvement Company; Martin, Morgan L.; Western Inland Lock Navigation Company
Canandaigua Treaty (1794), 24, 29, 31, 35, 101, 128, 150
Captain John. *See* John, Captain
Carron, Josette, 48, 56
Cass, Lewis, 31-32, 35, 63, 70, 75
Catlin, George, 6, 10, 62, 67
Cattaraugus Indian Reservation, 95
Cayuga Indians, 94
Chase, Salmon P., 149
Chase, Thomas, 159
Cha-wa-non (Menominee Indian), 46, 50
Cheno-ma-bee-mee (Menominee Indian), 75
Cherokee Indians, 66-67, 91-94
Cherokee Nation v. Georgia, 66-67
Chicago fire (1871), 158-159
Chiefs, Oneida. *See* Bread, Daniel; Cornelius, Jacob; Hill, Cornelius; Skenandoah; Shekandoah, Elijah
Chiefs Council, Oneida. *See* Political system, Oneida
Chippewa Indians, 53
Choctaw Indians, 67
Cholera, 95, 110
Chrisjohn/Christjohn. *See* Christian
Christ Episcopal Church (Green Bay, Wis.), 47-48
Christian (Oneida Indian), 20-21
Christian Daniel. *See* Bread, Daniel
Christian Party. *See* First Christian Party; Second Christian Party
Church of the Holy Apostles. *See* Holy Apostles Episcopal Church

Citizenship, U.S., 12, 104-105, 108, 112, 130, 148-49, 151, 157-58
Civil War, 8, 10-11, 40, 107, 129-30, 136-40, 142, 144-45, 149-51, 155. *See also* Fourteenth Wisconsin Volunteer Infantry
Clan Mothers, 7, 127. *See also* Women, Oneida
Clinton, De Witt, 32-33
Code of Handsome Lake. *See* Handsome Lake
Colman, Henry, 181n.29
Colton, Calvin, 50-51, 59-62, 66-67, 172n.19
Compromise Treaty. *See* Seneca Treaty of 1842
Condolence Council Ceremony, Iroquois, 122-25
Cooley, Dennis N., 139
Cope, Alfred, 117-20, 127, 146
Cornelius, Henry, 4
Cornelius, Jacob: cooperates with Daniel Bread to establish Wisconsin Oneida community, 102-103; efforts to stop Oneida Indian removal from Wisconsin, 109, 112-15; favors allotment of tribal lands, 156-57; helps overthrow Eleazer Williams, 90; leadership of Orchard Party, 13, 106, 128, 133-36, 146, 160; post-Civil War relationship with Bread, 141, 144, 146
Cornelius, John, 156
Corning, Erastus, 149
Crawford, T. Hartley, 106
Creek Indians, 67
Crime, 20, 22, 25, 133-35, 145-46, 154, 157
Cultural adaptation, Oneida (Wisconsin), 102-104, 110-11, 119-21, 123-26

Dairy Industry, Wisconsin, 148-49, 182n.14
Dallas, Alexander, 30-31
Davis, M. M., 137-38, 145, 150
Davis, Solomon, 10, 15, 28, 39, 11, 129-30, 169n.7

Dawes Act. *See* General Allotment Act (1887); Allotment pressures
Delaware Indians, 94
Denny, John, 30, 38, 108, 115
Denver, F. W., 134
Detroit, 34-35
Dispossession, Oneida (New York), 29-33, 37-40
Dodge, Henry, 104-106, 109, 112-15, 150, 160
Dole, William 137
Doty, James Duane: American Fur Company agent, 46-48, 57; appraises Daniel Bread, 10-11; attorney for Menominee Indians, 56-57; efforts to promote Oneida Indian removal from Wisconsin, 104-106, 109-10; Green Bay elite and, 44, 58; land speculation and transportation schemes, 58-59, 173n.31; mentioned, 91, 149; racist attitudes toward New York Indians, 59; relationship to Morgan L. Martin, 147. *See also* American Fur Company; Boundary Commission (1830), U.S.; Fox-Wisconsin River Improvement Company; Oshkosh; Stambaugh, Samuel C.; Wisconsin statehood
Duck Creek. *See* Oneida Indian Reservation, Wisconsin
Dutch Reformed religion, 91

Eaton, John, 54, 68
Economic conditions, Oneida: New York, 20, 22-26, 28-29; Wisconsin, 107-108, 110-11, 117-19, 131-35, 137-39, 143-47, 152-54
Education, Oneida. *See* Schools, Oneida
Ellis, Albert G.: appointed United States Indian Agent at Green Bay, 112; helps create Eleazer Williams myth in his writings, 10-12, 88-90; lumber interests of, 130; mentioned, 15, 109, 142, 150, 160; pushes Oneida Indian removal from Wisconsin as federal Indian agent, 112-15; Stambaugh treaties and, 65,

88. *See also* Boundary Commission (1830), U.S.; Green Bay; Williams, Eleazer.
Elm, Levi, 12
Elm, Peter, 3, 6
Epidemics, 20, 95, 110, 129, 153. *See also* cholera; smallpox
Episcopal religion. *See* Christ Episcopal Church; Davis, Solomon; First Christian Party, Oneida; Goodnough, Edward A.; Hobart Church; Holy Apostles Episcopal Church; Kemper, Jackson; Williams, Eleazer
Erie Canal, 47-48, 58, 94, 149, 160-61, 172n.12

Famines, 129, 134, 138, 143-44, 153
Federal Writers' Project, WPA. *See* Oneida Language and Folklore Project, WPA
Fenton, William N., 99, 122-24
First Christian Party, Oneida. *See* Archiquette, Neddy; Bread, Daniel; Hill, Cornelius; Hobart Church; Powless, Henry; Kirkland, Samuel; Skenandoah; Shekandore, Elijah; Williams, Eleazer
Fishing, Oneida, 18, 23-24, 29, 52, 138
Forest Lands, Oneida: in New York, 18, 22-24; in Wisconsin, 52, 110-11. *See also* Timber stripping
Fort Herkimer Treaty (1785), 29
Fort Howard, 44, 46, 117, 135
Fort Oswego, 3
Fort Schuyler Treaty (1788), 29
Fort Stanwix Treaty (1784), 24, 35
Foster, Nathaniel, 131
Four Legs (Winnebago Indian), 56
Fourteenth Wisconsin Volunteer Infantry, 138-39, 145
Fox River Portage Company, 148
Fox River Valley, Wis., 9, 34, 45, 47-48, 50, 57-58, 148-50. *See also* American Fur Company; Doty, James Duane; Fox-Wisconsin River Improvement Company; Green Bay; Martin, Morgan L.; Seymour, John; Whitney, Daniel

Index

Fox-Wisconsin River Improvement Company, 148-150, 172n.12
Franco-Menominees, 37, 43-45, 48, 55-58, 60, 65, 75, 88-89. See also Grignon, Augustin; Grignon, Charles G.
French, 44, 46, 55-56, 88. See also American Fur Company; Franco-Menominees; fur trade
Fur trade, 43-44, 48, 55, 57, 88. See also American Fur Company; Franco-Menominees; Astor, John Jacob; Doty, James Duane; Franco-Menominee; Grignon, Augustin; Grignon, Charles

Gaiwiio. See Handsome Lake
General Allotment Act (1887), 136
Genesee Turnpike. See Great Western Turnpike Road
Gillet, Ransom, 94
Good Peter (Oneida Indian), 25, 162
Good Word. See Handsome Lake
Goodnough, Edward A., 15, 135-37, 140-41, 143-47, 155, 181n.30, 182n.4
Goodnough, Ellen, 142, 151, 153-54, 159
Gospel Messenger, 90
Grand River (Ontario, Canada). See Six Nations Reserve
Great Britain. See American Revolution; Sandy Creek, Battle of; War of 1812
Great Chicago Fire. See Chicago fire (1871), 158-59
Great Law. See Great Binding Law, Iroquois
Great Peshtigo Fire. See Peshtigo Fire (1871)
Great Sioux Uprising. See Sioux War (1862)
Great Western Turnpike Road, 22-23, 28, 30
Green Bay (Wis.), 9, 14: description in 1830, 43-46; land office at, 103-104; lumber industry, 130-34; mentioned, 14, 17, 33, 37, 39-40, 44, 46-48, 50-51, 53, 60, 62, 69, 75-76, 90, 100-103, 154; power elite, 37, 46-48, 51-52, 55-59, 88, 107, 109, 116, 125, 140
Green Bay Advocate, xiii, 124-25, 159-60
Green Bay and Lake Pepin Railroad, 150
Greenwood, A. B., 133
Grignon, Augustin, 46, 75, 177n.28
Grignon, Charles G., 65, 75-76
Grizzly Bear (Menominee Indian), 75

Handsome Lake, xiii, 21-22
Hanyerry (Oneida Indian), 4
Hanyost (Oneida Indian), 4
Head, Orson, 149
Hill, Cornelius, 10, 15, 143, 147, 153-59
Hobart Church, 7, 8, 9, 12, 15, 107, 118, 141. See also Davis, Solomon; Goodnough, Edward A., Hill, Cornelius; Kemper, Jackson
Hobart, John Henry, 9, 31, 33
Ho-Chunk Indians. See Winnebago Indians
Holy Apostles Episcopal Church, xv, 8, 12. See also Hobart Church
"Homeless" Oneidas, 96, 145-47
Huebschmann, Francis, 132
Hunting, Oneida, 18, 29, 106, 138

Independence Day. See July 4th
Indian Removal Act (1830), 104
Indian Territory, 8, 11, 33, 93-95, 100, 104, 106-107, 109, 113-14, 137, 152, 178n.43. See also Buffalo Creek Treaty (1838); Kansas lands; Missouri Emigrating Party; Woodman Party
Iroquois Confederacy, 17-18, 21-22, 121, 123
Iroquois Indians. See Cayuga Indians; Iroquois Confederacy; Mohawk Indians; Oneida Indians; Onondaga Indians; Seneca Indians; Tuscarora Indians
Iron district, Wisconsin, 104
Irwin, A. I., 112

Jackson, Andrew: confronted by Daniel Bread, 69-73; mentioned, 11,

40, 54, 58, 62–63, 104, 160; promotes Stambaugh treaties, 66–69; pushes Schermerhorn treaty negotiations and, 91–94
Jenkins, Timothy, 38
John, Captain, 25
Johnson, Andrew, 155
Jones, David, 109–12
Jouett, Charles, 32
Jourdan, Mary, 89, 171n.36
July 4th, 8, 115, 118–19, 121–26

Kanaʔalóhaleʔ. See Oneida Castle
Kansas claims, 94–96
Kansas lands, 93–95
Kaunandauloonh (Oneida Indian). See Bread, Peter
Kemper, Jackson, 15, 107, 126, 142–43
King, Adam, 115
King, Metinus, 114
King, Stadler, 6–7, 12
Kirkland, Samuel, 6–7, 17, 19

La Baye. See Green Bay
Lacrosse, 12, 13, 18, 100, 103, 119, 124
Lafayette, Marquis de, 4, 128
Lakota Indians, 152. See also Sioux Indians
Land speculation. See Doty, James Duane; Fox-Wisconsin River Improvement Company; Ogden, David A.; Ogden, Thomas Ludlow; Ogden Land Company; Martin, Morgan L.; Whitney, Daniel
Language, Oneida, xv–xvi, 26. See also Oneida Language and Folklore Project, WPA; Oratory, Oneida
Lawe, John, 46–47
Lead mining, 68, 75
Lewis, David, 181n.29
Lincoln, Abraham, 149
Little Chute, 8–9, 52, 89, 92–93
Little Wave (Menominee Indian), 75
Livestock industry, Oneida, 118, 133
Logging. See Lumber industry; timber stripping
"Lost Dauphin" legend, 9–10
Louis XVI. See "Lost Dauphin" legend

Lumber industry, 130–34, 139–40. See also Arndt, John; Ellis, Albert; Foster, Nathaniel; Green Bay; timber stripping

McCall, James, 54, 59–60
McKenney, Thomas L., 63–64
Madison, James, 4
Madison, Wis., 58
Madison County, N.Y.: population statistics, 24. See also Oneida Indian Reservation (New York)
Manley, John, 154, 183n.30
Manypenny, George, 132
Martin, Morgan L.: background, 57, 147–49; federal Indian treaty commissioner promoting, 104; land and transportation schemes, 148–49; member of Green Bay elite, 44; mentioned, 59, 110, 144, 160, 177n.28, 182n.14, 183n.30; supports Stambaugh treaties, 68; urges allotment of Oneida Reservation (Wisconsin), 150–54. See also Doty, James Duane; Fox-Wisconsin River Improvement Company; Green Bay
Martin, Walter, 57
Mason, John S., 54, 60
Maude, John, 22–23
Medill, William 115
Menominee Indians, 32, 34–38, 45–48, 50, 63–76, 88, 95, 98, 106, 110, 117. See also American Fur Company; Bear Grease; Doty, James Duane; Franco-Menominee; Jourdan, Mary; Oshkosh; Stambaugh, Samuel C.; Treaty of 1821; Treaty of 1822; U.S.-Menominee Treaty of 1831 (Feb. 8); U.S.-Menominee Treaty of 1831 (Feb. 17); U.S.-Menominee Treaty of 1832
Methodist religion, 11, 12, 28, 118, 119, 129, 143, 181n.29. See also Cornelius, Jacob
Métis. See Franco-Menominees
Metoxen, John (Oneida Indian), 114
Metoxen, John (Stockbridge Indian), 51, 55, 60–61, 149

Index

Mexican War, 115
Michigan Territory, 9, 27, 31, 37, 39, 44, 50-51, 59, 61, 63, 68-69, 91
Military Trail (Wisconsin), 44
Milwaukee, 58, 148
Missouri Emigrating Party, 107-109, 113-15, 178n.32, 178n.43. *See also* Anthony, John
Mohawk Indians, 9, 21, 33-34, 71, 76, 93. *See also* Mohawk Prophet; Saint Regis Mohawk Reservation; Williams, Eleazer
Mohawk Prophet, 21
Mohican Indians. *See* Stockbridge Indians
Monroe, James, 31, 35, 49, 50, 61
Morgan, Lewis Henry, 26
Morse, Jedidiah, 9, 31-32, 35, 59
Munsee Indians. *See* Delaware Indians; Stockbridge Indians

Nanticoke Indians, 123
Nashotah Episcopal Seminary, 155
Navajo Indians, 152
Neddy, Nathaniel, 74, 76
Neddy, Thomas, 74
New Echota Treaty (1835), 91
"New York Indians." *See* Brothertown Indians; Oneida Indians, Wisconsin; Stockbridge Indians
New York State-Oneida Treaty of 1798, 29-30, 38-39
New York State-Oneida Treaty of 1802, 29-30
New York State-Oneida Treaty of 1809, 30
New York State-Oneida Treaty (1824), 33, 38, 89
New York State-Oneida Treaties (1829), 33, 38-39
Niemcewicz, Julian Ursyn, 22
Non-Intercourse Acts. *See* Trade and Intercourse Acts
Northern Missionary Society, 39
Northwest Ordinance (1787), 59

Ocquo-ne-naw (Menominee Indian). *See* Pine Shooter

Ogden, David A., 31-34, 36
Ogden, Thomas L., 63
Ogden Land Company, 31-34, 36, 50-53, 63, 89, 94-96
Oil Spring Reservation, 95
Ojibwa Indians, 45
Old Chiefs Council, Oneida. *See* Political system, Oneida (Wisconsin)
Old Oriske. *See* Oriskany
Oneida Castle. *See* Oneida Indian Reservation (New York)
Oneida Indian Reservation (New York): Daniel Bread's boyhood at, 16-19; dispossession of Oneidas at, 24-25, 29-30, 37-40; mentioned, 160; physical description of, 18, 22-24; religious life at, 19-22; social disintegration, 22-24, 28-30. *See also* agriculture, Oneida; dispossession, Oneida; forest lands, Oneida; fishing, Oneida; hunting; Kirkland, Samuel; Skenandoah; treaties
Oneida Indian Reservation (Wisconsin). *See* Amended Treaty of Buffalo Creek (Feb. 3, 1838); Bread, Daniel; Cornelius, Jacob; Davis, Solomon; Dodge, Henry; Doty, James Duane; economic conditions, Oneida; Hill, Cornelius; Goodnough, Edward A.; Hobart Church; Martin, Morgan L.; political system, Oneida; removal pressures; timber stripping; Treaty of 1821; Treaty of 1822; U.S.-Menominee Treaty of 1832
Oneida Indians, Canada. *See* Oneidas of the Thames; Six Nations Reserve
Oneida Indians, New York. *See* agriculture, Oneida; American Revolution; Bread, Daniel; dispossession, Oneida; Erie Canal; First Christian Party; Good Peter; Kirkland, Samuel; Madison County; Ogden Land Company; Oneida Castle; Oneida Reservation, New York; Pagan Party; political system,

Oneida; Skenandoah; treaties; Williams, Eleazer; women, Oneida
Oneida Indians, Wisconsin. *See* agriculture, Oneida; Anthony, John; Bread, Daniel; Cornelius, Jacob; cultural adaptation, Oneida; Davis, Solomon; economic conditions; Episcopal religion; First Christian Party; fishing, Oneida; Goodnough, Edward A.; Hill, Cornelius; Hobart Church; Hobart, John Henry; Kemper, Jackson; Oneida; Menominee Indians and; Methodist religion; Missouri Emigrating Party; Oneida Language and Folklore Project, WPA; Oneida Reservation, Wisconsin; Orchard Party; political system, Oneida; Second Christian Party; treaties; Williams, Eleazer; Winnebago Indians; women, Oneida; Woodman Party
Oneida Lake, 3, 16, 18-19, 23-24
Oneida Language and Folklore Project, WPA, xv-xvi, 6-7, 11-14
Oneidas of the Thames, 119, 126, 145-46
Onuhkwastkó (Big Medicine). *See* Hill, Cornelius
Oratory, Iroquois, 26-27, 44-45, 60-61, 121, 124-26, 155. *See also* July 4th
Orchard Party. See Cornelius, Jacob
Oriskany, Battle of, 3
Oriskany, N.Y., 19
Osage Indians, 67, 93
Oshkosh (Menominee Indian), 37, 48, 50, 88, 91, 177n.28. *See also* Doty, James Duane; Treaty of 1821; Treaty of 1822
Otsiquette. *See* Archiquette, Neddy
Ottawa Indians, 45

Pagan Party, 19, 33. *See also* Second Christian Party
"Pagan Peter." *See* Elm, Peter
Parker, Ely S., 141
Parrish, Jasper, 31
Peshtigo fire (1871), 158-59

Pe-wait-e-naw (Menominee Indian), 75
Pickering Treaty. *See* Canandaigua Treaty (1794)
Pine Shooter (Menominee Indian), 50
Pinetree chiefs, 6-7, 37, 120, 155
Political system, Oneida (New York), 7, 8, 24, 33-34; (Wisconsin), 78, 101-106, 127, 132-33, 135-36, 139-41, 150, 158, 160. *See also* Bread, Daniel; Clan mothers, Oneida; Cornelius, Jacob; cultural adaptations, Oneida; First Christian Party; Hill, Cornelius; Orchard Party; Pagan Party; Second Christian Party
Polk, James K., 112-13, 115
Popham, Stephen, 4-5
Population, Oneida, 23, 103
Population, Wisconsin, 105
Porlier family, 46
Porter, George B., 70-73, 75-76
Potawatomi Indians, 45
Powles. *See* Powless
Powlis. *See* Powless
Powless, Baptiste, 108, 114-15
Powless, Henry, 55, 60, 76, 100-101, 108, 136, 156, 158
Powless, Joseph, 159
Powless, Mrs. Mark, 11-12
Presbyterian religion, 6, 33
Prophets. *See* Handsome Lake; Mohawk Prophet

Quaker religion (Society of Friends), 95, 117, 138
Quapaw Indians, 67
Quinney, John, 51, 54, 65, 67, 76, 148-49

Railroads, 150
Removal pressures: from New York, 11, 15, 31-34, 44, 52, 91, 93, 151; from Wisconsin, 62, 99, 104-106, 109-15, 119. *See also* Buffalo Creek, Treaty of; Calhoun, John C.; Dodge, Henry; Doty, James Duane; Indian Removal Act; Jackson, Andrew; Martin, Morgan L.; Missouri Emigrating Party; Morse, Jedidiah;

Index

Ogden Land Company; Van Buren, Martin; Williams, Eleazer
Residence patterns, Oneida, 103
Revolutionary War. *See* American Revolution
Rohde, Fredrich, 23-24
Roman Catholicism, 45
Root, Erastus, 54, 60
Ross, John, 91-92
Runners, Iroquois, 27, 34

Sac and Fox Indians, 45, 94, 104
Sackets Harbor, 3-5
Saint Regis Mohawk Indians. *See* Mohawk Indians; Williams, Eleazer
Saint Regis Mohawk Reservation, 90
Sandy Creek, Battle of, 3-5, 128, 179n.5
Saponi Indians, 123
Saratoga, Battle of, 6
Schermerhorn, John C., 91-94
Schools, Oneida, 11, 15, 17, 38, 89-90, 93, 95, 103, 109, 114, 128, 133, 138, 143, 151, 155, 179n.6
Second Christian Party, 33
Seminole War (Second Seminole War), 91
Seneca Indians, 21-22, 91-95
Seneca Nation of Indians, 95
Seneca Turnpike. *See* Great Western Turnpike Road
Seymour, Horatio, 149, 172n.12
Seymour, Horatio, Jr., 172n.12
Seymour, John, 149, 172n.12
Shaw-e-no-geshig (Menominee Indian), 75
Shawnee Indians, 94
Sioux Indians, 45, 137. *See also* Lakota Indians
Sioux War (1862), 137
Sitting Bull, xiv
Six Nations. *See* Cayuga Indians; Mohawk Indians; Oneida Indians; Onondaga Indians; Seneca Indians; Tuscarora Indians
Six Nations Reserve, 12, 21
Skenandoah, 3, 19-20
Skenandoah, Adam, 3

Skenandoah (Skenando), John, 36
Skenandore, Elijah, 130, 136, 138-39, 156
Skenandore, John, 13-14
Smallpox, 129, 136-38, 144
Smith, Alice E., 43, 57-58
Society of Friends. *See* Quaker religion
Stambaugh, Samuel C.: appointed interim United States Indian Agent at Green Bay, 64; mentioned, 40, 91-92, 109, 148, 150, 160, 174n.16; urges reduction of Oneida lands in federal treaties with the Menominees, 65-69
Standing Stone Belief, 16-17
State Historical Society of Wisconsin, 10
Stevens, Cornelius, 55, 60, 74, 76
Stockbridge Indians: attempts to buy Oneida lands, 138, 145; Buffalo Creek Treaty (1838) and, 95; Chiefs Quinney and Metoxen go to Washington to lobby, 70, 73; efforts to make citizens causes tribal divisions, 100, 112-14; mentioned, 51, 54-55, 60-61, 65, 67, 76, 148-49. *See also* Boundary Commission (1830), U.S.; Metoxen, John; Quinney, John
Stockbridge-Munsee Indians. *See* Stockbridge Indians
Summer, Sarah, 12
Sundown, John. *See* Senny, John
Supplemental Treaty of 1842 (Seneca Treaty of 1842), 95
Sutcliff, Robert, 28
Swamp, Adam, 114, 145, 156

Taylor, Zachary, 64, 117
Tecumseh, xviii
Tega-wir-tiron. *See* Bread, Daniel
Tegawiatiron. *See* Bread, Daniel
Tekaweiatiron. *See* Bread, Daniel
Tekawyatiron. *See* Bread, Daniel
Tekayá·tilu. *See* Bread, Daniel
Timber stripping, Oneida, 20, 131-32, 139-40, 143-46, 152-54, 158-59

Tiro, Karim, 33–34
Tomah (Menominee Indian), 46
Tompkins, Daniel D., 20, 30–31
Tonawanda Band of Seneca Indians, 95
Tonawanda Indian Reservation, 95
Trade and Intercourse Acts [U.S.], 29–30
Treaty of 1821, 37, 48, 50–51, 52–60, 64–66, 73, 88–89, 98
Treaty of 1822, 37, 48, 50–51, 52–60, 64–66, 73, 88–89, 98
Treaties. See Amended Treaty of Buffalo Creek; Buffalo Creek, Treaty of; Butte des Morts Treaty; Canandaigua, Treaty of; Fort Herkimer, Treaty of; Fort Schuyler, Treaty of; Fort Stanwix, Treaty of (1784); New York State-Oneida Treaty of 1795; New York State-Oneida Treaty of 1798; New York State-Oneida Treaty of 1802; New York State-Oneida "Treaty" of 1809; New York State-Oneida "Treaty" of 1824; New York State-Oneida "Treaties" of 1829; Treaty of 1821; Treaty of 1822; U.S.-Menominee Treaty (Feb. 8, 1831); U.S.-Menominee Treaty (Feb. 17, 1831); U.S.-Menominee Treaty (1832); U.S.-Oneida Treaty of 1794
Troop, Enos, 69
Tuberculosis, 20
Tuscarora Indians, 93
Tutelo Indians, 123
Two Kettles Together (Oneida Indian), 4

U.S. v. Cook (1873), 154
U.S.-Menominee Treaty (Feb. 8, 1831), 65–66
U.S.-Menominee Treaty (Feb. 17, 1831), 66
U.S.-Menominee Treaty (Oct. 27, 1832), 74–77, 91, 96
U.S.-Oneida Treaty (1794), 24, 29, 35
U.S.-Oneida Treaty of 1838. See Amended Treaty of Buffalo Creek (Feb. 3, 1838)

U.S.-Tonawanda Treaty (1857), 95
U.S.S. Superior, 5

Van Buren, Martin, 38–39, 59, 91, 104–105
Van Hoeven, James, 91

Wampum, 27, 55
War of 1812, 3–5, 16, 26, 31, 45–46, 179n.5. See also Sandy Creek, Battle of
Wars. See American Revolution; Black Hawk's War; Civil War; War of 1812
Washington, George, 77, 113, 121, 125, 128
Weed, Thurlow, 28–29
Western Inland Lock Navigation Company, 22–23
Wheelock, Isaac, 115
Williams, Eleazer: Albert Ellis perpetuates myths about, 9–12; deposed as missionary to Oneidas, 31–40, 89–90; meets with President Jackson, 71–74; Jourdan, Mary; mentioned, 33–34, 36–39, 55, 71–72, 74, 170n.26, 171n.36, 175n.3; supports Schermerhorn efforts leading up to Buffalo Creek Treaty (1838), 88–90, 92, 94–95. See also Ellis, Albert G.; Stambaugh, Samuel; Treaty of 1821; Treaty of 1822
Winnebago (Ho-Chunk) Indians, 32, 36, 45, 47–48, 50–57, 60, 66, 73, 104, 106, 110, 117, 172n.19. See also Treaty of 1821; Treaty of 1822
Wisconsin statehood, xiii, 10–11, 51, 57, 104, 106–107, 147, 149, 172n.19
Wisconsin Territory, 94, 103–104, 114. See also American Fur Company; Doty, James Duane; Fox River Valley; Fox-Wisconsin River Improvement Company; Green Bay; lumber industry; Martin, Morgan L.; Whitney, Daniel
Wistar, Thomas, 117

Whitney, Daniel, 44, 46-48, 104, 109, 111-13, 148-50.
Women, Oneida, 7, 22-23, 29, 117, 127, 143
Woodman Party, 107-109, 146-47
Woodman, William, 107
Woolsey, Melancthon, 4-5

Wovoka, xiii
WPA. *See* Oneida Language and Folklore Project, WPA
Wright, Silas, 39, 94

Yellow fever, 20

www.ingramcontent.com/pod-product-compliance
Lightning Source LLC
Chambersburg PA
CBHW021818300125
21133CB00007B/726